The Chicago Guide to Writing about Numbers

Chicago Guides
to *Writing,* Editing,
and Publishing

The Chicago Guide to Writing about Numbers

JANE E. MILLER

The University of Chicago Press
Chicago and London

Jane E. Miller is associate professor in the Institute for Health, Health Care Policy, and Aging Research and the Edward J. Bloustein School of Planning and Public Policy at Rutgers University. Trained as a demographer at the University of Pennsylvania, she has taught research methods and statistics for more than a decade.

The University of Chicago Press, Chicago 60637
The University of Chicago Press, Ltd., London
© 2004 by The University of Chicago
All rights reserved. Published 2004
Printed in the United States of America

13 12 11 10 09 08 07 06 05 04   1 2 3 4 5

ISBN: 0-226-52630-5 (cloth)
ISBN: 0-226-52631-3 (paper)

Library of Congress Cataloging-in-Publication Data
Miller, Jane E., Ph. D.
   The Chicago guide to writing about numbers / Jane E. Miller.
       p.   cm. — (Chicago guides to writing, editing, and publishing)
   Includes bibliographical references and index.
   ISBN 0-226-52630-5 (alk. paper) — ISBN 0-226-52631-3 (pbk. : alk. paper)
   1. Technical writing.   I. Title.   II. Series.
T11.M485 2004
808′.0665 — dc22   2004000204

For a study guide containing problem sets and suggested course extensions for *The Chicago Guide to Writing about Numbers,* please see www.press.uchicago.edu/books/Miller.

To my parents,

for nurturing my love of numbers

CONTENTS

TABLES

FIGURES

BOXES

ACKNOWLEDGMENTS

This book is the product of my experience as a student, practitioner, and teacher of quantitative analysis and presentation. Thinking back on how I learned to write about numbers, I realized that I acquired most of the ideas from patient thesis advisors and collaborators who wrote comments in the margins of my work to help me refine my presentation of quantitative information. This book was born out of my desire to share the principles and tools for writing about numbers with those who don't have access to that level of individualized attention.

Foremost, I would like to thank my doctoral dissertation committee from the University of Pennsylvania, who planted the seeds for this book nearly two decades ago. Samuel Preston was the source of several ideas in this book and the inspiration for others. He, Jane Menken, and Herbert Smith not only served as models of high standards for communicating quantitative material to varying audiences, but taught me the skills and concepts needed to meet those standards.

Many colleagues and friends offered tidbits from their own experience that found their way into this book, or provided thoughtful feedback on early drafts. In particular, I would like to thank Ellen Idler, Diane (Deedee) Davis, Louise Russell, Don Hoover, Deborah Carr, Julie McLaughlin, Tami Videon, Dawne Harris, Usha Sambamoorthi, and Lynn Warner. Susan Darley and Ian Miller taught me a great deal about effective analogies and metaphors. Jane Wilson and Charles Field gave invaluable advice about organization, writing, and graphic design; and four reviewers offered insightful suggestions of ways to improve the book. Kathleen Pottick, Keith Wailoo, and Allan Horwitz provided indispensable guidance and support for bringing this project to fruition. As the director of the Institute for Health, Health Care Policy, and Aging Research, David Mechanic generously granted me the time to work on this venture.

Finally, I would like to thank my students for providing a steady stream of ideas about what to include in the book, as well as opportunities to test and refine the methods and materials.

Why Write about Numbers?

Writing about numbers is an essential skill, an important tool in the repertoire of expository writers in many disciplines. For a quantitative analysis, presenting numbers and patterns is a critical element of the work. Even for works that are not inherently quantitative, one or two numeric facts can help convey the importance or context of your topic. An issue brief about educational policy might include a statistic about the prevalence of school voucher programs and how that figure has changed since the policy was enacted. Or, information could be provided about the impact of vouchers on students' test scores or parents' participation in schools. For both qualitative and quantitative works, communicating numeric concepts is an important part of telling the broader story.

As you write, you will incorporate numbers in several different ways: a few carefully chosen facts in a short article or a nonquantitative piece, a table in the analytic section of a scientific report, a chart of trends in the slides for a speech, a case example in a policy statement or marketing report. In each of these contexts, the numbers support other aspects of the written work. They are not taken in isolation, as in a simple arithmetic problem. Rather, they are applied to some larger objective, as in a math "word problem" where the results of the calculations are used to answer some real-world question. Instead of merely calculating average out-of-pocket costs of prescription medications, for instance, the results of that calculation would be included in an article or policy statement about insurance coverage for prescription medications. Used in that way, the numbers generate interest in the topic or provide evidence for a debate on the issue.

In many ways, writing about numbers is similar to other kinds of expository writing: it should be clear, concise, and written in a logical order. It should start by stating an idea or proposition, then provide evidence to support that thesis. It should include examples that the expected audience can relate to and descriptive language that enhances their understanding of how the evidence relates to the question. It should be written at a level of detail that is consistent with its expected use. It should set the context and define terms the audience might not be expected to know, but do so in ways that distract as little as possible from the main thrust of the work. In short, it will follow many of the principles of good writing, but with the addition of quantitative information.

When I refer to writing about numbers, I mean "writing" in a broad sense: preparation of materials for oral or visual presentation as well as materials to be read. Most of the principles outlined in this book apply equally to speech writing and the accompanying slides or to development of a Web site or an educational or advertising booth with an automated slide show.

Writing effectively about numbers also involves *reading* effectively about numbers. To select and explain pertinent quantitative information for your work, you must understand what those numbers mean and how they were measured or calculated. The first few chapters provide guidance on important features such as units and context to watch for as you garner numeric facts from other sources.

■ WHO WRITES ABOUT NUMBERS?

Numbers are used everywhere. In daily life, you encounter numbers in stock market reports, recipes, sports telecasts, the weather report, and many other places. Pick up a copy of your local newspaper, turn on the television, or connect to the Internet and you are bombarded by numbers being used to persuade you of one viewpoint or another. In professional settings, quantitative information is used in laboratory reports, research papers, books, and grant proposals in the physical and social sciences, in the policy arena, marketing and finance, and popular journalism. Engineers, architects, and other applied scientists need to communicate with their clients as well as with highly trained peers. In all of these situations, for numbers to accomplish their purpose, writers must succinctly and clearly convey quantitative ideas. Whether you are a policy analyst or an engineer, a journalist or a consultant, a college student or a research scientist, chances are you need to write about numbers.

Despite this apparently widespread need, few people are formally trained to write about numbers. Communications specialists learn to write for varied audiences, but rarely are taught specifically to deal with numbers. Scientists and others who routinely work with numbers learn to calculate and interpret the findings, but rarely are taught to describe them in ways that are comprehensible to audiences with different levels of quantitative expertise or interest. I have seen poor communication of numeric concepts at all levels of training and experience, from papers by undergraduates who were shocked at the very concept of putting numbers in sentences, to presentations by business consultants, policy analysts, and scientists, to publications by experienced researchers in elite, peer-reviewed journals. This book is intended to bridge the gap between correct quantitative analysis and good expository writing, taking into account the intended objective and audience.

■ TAILORING YOUR WRITING TO ITS PURPOSE

A critical first step in any writing process is to identify the purpose of the written work.

Objectives

What are the objectives of the piece? To communicate a simple point in a public service announcement? To use statistics to persuade magazine readers of a particular perspective? To serve as a reference for those who need a regular source of data for comparison and calculation? To test hypotheses using the results of a complex statistical analysis?

Audience

Who is your audience? An eighth grade civics class? A group of legislators who need to be briefed on an issue? A panel of scientific experts?

Address these two fundamental questions early in the writing process to guide your choice of vocabulary, depth, length, and style, as well as the selection of appropriate tools for communicating quantitative information. Throughout this book, I return often to issues about audience and objectives as they relate to specific aspects of writing about numbers.

■ A WRITER'S TOOLKIT

Writing about numbers is more than simply plunking a number or two into a sentence. You may want to provide a general image of a pattern or you may need specific, detailed information. Sometimes you will be reporting a single number, other times many numbers. Just as a carpenter selects among different tools depending on the job, those who write about numbers have an array of tools to use for different purposes. Some tools do not suit certain jobs, whether in carpentry (e.g., welding is not used to join pieces of wood), or in writing about numbers (e.g., a pie chart cannot be used to show trends). And just as there may be several appropriate tools for a task in carpentry (e.g., nails, screws, glue, or dowels to fasten together wooden components), in many instances any of several tools could be used to present numbers.

There are three basic tools in a writer's toolkit for presenting quantitative information: prose, tables, and charts.

Prose

Numbers can be presented as a couple of facts or as part of a detailed description of an analytic process or findings. A handful of numbers can be described in a sentence or two, whereas a complex statistical analysis can require a page or more. In the main body of the text, numbers are incorporated into full sentences. In slides, in the executive summary of a report, or on an information kiosk, numbers may be included in a bulleted list, with short phrases used in place of complete sentences. Detailed background information is often given in footnotes (for a sentence or two) or appendixes (for longer descriptions).

Tables

Tables use a grid to present numbers in a predictable way, guided by labels and notes within the table. A simple table might present high school graduation rates in each of several cities. A more complicated table might show relationships among three or more variables such as graduation rates by city over a 20-year period, or results of one or more statistical models analyzing graduation rates. Tables are often used to organize a detailed set of numbers in appendixes, to supplement the information in the main body of the work.

Charts

There are pie charts, bar charts, and line charts and the many variants of each. Like tables, charts organize information into a predictable format: the axes, legend, and labels of a well-designed chart lead the audience through a systematic understanding of the patterns being presented. Charts can be simple and focused, such as a pie chart of the distribution of current market share across the major Internet service providers. Or, they can be complex, such as "high/low/close" charts illustrating stock market activity across a week or more.

As an experienced carpenter knows, even when any of several tools could be used for a job, often one of those options will work better in a specific situation. If there will be a lot of sideways force on a joint, glue will not hold well. If your listening audience has only 30 seconds to grasp a numerical relationship, a complicated table will be overwhelming. If kids will be playing floor hockey in your family room, heavy-duty laminated flooring will hold up better than parquet. If your audience needs many detailed numbers, a table will organize those numbers better than sentences.

With experience, you will learn to identify which tools are suited to different aspects of writing about numbers, and to choose among the different workable options. Those of you who are new to writing about numbers can consider this book an introduction to carpentry — a way to familiarize yourself with the names and operations of each of the tools and the principles that guide their use. Those of you who have experience writing about numbers can consider this a course in advanced techniques, with suggestions for refining your approach and skills to communicate quantitative concepts more clearly and systematically.

■ IDENTIFYING THE ROLE OF THE NUMBERS YOU USE

When writing about numbers, help your readers see where those numbers fit into the story you are telling — how they answer some question you have raised. A naked number sitting alone and uninterpreted is unlikely to accomplish its purpose. Start each paragraph with a topic sentence or thesis statement, then provide evidence that supports or refutes that statement. A short newspaper article on wages might report an average wage and a statistic on how many people earn the minimum wage. Longer, more analytic pieces might have several paragraphs or sections, each addressing a different question related to the main topic. A report on wage patterns might report overall wage levels, then examine how they vary by educational attainment, work experience, and other factors. Structure your paragraphs so your audience can follow how each section and each number contributes to the overall scheme.

To tell your story well, you, the writer, need to know *why* you are including a given fact or set of facts in your work. Think of the numbers as the answer to a word problem, then step back and identify (for yourself) and explain (to your readers) both the question and the answer. This approach is much more informative for the reader than encountering a number without knowing why it is there. Once you have identified the objective and chosen the numbers, convey their purpose to your readers. Provide a context for the numbers by relating them to the issue at hand. Does a given statistic show how large or common something is? How small or infrequent? Do trend data illustrate stability or change? Do those numbers represent typical or unusual values? Often, numerical benchmarks such as thresholds, historical averages, highs, or lows can serve as useful contrasts to help your readers grasp your point more effectively: compare current average wages with the "living wage" needed to exceed the poverty level, for example.

■ ITERATIVE PROCESS IN WRITING

Writing about numbers is an iterative process. Initial choices of tools may later prove to be less effective than some alternative. A table layout may turn out to be too simple or too complicated, or you may conclude that a chart would be preferable. You may discover as you write a description of the patterns in a table that a different table layout would highlight the key findings more efficiently. You may need to condense a technical description of patterns for a research report into bulleted statements for an executive summary, or simplify them into charts for a speech or a compendium of annotated figures such as a chartbook.

To increase your virtuosity at writing about numbers, I introduce a wide range of principles and tools to help you plan the most effective way to present your numbers. I encourage you to draft tables and charts with pencil and paper before creating the computerized version, and to outline key findings before you describe a complex pattern, allowing you to separate the work into distinct steps. However, no amount of advance analysis and planning can envision the perfect final product, which likely will emerge only after several drafts and much review. Expect to have to revise your work, along the way considering the variants of how numbers can be presented.

■ OBJECTIVES OF THIS BOOK

How This Book Is Unique

Writing about numbers is a complex process: it involves finding pertinent numbers, identifying patterns, calculating comparisons, organizing ideas, designing tables or charts, and finally, writing prose. Each of these tasks alone can be challenging, particularly for novices. Adding to the difficulty is the final task of integrating the products of those steps into a coherent whole while keeping in mind the appropriate level of detail for your audience. Unfortunately, these steps are usually taught separately, each covered in a different book or course, discouraging authors from thinking holistically about the writing process.

This book integrates all of these facets into one volume, pointing out how each aspect of the process affects the others; for instance, the patterns in a table are easier to explain if that table was designed with both the statistics and writing in mind. An example will work better if the objective, audience, and data are considered together. By teaching all of these steps in a single book, I encourage alternating perspectives between the "trees" (the tools, examples, and sentences) and the "forest" (the main focus of your work, and its context). This approach will yield a clear, coherent story about your topic, with numbers playing a fundamental but unobtrusive role.

What This Book Is Not

Although this book deals with both writing and numbers, it is neither a writing manual nor a math or statistics book. Rather than repeating principles that apply to other types of writing, I concentrate on those that are unique to writing about numbers and those that require some translation or additional explication. I assume a solid grounding in basic expository writing skills such as organizing ideas into a logical paragraph structure and using evidence to support a thesis statement. For good general guides to expository writing, see Strunk and White (1999) or Zinsser (1998). Other excellent resources include Lanham (2000) for revising prose, and Montgomery (2003) for writing about science.

I also assume a good working knowledge of elementary quantitative concepts such as ratios, percentages, averages, and simple statistical tests, although I explain some mathematical or statistical issues along the way. See Kornegay (1999) for a dictionary of mathematical terms, Utts (1999) or Moore (1997) for good introductory guides to statistics, and Schutt (2001) or Lilienfeld and Stolley (1994) on study design. Those of you who write about multivariate analyses might prefer the more advanced version of this book; see Miller (forthcoming).

How This Book Is Organized

This book encompasses a wide range of material, from broad planning principles to specific technical details. The first section of the book, "Principles," lays the groundwork, describing a series of basic principles for writing about numbers that form the basis for planning and evaluating your writing about numbers. The next section, "Tools," explains the nuts-and-bolts tasks of selecting, calculating, and presenting the numbers you will describe in your prose. The final section, "Pulling It All Together," demonstrates how to apply these principles and tools to write full paragraphs, sections, and documents, with examples of writing for, and speaking to, both scientific and nonscientific audiences.

Principles

PART I

In this section, I introduce a series of fundamental principles for writing about numbers, ranging from setting the context to concepts of statistical significance to more technical issues such as types of variables and use of standards. To illustrate these principles, I include "poor/better/best" versions of sentences — samples of ineffective writing annotated to point out weaknesses, followed by concrete examples and explanations of improved presentation. The "poor" examples are adapted from ones I have encountered while teaching research methods, writing and reviewing research papers and proposals, or attending and giving presentations to academic, policy, and business audiences. These examples may reflect lack of familiarity with quantitative concepts, poor writing or design skills, indoctrination into the jargon of a technical discipline, or failure to take the time to adapt materials for the intended audience and objectives. The principles and "better" examples will help you plan and evaluate your writing about numbers to avoid similar pitfalls in your own work.

Seven Basic Principles

In this chapter, I introduce seven basic principles to increase the precision and power of your quantitative writing. I begin with the simplest, most general principles, several of which are equally applicable to other types of writing: setting the context; choosing simple, plausible examples; and defining your terms. I also introduce criteria for choosing among prose, tables, and charts. Lastly, I cover several principles that are more specific to quantitative tasks: reporting and interpreting numbers, specifying direction and magnitude of associations, and summarizing patterns. I accompany each of these principles with illustrations of how to write (and how not to write) about numbers.

▉ ESTABLISH THE CONTEXT FOR YOUR FACTS

"The W's"

Context is essential for all types of writing. Few stories are told without somehow conveying "who, what, when, and where," or what I call the W's. Without them your audience cannot interpret your numbers and will probably assume that your data describe everyone in the current time and place (e.g., the entire population of the United States in 2003). This unspoken convention may seem convenient. However, if your numbers are read later or in a different situation without information about their source they can be misinterpreted. Don't expect your readers to keep track of when a report was issued to establish the date to which the facts pertain. Even using such tricks, all they can determine is that the information predated publication, which leaves a lot of room for error. If you encounter data without the W's attached, either track down the associated contextual information and report it, or don't use those facts.

To include all of the W's, some beginners write separate sentences

Box 2.1. Named Periods and Cohorts

Some time periods or cohorts are referred to by names such as "the Great Depression," "the post-war baby boom," or "Generation X," the dates varying from source to source. Generation X is loosely defined as the generation following the baby boom, but has been variously interpreted as "those born between 1965 and 1980," "those raised in the 1970s and 1980s," or even "those born since the mid-1960s" (scary, since it is lacking an end date, unless you look at when the article was published) (Jochim 1997). When reporting numbers about a "named" period for general background purposes, varying definitions probably don't matter very much. However, if your readers need precise comparisons, specify the range of dates. If you directly compare figures from several sources, point out any variation in the definitions.

for each one, or write them in a stilted list: "The year was 2000. The place was the United States. The numbers reported include everyone of all ages, racial groups, and both sexes. [Then a sentence reporting the pertinent numbers]." Setting the context doesn't have to be lengthy or rote. In practice, each of the W's requires only a few words or a short phrase that can be easily incorporated into the sentence with the numbers. Suppose you want to include some mortality statistics in the introductory section of a paper about the Black Plague in fourteenth-century Europe.

Poor: "There were 25 million deaths."
   This statement lacks information about when and where these deaths occurred, or who was affected (e.g., certain age groups or locales). It also fails to mention whether these deaths were from Black Plague alone or whether other causes also contributed to that figure.
Better: "During the fourteenth century, 25 million people died in Europe."
   Although this statement specifies the time and place, it still does not clarify whether the deaths were from all causes or from the plague alone.
Best: "When the Black Plague hit Europe in the latter half of the fourteenth century, it took the lives of 25 million people, young and old, city dwellers and those living in the countryside. The disease killed about one-quarter of Europe's total population at the time (Mack, n.d.)."

This sentence clearly conveys the time, place, and attributes of the
people affected by the plague, and provides information to convey the
scale of that figure.

Despite the importance of specifying context, it is possible to take this principle too far: in an effort to make sure there is absolutely no confusion about context, some authors repeat the W's for every numeric fact. I have read papers that mention the date, place, and group literally in every sentence pertaining to numbers — a truly mind-numbing experience for both writer and reader. Ultimately, this obscures the meaning of the numbers because those endless W's clutter up the writing. To avert this problem, specify the context for the first number in a paragraph, then mention it again in that paragraph only if one or more aspects of the context change.

"When the Black Plague hit Europe in the latter half of the
fourteenth century, it took the lives of 25 million people. The
disease killed about one-quarter of Europe's total population
at the time." [*Add*] "Smaller epidemics occurred from 1300
to 1600."]
The last sentence mentions new dates but does not repeat the place or
cause of death, implying that those aspects of the context remain the
same as in the preceding sentences.

If you are writing a description of numeric patterns that spans several paragraphs, occasionally mention the W's again. For longer descriptions, this will occur naturally as the comparisons you make vary from one paragraph to the next. In a detailed analysis of the plague, you might compare mortality from the plague to mortality from other causes in the same time and place, mortality from the plague in other places or other times, and a benchmark statistic to help people relate to the magnitude of the plague's impact. Discuss each of these points in separate sentences or paragraphs, with introductory topic phrases or sentences stating the purpose and context of the comparison. Then incorporate the pertinent W's in the introductory sentence or in the sentence reporting and comparing the numbers.

Units

An important aspect of "what" you are reporting is the units in which it was measured. There are different systems of measurement for virtually everything we quantify — distance, weight, volume, temperature, monetary value, and calendar time, to name a few. Although most Americans continue to be brought up with the British system of measurement — distance in feet and inches; weight in pounds and ounces; liquid volume in cups, pints, and gallons; temperature in degrees Fahrenheit — most other countries use the metric system — meters, grams, liters, and degrees Celsius, respectively. Different cultural and religious groups use many different monetary and calendar systems.

Scale of measurement also varies, so that population statistics may be reported in hundreds, thousands, millions, or even billions of people, according to whether one is discussing local, national, or international figures. Because of these variations, if the units of measurement are not reported along with a fact, a number alone is virtually useless, as you will see in some amusing examples in chapter 4, where I discuss this important principle in depth.

■ PICK SIMPLE, PLAUSIBLE EXAMPLES

As accomplished speakers know, one strong intuitive example or analogy can go a long way toward helping your audience grasp quantitative concepts. If you can relate calories burned in a recommended exercise to how many extra cookies someone could eat, or translate a tax reduction into how many dollars a typical family would save, you will have given your readers a familiar basis of comparison for the numbers you report.

Most people don't routinely carry scales, measuring cups, or radar guns with them, so if you refer to dimensions such as weight, volume, or speed, provide visual or other analogies to explain particular values. In a presentation about estimating the number of people attending the Million Man March, Joel Best[1] held up a newspaper page to portray the estimated area occupied by each person (3.6 square feet). This device was especially effective because he was standing behind the page as he explained the concept, making it easy for his audience to literally see whether it was a reasonable approximation of the space he — an average-size adult — occupied.

The choice of a fitting example or analogy is often elusive. Finding one depends on both the audience and the specific purpose of your example.

Objectives of Examples

Most examples are used to provide background information that establishes the importance of the topic, to compare findings with earlier ones, or to illustrate the implications of results. Your objectives will determine the choice of an example. For introductory information, a couple of numerical facts gleaned from another source usually will do. For a detailed scientific report, examples often come from your own analyses and appropriate contrasts within your own data or comparisons with findings from other sources become critical issues. Below I outline a set of criteria to get you started thinking about how to choose effective examples for your own work.

The logic behind choosing numeric illustrations is similar to that for selecting excerpts of prose in an analysis of a literary work or case examples in a policy brief. Some examples are chosen to be representative of a broad theme, others to illustrate deviations or exceptions from a pattern. Make it clear whether an example you are writing about is typical or atypical, normative or extreme. Consider the following ways to describe annual temperature:

Poor: "In 2001, the average temperature in the New York City area was 56.3 degrees Fahrenheit."
From this sentence, you cannot tell whether 2001 was a typical year, unusually warm or unusually cool.
Better: "In 2001, the average temperature in the New York City area was 56.3 degrees Fahrenheit, 1.5 degrees above normal."
This version clarifies that 2001 was a warm year, as well as reporting the average temperature.
Best: "In 2001, the average temperature in the New York City area was 56.3 degrees Fahrenheit, 1.5 degrees above normal, making it the seventh warmest year on record for the area."
This version points out not only that temperatures for 2001 were above average, but also just how unusual that departure was.

Principles for Choosing Examples

The two most important criteria for choosing effective examples are that they be simple and plausible.

Simplicity

The oft-repeated mnemonic KISS — "Keep It Simple, Stupid" — applies to both the choice and explication of examples and analogies. Although the definition of "simple" will vary by audience and length of the work, your job is to design and explain examples that are straightforward and familiar. The fewer terms you have to define along the way, and the fewer logical or arithmetic steps you have to walk your readers through, the easier it will be for them to understand the example and its purpose. The immensity of the Twin Towers was really driven home by equating the volume of concrete used in those buildings to the amount needed to build a sidewalk from New York City to Washington, D.C. (Glanz and Lipton 2002) — especially to someone who recently completed the three-hour train ride between those two cities.

Plausibility

A comparison example must be plausible: the differences between groups or changes across time must be feasible biologically, behaviorally, politically, or in whatever arena your topic fits. If you calculate the beneficial effects of a 20-pound weight loss on chances of a heart attack but the typical dieter loses only 10 pounds, your projection will not apply to most cases. If voters are unlikely to approve more than a 0.7% increase in local property taxes, projecting the effects of a 1.0% increase will overestimate potential revenue.

This is an aspect of choosing examples that is ripe for abuse: advocates can artificially inflate apparent benefits (or understate liabilities) by using unrealistically large or small differences in their examples. For example, sea salt aficionados tout the extra minerals it provides in comparison to those found in regular ol' supermarket salt. Although sea salt does contain trace amounts of several minerals, closer examination reveals that you'd have to eat about a quarter pound of it to obtain the amount of iron found in a single grape (Wolke 2002). The fact that two pounds of salt can be fatal provides additional perspective on just how problematic a source of iron it would be.

Other factors to consider include relevance, comparability, target audience, and how your examples are likely to be used, as well as a host of measurement issues. Because the choice of examples has many nuances, I devote the whole of chapter 8 to that subject.

■ **SELECT THE RIGHT TOOL FOR THE JOB**

The main tools for presenting quantitative information — prose, charts, and tables — have different, albeit sometimes overlapping, advantages and disadvantages. Your choice of tools depends on several things, including how many numbers are to be presented, the amount of time your audience has to digest the information, the importance of precise versus approximate numeric values, and, as always, the nature of your audience. Chapters 6 and 7 provide detailed guidelines and examples. For now, a few basics.

How Many Numbers?

Some tools work best when only a few numbers are involved; others can handle and organize massive amounts of data. Suppose you are writing about how unemployment has varied by age group and region of the country in recent years. If you are reporting a few numbers to give a sense of the general pattern of unemployment for a short piece or an introduction to a longer work, a table or chart would probably be overkill. Instead, use a sentence or two:

> "In December 2001, the unemployment rate for the United States was 5.8%, up from 3.9% a year earlier. Unemployment rates in each of the four major census regions also showed a substantial increase over that period (U.S. Bureau of Labor Statistics 2002a)."

If you need to include 10 years' worth of unemployment data on three age groups for each of four census regions, a table or chart is efficient and effective.

How Much Time?

When a presentation or memo must be brief, a chart, simple table, or series of bulleted phrases is often the quickest way of helping your audience understand your information. Avoid large, complicated tables: your audience won't grasp them in the limited time. For a memo or executive summary, write one bullet for each point in lieu of tables or charts.

Are Precise Values Important?

If in-depth analysis of specific numeric values is the point of your work, a detailed table is appropriate. For instance, if your readers need to see the fine detail of variation in unemployment rates over a decade or more, a table reporting those rates to the nearest tenth of a percentage point would be a good choice. Conversely, if your main objective is to show the general pattern of unemployment over that period, a chart would work better: all those numbers (and extra digits) in a table can distract and confuse.

"A chart is worth a thousand words," to play on the cliché. It can capture vast amounts of information far more succinctly than prose, and illustrate the size of a difference or the direction of a trend more powerfully than a sentence or a table. There is a tradeoff, however: it is difficult to ascertain exact values from a chart. Avoid them if that is your objective.

Mixing Tools

In most situations, you will use a combination of tables, charts, and prose. Suppose you were writing a scholarly paper on unemployment patterns. You might include a few statistics on current unemployment rates in your introduction, a table to show how current unemployment varies by age group and region, and some charts to illustrate 10-year trends in unemployment by age group and region. To explain patterns in the tables or charts and relate those findings to the main purpose of the paper, describe those patterns in prose. For oral presentations, chartbooks, or automated slide shows, use bulleted phrases next to each chart or table to summarize the key points. Examples of these formats appear in later chapters.

As a general rule, don't duplicate information in both a table and a chart; you will only waste space and test your readers' patience. For instance, if I were to see both a table and a chart presenting unemployment rates for the same three age groups, four regions, and 10-year period, I would wonder whether I had missed some important point that one but not the other vehicle was trying to make. And I certainly wouldn't want to read the explanation of the same patterns twice — once for the table and again for the chart.

There are exceptions to every rule, and here are two. First, if both a quick sense of a general pattern *and* access to the full set of exact numbers matter, you might include a chart in the text and tables in an appendix to report the detailed numbers from which the chart is constructed. Second, if you are presenting the same information to different audiences or in different formats, make both table and chart versions of the same data. You might use a table of unemployment statistics in a detailed academic journal article but show the chart in a presentation to your church's fundraising committee for the homeless.

■ DEFINE YOUR TERMS (AND WATCH FOR JARGON)

Why Define Terms?

Quantitative writing often uses technical language. To make sure your audience comprehends your information, define your terms, acronyms, and symbols.

Box 2.2. Names for Numbers.

In addition to some of the more obvious jargon, other numeric terminology can confuse your audience. You might want to spice up your writing by using phrases such as "a century" instead of "100 years" or "the age of majority" instead of "age 18." Some of those phrases are widely understood, others a part of cultural literacy that depends on what culture you are from. That "a dozen" equals 12 is common knowledge in the United States, but the idea that "a baker's dozen" equals 13 is less universal. Writing for a modern American audience, I would hesitate to use terms such as "a fortnight" (14 nights or two weeks), "a stone" (14 pounds) or "a score" (20) without defining them. A British author or a historian could probably use them with less concern. Think carefully about using terms that require a pause (even a parenthetical pause), to define them, as it can interrupt the rhythm of your writing.

Unfamiliar Terms

Don't use phrases such as "opportunity cost" or "standardized mortality ratio" with readers who are unfamiliar with those terms. Ditto with abbreviations such as "SES," "LBW," or "PSA." If you use technical language without defining it first, you run the risk of intimidating your audience and losing them from the outset. Or, if they try to figure out the meaning of new words or acronyms while you are speaking, they will miss what you are saying. If you don't define terms in written work, you either leave your readers in the dark or send them scurrying for a textbook or a dictionary.

Terms That Have More Than One Meaning

A more subtle problem occurs with words or abbreviations that have different meanings in other contexts. If you use a term that is defined differently in lay usage or in other fields, people may *think* they know what you are referring to when they actually have the wrong concept.

- To most people, a "significant difference" means a large one, rather than a difference that meets certain criteria for inferential statistical tests.[2] Because of the potential for confusion about the meaning of "significant," restrict its use to the statistical sense when describing statistical results.

Many other adjectives such as "considerable," "appreciable," or even "big" can fill in ably to describe "large" differences between values.

- Depending on the academic discipline and type of analysis, the Greek symbol α (alpha) may denote the probability of Type I error, inter-item reliability, or the intercept in a regression model — three completely different concepts (Agresti and Finlay 1997).

- The acronym PSA means "public service announcement" to people in communications, "prostate specific antigen" to health professionals, "professional services automation" in the business world, among 81 other definitions according to an online acronym finder.

These examples probably seem obvious now, but can catch you unaware. Often people become so familiar with how a term or symbol is used in a particular context that they forget that it could be confused with other meanings. Even relative newcomers to a field can become so immersed in their work that they no longer recognize certain terms as ones they would not have understood a few months before.

Different Terms for the Same Concept

People from different fields of study sometimes use different terms for the same quantitative concept. For example, the term "scale" is sometimes referred to as "order of magnitude," and what some people call an "interaction" is known to others as "effect modification." Even with a quantitatively sophisticated audience, don't assume that people will know the equivalent vocabulary used in other fields. The journal *Medical Care* recently published an article whose sole purpose was to compare statistical terminology across various disciplines involved in health services research, so that people could understand one another (Maciejewski et al. 2002). After you define the term you plan to use, mention the synonyms from other fields represented in your audience to make sure everyone can relate your methods and findings to those from other disciplines.

To avoid confusion about terminology, scan your work for jargon before your audience sees it. Step back and put yourself in your readers' shoes, thinking carefully about whether they will be familiar with the quantitative terms, concepts, abbreviations, and notation. Show a draft of your work to someone who fits the profile of one of your future readers in terms of education, interest level, and likely use of the numbers and ask the reader to flag anything he or she is unsure about. Then evaluate whether those potentially troublesome terms are necessary for the audience and objectives.

Do You Need Technical Terms?

One of the first decisions to make when writing about numbers is whether quantitative terminology or mathematical symbols are appropriate for a particular audience and objective. For all but the most technical situations, *you* need to know the name and operation of the tools you are using to present numeric concepts, but your readers may not. When a carpenter builds a deck for your house, she doesn't need to name or explain to you how each of her tools works as long as she knows which tools suit the task and is proficient at using them. You use the results of her work but don't need to understand the technical details of how it was accomplished.

To demonstrate their expertise, some writers, particularly novices to scientific or other technical fields, are tempted to use only complex quantitative terms. However, some of the most brilliant and effective writers are so brilliant and effective precisely because they can make a complicated idea easy to grasp. Even for a quantitatively adept audience, a well-conceived restatement of a complex numeric relation underscores your familiarity with the concepts and enlightens those in the audience who are too embarrassed to ask for clarification.

When to Avoid Jargon Altogether

For nonscientific audiences or short pieces where a new term would be used only once, avoid jargon altogether. There is little benefit to introducing new vocabulary or notation if you will not be using it again. And for nonstatisticians, equations full of Greek symbols, subscripts, and superscripts are more likely to reawaken math anxiety than to promote effective communication. The same logic applies to introductory or concluding sections of scientific papers: using a new word means that you must define it, which takes attention away from your main point. If you will not be repeating the term, find other ways to describe numeric facts or patterns. Replace complex or unfamiliar words, acronyms, or mathematical symbols with familiar synonyms, and rephrase complicated concepts into more intuitive ones.

Suppose an engineering firm has been asked to design a bridge between Littletown and Midville. To evaluate which materials last the longest, they use a statistical technique called failure time analysis (also known as hazards analysis, survival modeling, and event history analysis). They are to present their recommendations to local officials, few of whom have technical or statistical training.

Poor: "The relative hazard of failure for material C was 0.78."
  The key question — which material will last longer — is not answered in ways that the audience will understand. Also, it is not clear which material is the basis of comparison.
Better: "Under simulated conditions, the best-performing material (material C) lasted 1.28 times as long as the next best choice (material B)."
  This version presents the information in terms the audience can comprehend: how much longer the best-performing material will last. Scientific jargon that hints at a complicated statistical method has been translated into common, everyday language.
Best: "In conditions that mimic the weather and volume and weight of traffic in Littletown and Midville, the best-performing material (material C) has an average expected lifetime of 64 years, compared with 50 years for the next best choice (material B)."
  In addition to avoiding statistical terminology related to failure time analysis, this version gives specific estimates of how long the materials can be expected to last, rather than just reporting the comparison as a ratio. It also replaces "simulated conditions" with the particular issues involved — ideas that the audience can relate to.

When to Use and Then Paraphrase Jargon

Many situations call for one or more scientific terms for numeric ideas. You may refer repeatedly to unfamiliar terminology. You may use a word or symbol that has several different meanings. You may refer to a concept that has different names in different disciplines. Finally, you may have tried to "explain around" the jargon, but discovered that explaining it in nontechnical language was too convoluted or confusing. In those instances, use the new term, then define or rephrase it in other, more commonly used language to clarify its meaning and interpretation. Suppose a journalist for a daily newspaper is asked to write an article about international variation in mortality.

Poor: "In 1999, the crude death rate (CDR) for Sweden was 11 deaths per 1,000 people and the CDR for Ghana was 10 deaths per 1,000 people (World Bank 2001a). You would think that Sweden — one of the most highly industrialized countries — would have lower mortality than Ghana — a less developed country. The reason is differences in the age structure, so I calculated life expectancy for each of the two countries. To calculate life expectancy, you apply age-specific death rates for every age group to a cohort of . . . [You get the idea . . .] Calculated life expectancy estimates for Sweden and Ghana were 78 years and 58 years."

This explanation includes a lot of background information and jargon that the average reader does not need, and the main point gets lost among all the details. Using many separate sentences, each with one fact or definition or calculation, also makes the presentation less effective.

Better (For a nontechnical audience): "In 1999, people in Ghana could expect to live until age 58, on average, compared to age 78 in Sweden. These life expectancies reflect much lower mortality rates in Sweden (World Bank 2001a)."

This version conveys the main point about differences in mortality rates without the distracting detail about age distributions and how to calculate life expectancy.

Better (For a longer, more technical article): "In 1999, the crude death rate (CDR) for Sweden was 11 deaths per 1,000 people and the CDR for Ghana was 10 deaths per 1,000 people, giving the appearance of slightly more favorable survival chances in Ghana (World Bank 2001a). However, Sweden has a much higher share of its population in the older age groups (17% aged 65 and older, compared to only 3% in Ghana), and older people have higher death rates. This difference pulls up the average death rate for Sweden. Life expectancy — a measure of mortality that corrects for differences in the age distribution — shows that in fact survival chances are much better in Sweden, where the average person can expect to live for 78 years, than in Ghana (58 years)."

This version conveys the main point about why life expectancy is the preferred measure and rephrases it in ways that introduce the underlying concepts (that older people have higher mortality, and that Sweden has a higher share of older people).

When to Rely on Technical Language

Although jargon can obscure quantitative information, equations and scientific phrasing are often useful, even necessary. When tradesmen talk to one another, using the specific technical names of their tools and supplies makes their communication more precise and efficient, which is the reason such terms exist. Being familiar with a "grade 8 hex cap bolt," they know immediately what supplies they need. A general term such as "a bolt" would omit important information. Likewise, if author and audience are proficient in the same field, the terminology of that discipline facilitates communication. If you are defending your doctoral dissertation in economics, using the salient terminology demonstrates that you are qualified to earn your PhD. And an equation with conventional symbols and abbreviations provides convenient shorthand for communicating statistical relationships, model specifications, and findings to audiences that are conversant with the pertinent notation.

Even for quantitatively sophisticated audiences, I suggest paraphrasing technical language in the introductory and concluding sections of a talk or paper, saving the heavy-duty jargon for the methodological and analytic portions. This approach reminds the audience of the purpose of the analyses, and places the findings back in a real-world context — both important parts of telling your story with numbers.

■ REPORT *AND* INTERPRET

Why Interpret?

Reporting the numbers you work with is an important first step toward effective writing about numbers. By including the numbers in the text, table, or chart, you give your readers the raw materials with which to make their own assessments. After reporting the raw numbers, interpret them. An isolated number that has not been introduced or explained leaves its explication entirely to your readers. Those who are not familiar with your topic are unlikely to know which comparisons to make or to have the information for those comparisons immediately at hand. To help them grasp the meaning of the numbers you report, provide the relevant data and explain the comparisons. Consider an introduction to a report on health care costs in the United States, where you want to illustrate why these expenditures are of concern.

Poor: "In 1998, total expenditures on health care in the United States were estimated to be more than $1.1 trillion (Centers for Medicare and Medicaid Services 2004)."
From this sentence, it is difficult to assess whether total U.S. expenditures on health care in the are high or low, stable or changing quickly. To most people, $1.1 trillion sounds like a lot of money, but a key question is

"compared to what"? If they knew the total national budget, they could do a benchmark calculation, but you will make the point more directly if you do that calculation for them.

Better: "In 1998, total expenditures on health care in the United States were estimated to be more than $1.1 trillion, equivalent to $4,178 for every man, woman, and child in the nation (Centers for Medicare and Medicaid Services 2004)."

This simple translation of total expenditures into a per capita figure takes a large number that is difficult for many people to fathom and converts it into something that they can relate to. Readers can compare that figure with their own bank balance or what they have spent on health care recently to assess the scale of national health care expenditures.

Best (To emphasize trend): "Between 1990 and 1998, the total costs of health care in the United States rose to $1,150 billion from $699 billion — an increase of 65%. Over that same period, the share of gross domestic product (GDP) spent for health care increased to 13.1% from 12.0% (Centers for Medicare and Medicaid Services 2004)."

By discussing how health care expenditures have changed across time, this version points out that the expenditures have risen markedly in recent years. The sentence on share of GDP spent on health care shows that these expenditures comprise a substantial portion of the national budget — another useful benchmark.

Best (To put the United States in an international context): "In the United States, per capita health expenditures averaged $4,108 in the 1990s, equivalent to 13.0% of gross domestic product (GDP) — a higher share of GDP than in any other country in the same period. In comparison, Switzerland — the country with the second highest per capita health expenditures — spent approximately $3,835 per person, or 10.4% of GDP. No other country exceeded $3,000 per capita on health expenditures (World Bank 2001b)."

This description reveals that health care expenditures in the United States were the highest of any country and reports how much higher compared to the next highest country. By using percentage of GDP as the measure, this comparison avoids the issue that countries with smaller populations would be expected to spend fewer total dollars but could still have higher per capita or percentage of GDP expenditures on health.

Why Report the Raw Numbers?

Although it is important to interpret quantitative information, it is also essential to report the numbers. If you *only* describe a relative difference or percentage change, for example, you will have painted an incomplete picture. Suppose that a report by the local department of wildlife states that the density of the deer population in your town is 30% greater than it was five years ago but does not report the density for either year. A 30% difference is consistent with many possible combinations: 0.010 and 0.013 deer per square mile, or 5.0 and 6.5, or 1,000 and 1,300, for example. The first pair of numbers suggests a very sparse deer population, the last pair an extremely high concentration. Unless the densities themselves are mentioned, you can't determine whether the species has narrowly missed extinction or faces an overpopulation problem. Furthermore, you can't compare density figures from other times or places.

■ SPECIFY DIRECTION AND MAGNITUDE OF AN ASSOCIATION

Writing about numbers often involves describing relationships between two or more variables. To interpret an association, explain both its shape and size rather than simply stating whether the variables are correlated.[3] Suppose an educational consulting firm is asked to compare the academic and physical development of students in two school districts, one of which offers a free breakfast program. If the consultants do their job well, they will report which group is bigger, faster, and smarter, as well as *how much* bigger, faster, and smarter.

Direction of Association

Variables can have a *positive* or *direct* association — as the value of one variable increases, the value of the other variable also increases — or a *negative* or *inverse* association — as one variable increases, the other decreases. Physical gas laws state that as the temperature of a confined gas rises, so does pressure; hence temperature and pressure are positively related. Conversely, as the price of a pair of jeans rises, the demand for jeans falls, so price and demand are inversely related.

For nominal variables such as gender, race, or religion that are classified into categories that have no inherent order, describe direction of association by specifying which category has the highest or lowest value (see chapter 4 for more about nominal variables, chapter 9 for more on prose descriptions). "Religious group is negatively associated with smoking" cannot be interpreted. Instead, write "Mormons were the group least likely to smoke," and mention how other religious groups compare.

Size of Association

An association can be large — a given change in one variable is associated with a big change in the other variable — or small — a given change in one variable is associated with a small change in the other. A $10 increase in the price of jeans might reduce demand by 25% or by only 5%, depending on initial price, trendiness, and other factors. If several factors each reduce demand for jeans, knowing which make a big difference can help the manufacturer increase sales.

To see how these points improve a description of a pattern, consider the following variants of a description of the association between age and mortality. Note that describing direction and magnitude can be accomplished with short sentences and straightforward vocabulary.

Poor: "Mortality and age are correlated."
This sentence doesn't say whether age and mortality are positively or negatively related or how much mortality differs by age.
Better: "As age increases, mortality increases."
Although this version specifies the direction of the association, the size of the mortality difference by age is still unclear.
Best: "Among the elderly, mortality roughly doubles for each successive five-year age group."
This version explains both the direction and the magnitude of the age/ mortality association.

Specifying direction of an association can also strengthen statements of hypotheses: state which group is expected to have the more favorable outcome, not just that the characteristic and the outcome are expected to be related. "Persons receiving Medication A are expected to have fewer symptoms than those receiving a placebo" is more informative than "symptoms are expected to differ in the treatment and control groups." Typically, hypotheses do not include precise predictions about the size of differences between groups.

■ SUMMARIZE PATTERNS

The numbers you present, whether in text, tables, or charts, are meant to provide evidence about some issue or question. However, if you merely provide a table or chart, you leave it to your readers to figure out for themselves what that evidence says. Instead, digest the patterns to help readers see the general relationship in the table or chart.

When asked to summarize a table or chart, inexperienced writers often make one of two opposite mistakes: (1) they report every single number from the table or chart in the text, or (2) they pick a few arbitrary numbers to contrast in sentence form without considering whether those numbers represent an underlying general pattern. Neither approach adds much to the information presented in the table or chart and both can confuse or mislead the audience. Paint the big picture, rather than reiterating all of the little details. If readers are interested in specific values within the pattern you describe they can look them up in the accompanying table or chart.

Why Summarize?

Summarize to relate the evidence back to the substantive topic. Do housing prices change across time as would be expected based on changing economic conditions? Are there appreciable differences in housing prices across regions? Summarize broad patterns with a few simple statements instead of writing piecemeal about individual numbers or comparing many pairs of numbers. For example, answering a question such as "Are housing prices rising, falling, or remaining stable?" is much more instructive than responding to "What were housing prices in 1980, 1981, 1982 . . . 1999, 2000 in the Northeast?" or "How much did housing prices in the Northeast change between 1980 and 1981? Between 1981 and 1982? . . ."

Generalization, Example, Exceptions — An Approach to Summarizing Numeric Patterns

Here is a mantra I devised to help guide you through the steps of writing an effective description of a pattern involving three or more numbers: "generalization, example, exceptions," or GEE for short. The idea is to identify and describe a pattern in general terms, give a representative example to illustrate that pattern, and then explain and illustrate any exceptions.

Generalization

For a generalization, come up with a description that characterizes a relationship among most, if not all, of the numbers. In figure 2.1, is the general trend in most regions rising, falling, or stable? Does one region consistently have the highest housing prices over the years?

Median sales price of new single-family homes, by region, United States, 1980–2000

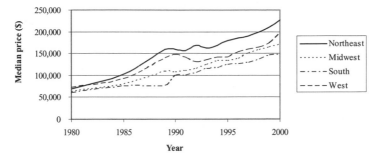

Figure 2.1. Generalizing patterns from a multiple-line trend chart.
Source: U.S. Census Bureau 2001a.

Start by describing one such pattern (e.g., trends in housing prices in the Northeast) then consider whether that pattern applies to the other regions as well. Or, figure out which region had the highest housing prices in 1980 and see whether it is also the most expensive region in 1990 and 2000. If the pattern fits most of the time and most places, it is a generalization. For the few situations it doesn't fit, you have an *exception* (see below).

> "As shown in figure 2.1, the median price of a new single-family home followed a general upward trend in each of the four major census regions between 1980 and 2000. This trend was interrupted by a leveling off or even a decline in prices around 1990, after which prices resumed their upward trajectory. Throughout most of the period shown, the highest housing prices were found in the Northeast, followed by the West, Midwest, and South (U.S. Census Bureau 2001a)."
>
> *This description depicts the approximate shape of the trend in housing prices (first two sentences), then explains how the four regions compare to one another in terms of relative price (last sentence). There are two generalizations: the first about how prices changed across time, the second about regional differences in price. Readers are referred to the accompanying chart, which depicts the relationships, but no precise numbers have been reported yet.*

"Example"
Having described your generalizable pattern in intuitive language, illustrate it with numbers from your table or chart. This step anchors

your generalization to the specific numbers upon which it is based. It ties the prose and table or chart together. By reporting a few illustrative numbers, you implicitly show your readers where in the table or chart those numbers came from as well as the comparison involved. They can then test whether the pattern applies to other times, groups, or places using other data from the table or chart. Having written the above generalizations about figure 2.1, include sentences that incorporate examples from the chart into the description.

> (To follow the trend generalization): "For example, in the Northeast region, the median price of a new single-family home rose from $69,500 in 1980 to $227,400 in 2000, more than a three-fold increase in price."

> (To follow the across-region generalization): "In 2000, the median prices of new single-family homes were $227,400, $196,400, $169,700, and $148,000 in the Northeast, West, Midwest, and South, respectively."

Exceptions

Life is complicated: rarely will anything be so consistent that a single general description will capture all relevant variation in your data. Tiny blips can usually be ignored, but if some parts of a table or chart depart substantially from your generalization, describe those departures. When portraying an exception, explain its overall shape and how it differs from the generalization you have described and illustrated in your preceding sentences. Is it higher or lower? By how much? If a trend, is it moving toward or away from the pattern you are contrasting it against? In other words, describe both the direction and magnitude of change or difference between the generalization and the exception. Finally, provide numeric examples from the table or chart to illustrate the exception.

> "In three of the four regions, housing prices rose throughout the 1980s. In the South, however, housing prices did not begin to rise until 1990, after which they rose at approximately the same rate as in each of the other regions."
>
> *The first sentence describes a general pattern that characterizes most of the regions. The second sentence describes the exception and identifies the region to which it applies. Specific numeric examples to illustrate both the generalization and the exception could be added to this description.*

Other types of exceptions include instances where prices in all four regions were rising but at a notably slower rate in some regions, or where prices rose over a sustained period in some regions but fell appreciably in others. In other words, an exception can occur in terms of magnitude (e.g., small versus large change over time) as well as in direction (e.g., rising versus falling, or higher versus lower).

Because learning to identify and describe generalizations and exceptions can be difficult, in appendix A you will find additional guidelines about recognizing and portraying patterns, and organizing the ideas for a GEE into paragraphs, with step-by-step illustrations from several different tables and charts.

■ CHECKLIST FOR THE SEVEN BASIC PRINCIPLES

- Set the context for the numbers you present by specifying the W's.
- Choose effective examples and analogies:
    - Use simple, familiar examples that your audience will be able to understand and relate to.
    - Select contrasts that are realistic under real-world circumstances.
- Choose vocabulary to suit your readers:
    - Define terms and mention synonyms from related fields for statistical audiences.
    - Replace jargon and mathematical symbols with colloquial language for nontechnical audiences.
- Decide whether to present numbers in text, tables, or figures:
    - Decide how many numbers you need to report.
    - Estimate how much time your audience has to grasp your data.
    - Assess whether your readers need exact values.
- Report and interpret numbers in the text:
    - Report them and specify their purpose.
    - Interpret and relate them back to your main topic.
- Specify both the direction and size of an association between variables:
    - If a trend, is it rising or falling?
    - If a difference across groups or places, which has the higher value and by how much?
- To describe a pattern involving many numbers, summarize the overall pattern rather than repeating all the numbers:
    - Find a generalization that fits most of the data.
    - Report a few illustrative numbers from the associated table or chart.
    - Describe exceptions to the general pattern.

3

Causality, Statistical Significance, and Substantive Significance

A common task when writing about numbers is describing a relationship between two or more variables, such as the association between math curriculum and student performance, or the associations among diet, exercise, and heart attack risk. After you portray the shape and size of the association, interpret the relationship, assessing whether it is "significant" or "important."

Although many people initially believe that importance is based only on the size of an association — the bigger the difference across groups, the more important the association — in practice, this appraisal involves a bit more thought. There are three key questions to consider. First, is the association merely a spurious correlation, or is there an underlying *causal* relationship between the variables? Second, is that association *statistically* significant? And third, is it *substantively* significant or meaningful? Only if all three criteria are satisfied does it make sense to base programs or policy on that association, seeking to improve student performance by changing math curriculums, for example. To provide a common basis for understanding these principles, below I review some needed statistical terms and concepts of study design and provide references that treat these concepts in greater depth.

■ CAUSALITY

Many policy issues or applied scientific topics address questions such as, If we were to change *X*, would *Y* get better? Will a new type of antifreeze have a less detrimental environmental impact than those currently in use? If we dye white-haired people's hair some other color, will it increase their life spans? For permanent characteristics like gender, the question is slightly different: Is the difference across groups real, such that targeting cases based on those traits would be an appropriate strategy? Is it really gender that explains lower average income among women (implying gender discrimination), or are differences in work experience the cause?

Explanations for Associations

Anyone with even a passing acquaintance with statistics has probably heard the phrase "correlation does not necessarily mean causation." If an association between two variables X and Y is statistically significant (see below), that does not necessarily mean that X caused Y or that Y caused X. An association between two variables can be due to causality, confounding, bias, or simple happenstance.

Causal Associations and Reverse Causation

A causal association means that if the ostensible cause ("predictor" or "independent" variable) is changed, the hypothesized effect ("outcome" or "dependent" variable) will change in response. If a new curriculum is really the cause of better math performance, then adopting that curriculum should improve test scores. Establishing a plausible mechanism by which the first variable could affect the second helps build the case for a causal association. If you can show that the new math curriculum improves test scores by addressing previously neglected math facts or skills, that information strengthens the argument that the new curriculum is the reason for the better performance. To identify such mechanisms, know the theoretical context and base of existing knowledge for your topic.

Reverse causation occurs when what was believed to be the cause is actually the effect. For example, newspaper vendors are among the least healthy of all workers. How could that be? Selling newspapers doesn't seem like a very risky enterprise. It turns out that people who are too ill or disabled to perform other jobs are more likely than other people to become newspaper vendors because they are able to sell papers despite health problems that would prevent them from doing other jobs. Hence the ill health is what causes the occupation choice, not the reverse. To detect reverse causation, consider the time sequence of the two variables: which occurred first?

Confounding

If two variables are associated because of their mutual association with another variable, that relationship is *confounded* by that third variable (Abramson 1994). In some relationships affected by confounding, the third variable completely explains the association between the other two, in which case we say that association is *spurious*. People with white hair have higher mortality than people with other hair colors, but dyeing their hair black or blond is unlikely to improve their survival chances. Why? Because both the white hair and higher mortality are caused by old age (with some variation, of course), so the association between hair color and mortality is spurious rather than causal — it is wholly explained by the fact that both are associated with age.

In other associations, confounding is only a partial explanation: taking into account one or more confounding factors reduces the size of the association between a predictor and outcome, but the predictor retains some explanatory role. For example, both a high salt diet and a lack of exercise are associated with higher risk of a heart attack, but diet and exercise are correlated. Thus when both are considered simultaneously, the size of the association between each predictor and heart attack risk is reduced; each of those variables confounds the relationship between the other predictor and heart attacks. Again, consider the theoretical and empirical context of your topic to assess whether confounding might be occurring.

Bias

Bias is a systematic error in the observed patterns of one or more variables relative to their true values. In contrast to random error, where some measured values are higher than their actual values and some are lower, bias means that measurements consistently deviate from the true value in the same direction (Moore 1997). Bias can occur for several reasons, broadly classified into problems related to sampling and those related to measurement.

Sampling issues affect how cases are selected for a study. For instance, low-income families are less likely to have telephones. Thus studies that collect data using a telephone survey often underrepresent poor people, leading to biased estimates of knowledge, health, and other outcomes related to socioeconomic status. Another example: people who volunteer and qualify for a study are often different from nonparticipants. To be eligible for the Women's Health Initiative study of hormone replacement therapy (HRT), participants had to be free of heart disease at the start of the study, never have used HRT previously, and be willing to take HRT for several years — much longer than is typically prescribed (Kolata 2003). Hence the study findings might not apply to all women considering HRT. In these situations, the apparent association does not reflect the real pattern because the sample is not representative of the population of interest (see "Representativeness" in chapter 10).

Measurement problems relate to the ways data are collected, whether due to subjective reporting or bias in objective measurement. Respondents may shape their answers to more closely conform to social norms — playing down stigmatizing traits such as mental illness or exaggerating desirable attributes like income, for example. Or, an improperly calibrated scale might falsely add to the measured weights of every specimen.

As you assess an association between two or more variables, be alert to possible sampling or measurement biases that might cause the observed association to differ from the pattern in the population from which your sample is drawn. See Schutt (2001) or Moore (1997) for more on bias.

Assessing Causality

How can you tell whether a relationship between two or more variables is causal? In the mid-1960s an advisory committee to the surgeon general agreed upon five criteria for establishing causality in epidemiologic studies (Morton, Hebel, and McCarter 2001). Four of those criteria are applicable to evaluating associations in other disciplines,[1] and similar principles have been established for the social sciences and other disciplines (Schutt 2001).

- *Consistency of association.* The association is observed in several different populations using different types of study design.
- *Strength of association.* A bigger difference in outcomes between cases with and without the purported causal factor indicates a stronger association.
- *Temporal relationship.* The cause preceded the effect. A correlation between two variables measured at the same time gives weaker evidence than one measuring the relationship between changes in the supposed cause and subsequent responses in the outcome.
- *Mechanism.* There is a plausible means by which the alleged cause could affect the outcome.

Much scientific research aims to assess whether relationships are causal, using empirical evidence as the basis of evaluation. Certain types of data are better for evaluating a potentially causal relationship. Data from a randomized experiment or other "before and after" design provide more convincing evidence of a causal relationship than data where both the hypothesized cause and the hypothesized effect are measured at the same time ("cross-sectional" data). See Lilienfeld and Stolley (1994), Davis (1985) or Morton et al. (2001) for a thorough discussion of study design and causal inference.

- An experimental study comparing math scores from schools with similar demographic and social makeup can provide convincing causal evidence. In an experiment, schools are randomly assigned into either the new or the old math curriculum, using a coin toss, lottery, or random number table to decide which schools get which curriculum. Random assignment ensures that other possible causes of improved math scores are equally distributed among schools with both new and old curriculums, so those other factors cannot explain differences in observed test scores.

- Even in the absence of an experimental study, an improvement in math test scores after introduction of a new curriculum can lend support for the curriculum as the reason for better performance. The time sequence (temporal relationship) of curriculum adoption and math performance is unambiguous. However, other concurrent changes such as a decrease in class size or increase in teacher experience could be the reason for the better scores, so those factors should be taken into account before inferring cause.

- A cross-sectional comparison of math scores for two schools, each of which happens to use one type of math curriculum, is less compelling because other factors that affect test scores could affect curriculum choice: an innovative school with involved parents or a larger budget might be more likely to adopt the new curriculum *and* to have better math scores regardless of curriculum, confounding the association between curriculum and math performance.

For situations in which random assignment isn't possible, "quasi-experimental" conditions are simulated by taking into consideration measures of possible confounding or mediating factors. For example, observational studies of different math curriculums compare performance differences by controlling statistically for other possible causal factors such as parental involvement and school budget (Allison 1999; Miller forthcoming). Because it is impossible to measure all ways in which schools differ, however, evidence of causality from quasi-experimental studies is weaker than evidence from randomized experiments.

Causality as the Basis for Interventions

If confounding, bias, or reverse causality explains a correlation between variables, that association is not a good basis for policies or interventions aimed at changing the outcome. However, if a residual association remains after you take confounding, bias, and reverse causation into account, then evaluate both the substantive and statistical significance of the remaining association to determine its policy relevance. For example, if exercise retains a large, statistically significant association with lowered heart attack risk even after the effect of diet has been considered, exercise programs could be an appropriate intervention against heart attacks.

Writing about Causality

How does knowledge about causality affect the way you write about relationships among the concepts under study? For analyses intended to inform policy or other interventions, convey whether the association is causal and describe possible causal mechanisms. Discuss alternative explanations such as bias, confounding, or reverse causation, indicating whether or not they are taken into account in your statistical analysis. For noncausal relationships, explain the confounders, biases, or reverse causation that gave rise to the observed association.

Vocabulary Issues

Carefully select the words you use to describe associations: verbs such as "affect" or "cause" and nouns such as "consequences" or "effects" all imply causality. "Correlated" or "associated" do not.

Poor: "The effect of white hair on mortality was substantial, with five times the risk of any other hair color."

Poor (version 2): "White hair increased the risk of dying by 400%."
The active verb ("increased") suggests that white hair brought about the higher mortality. The phrase "effect of X [white hair] on Y [mortality]" also implies causality. Avoid such wording unless you have good reason to suspect a causal association.

[Slightly] Better: "The whiter the hair, the higher the mortality rate" or "As hair gets whiter, mortality increases."
These versions are written in neutral, purely descriptive language, failing to provide guidance about whether these patterns are thought to be causal.

Better: "People with white hair had considerably higher mortality rates than people with a different color hair. However, most

people with white hair were over age 60 — a high-mortality age group — so the association between white hair and high mortality is probably due to their mutual association with older age."
Both the more neutral verb ("had") and linking both white hair and high mortality with old age help the audience grasp that white hair is not likely to be the cause of higher mortality. In this explanation, the focus is shifted from the attribute (white hair) to other possible differences between people who do and do not have that attribute that could explain (confound) the hair color/mortality pattern.

Similar considerations apply to statement of hypotheses: phrase your statement to convey whether you believe the relationship to be causal or merely a correlation.

Poor: "We expect that the new math curriculum will be associated with higher math scores."
In the absence of a statement to the contrary, most readers will interpret this to mean that the new curriculum is expected to cause better math performance.

Better: "We expect that adoption of the new mathematics curriculum will improve math scores."
By using an active verb ("improve"), this statement explicitly conveys that the curriculum change is an expected cause of better math performance.

Limitations of Study Design for Demonstrating Causality

While causality can be disproved by showing that even one of the causal criteria listed above is *not* true, it is much more difficult for one study to simultaneously show that all four criteria *are* true. It may be impossible to establish which event or condition occurred first, and often there are numerous potential unmeasured confounders and biases. For study designs that do not allow a cause-effect pattern to be tested well, point out those weaknesses and their implications for inferring causality (see "Data and Methods in the Discussion Section" in chapter 10 for additional guidelines).

Poor: "In 1999, School Q, which adopted the new math curriculum two years ago, averaged 10 percentiles higher on a standardized math test than did School R, which continued to use an older curriculum."
By omitting any reference to the way the study was conducted and how that might affect interpretation of the data, this explanation implies that the new curriculum is the cause of Q's better performance.

Better: "In 1999, School Q, which adopted the new math curriculum two years ago, averaged 10 percentiles higher on a standardized math test than School R, which continued to use an older curriculum. However, School Q is in a higher income district which could afford the new curriculum and has smaller average class sizes and more experienced teachers than School R. Consequently, School Q's better performance cannot be attributed exclusively to the new curriculum."

By mentioning alternative explanations for the observed cross-sectional differences in math performance, this version explains that the evidence for beneficial effects of the new curriculum is relatively weak. A discussion of other study designs that could better assess causality would further strengthen this explanation.

■ STATISTICAL SIGNIFICANCE

Statistical significance is a formal way of assessing whether observed associations are likely to be explained by chance alone. It is an important consideration for most descriptions of associations between variables, particularly in scientific reports or papers. In the absence of disclaimers about lack of statistical significance, readers tend to interpret reported associations as "real" and may use them to explain certain patterns or to generate solutions to problems. This is especially true if the association has already been shown to be causal.

For most of your quantitative writing, you can avoid a complicated statistical discussion. Your statistics professor aside, many readers neither want nor need to hear how you arrived at your conclusions about statistical significance. As in the carpenter analogy, the quality of the final product is affected by work done behind the scenes, but consumers don't want to see the details of that messy work. It is up to you — the tradesperson — to ensure that appropriate steps were done correctly. For statistically oriented audiences, you might enhance their faith in your work by naming the statistical tests you used, just as a carpenter might try to boost confidence in his work by mentioning that he used Pella windows or Owens Corning insulation.

An Aside on Descriptive and Inferential Statistics

How is statistical significance assessed? Here's a quick review of the logic behind statistical tests, to familiarize you with vocabulary you may encounter and how the concepts are used to test the question of whether an observed difference can be attributed to chance.

For a more thorough grounding in these concepts, consult Moore (1997) or Utts (1999). See Miller (forthcoming) for a discussion of ways to present statistical information to different audiences.

Even if you have not studied statistics, you have probably encountered *descriptive statistics,* such as the mean, median, mode, and range in math scores among elementary school students. *Inferential statistics* take things a step further, testing whether differences between groups are statistically significant — not likely to occur by chance alone if there were no real association — as a way of formally comparing average math scores between schools, for example.

Inferential statistical tests evaluate how likely it would be to obtain the observed difference or a larger difference between groups under the assumption that there is no difference. In statistical lingo, the assumption of "no difference" is called the *null hypothesis.* In the math example, the null hypothesis would state that average test scores for schools using the new and old math curriculums are equal. Most studies are based on a sample or subset of all possible cases; thus random error affects estimates of average test scores and must be taken into account when assessing differences between groups. For example, inferences about the benefits of the math curriculum might be based on comparison of scores from a random sample of students rather than from all students following those curriculums. Because of random variation, the average scores in each of the curriculum groups will vary from one sample to the next. The extent of variation around the sample average is measured by the standard error of that estimate, which is affected by the number of cases used in the calculation (see below).

In a twist of logic that many novice statisticians find perplexing, the next step in inferential statistics is to try to *reject* the null hypothesis by posing the question "If the null hypothesis is really true, how likely would it be to observe associations as large as or larger than those seen in the current analysis simply by chance alone?" To answer this question, a *test statistic* such as the *t*-test statistic or chi-square statistic is computed from the estimate and its standard error. A *p-value* is then obtained by comparing the test statistic against the pertinent statistical distribution.

The *p*-value gives the probability of obtaining a score difference at least as large as that observed in the sample, if in fact there is no difference between all students following the two curriculums. The lower the *p*-value, the lower the chance of falsely rejecting the null hypothesis. Put differently, a very small *p*-value corresponds to a very low probability of incorrectly concluding that there is a difference in achievement under the new versus old curriculum if in reality the two yield the same student performance. So, to conclude that a difference is statistically significant, we want a low p-value.

The "p < 0.05 Rule"

The standard criterion for "statistically significant" is a p-value $<$ 0.05 on the pertinent statistical test, although this cutoff varies somewhat by discipline. That $p < 0.05$ means that if the null hypothesis were true, we would observe a difference as large as or larger than the sample value in fewer than 5 out of 100 samples (less than 5%) drawn from the same population. Suppose a study of the two math curriculums obtained a p-value of 0.001. This means that if in truth there was no real difference in math performance between the old and new curriculums and we were to obtain 1,000 different samples, in only *one* of these samples would the score differences be as large or larger than in the sample we studied. This p-value of 0.001 is less than 0.05, so by the $p < 0.05$ rule we reject the null hypothesis of no difference between old and new curriculums. In other words, this p-value suggests that it is extremely unlikely that the observed difference in test scores could be due only to random variation between samples, lending support to the idea that there is a "real" difference in how the students perform under the two different curriculums.

Sample Size and Statistical Tests

The number of cases affects the related statistical tests: the more cases used to calculate the average score, the smaller the standard error of that average. A smaller standard error reflects less chance variability in the estimate. Hence a two-point difference in average test scores between two groups might not be statistically significant if only a few students in each school were involved in the study, but the same two-point difference might be statistically significant if more students were tested.

Confidence Intervals

An alternative way of expressing results of a statistical test is to present the *confidence interval* around the estimate. The 95% confidence interval (abbreviated "95% CI") is a range of values such that in 95 out of every 100 samples drawn from the same population, the sample mean will fall within two standard errors of the true population mean.[2] Suppose our sample yields a mean math test score of 73.1 points with a standard error of 2.1 points. The 95% CI is 73.1 ± (2 × 2.1), so we can be 95% sure that the average test score for the population falls between 68.9 and 77.3 points. Conceptually, a 95% confidence interval corresponds to a $p < 0.05$ for the statistical test.[3]

How Statistical Significance (or Lack Thereof) Affects Your Writing

How should you write about results of statistical tests? The answer depends on statistical significance of findings, your audience, and the length and detail of the work.

Statistically Significant Results

Many academic journals specify that you use a table to report statistical test results for all variables, but then limit your text description to only those results that are statistically significant, in most cases using $p < 0.05$ as the criterion. The $p < 0.05$ rule of thumb also applies for other audiences, although you will use and present the statistical information differently (see below). Emphasizing statistically significant findings is especially important if you are investigating several different factors, such as how gender, race, class size, teacher experience, and teacher's major field of study each affected students' math test scores. If only some traits associated with math scores are statistically significant, focus your discussion on those rather than giving equal prominence to all factors. This approach helps readers answer the main question behind the analysis: which factors can help improve math performance the most?

When to Report Results That Are Not Statistically Significant

The "$p < 0.05$ rule" notwithstanding, a nonstatistically significant finding can be highly salient if that result pertains to the main topic you are investigating: if the lack of statistical significance runs contrary to theory or previously reported results, report the numbers, size of the association, and the lack of statistical significance. In such situations, the lack of a difference between groups answers a key question in the analysis, so highlight it in the concluding section of the work (see "Numeric Information in a Concluding Section" in chapter 11).

Suppose earlier studies showed that students in School A were more likely to pass a standardized math test than students in School B.

After a new math curriculum was implemented in School B, you find no difference between math scores in the two schools, or that the observed difference is not statistically significant. Mention the change in both size and statistical significance of the difference between the schools' scores compared to before the curriculum change, then explicitly relate the new finding back to theoretical expectations and results of previous studies. This approach applies to a short newspaper article or a policy brief as well as to scientific reports or papers.

"Borderline" Statistical Significance

A controversial issue is what to do if the p-value is only slightly above 0.05, say $p = 0.06$ or $p = 0.08$. Such values fall in a gray area: strictly speaking they are not statistically significant according to conventional criteria, but they seem oh-so-close that they are difficult to ignore. How you handle such findings depends on several factors that influence statistical tests:

- The effect size
- The sample size
- The value of the test statistic and its associated p-value

If the effect size (e.g., difference in math test scores between two schools or correlation between exercise and heart attacks) is very small, a larger number of cases is unlikely to increase the statistical significance of the association. Such associations are unlikely to be of substantive interest even if they are real and causal (see "substantive significance" below), so treat them as if they were not statistically significant. On the other hand, if the effect size is moderate to large, the p-value is in the gray area between $p < 0.05$ and $p < 0.10$, *and* the sample size is small, report the effect and its p-value, and mention the small sample size and its effect on the standard error. Unfortunately, all of these criteria are subjective (What is a "moderate effect size?" A "small sample size?") and opinions vary by discipline, so learn the conventions used in your field.

Writing about Statistical Significance

Tailor your description of statistical significance to meet the needs and abilities of your audience.

Nontechnical Audiences

For most nontechnical audiences, keep discussion of statistical significance very simple or omit it entirely. No matter how carefully you try to phrase it, a discussion of the purpose and interpretation of statistical tests may confuse readers who are not trained in statistics. Instead of reporting *p*-values or test statistics, use statistical tests and consideration of causality as screens for what you report and how you discuss findings, or paraphrase the concepts behind the statistics into everyday language.

Poor (unless you are teaching introductory statistics): "In 1997, the mean score on the mathematics test for fourth graders in School A was 62.7% correct. The mean score on the same test in School B was 72.0% correct. The standard error of the difference in means was 2.9. Because the differences in means (9.3 percentage points) is more than twice the standard error of the difference, we conclude that the difference cannot be attributed to random variation in scores at the two schools." *This description puts too much emphasis on the logic behind the statistical test. Skip the statistics lesson and just report whether the difference between the two schools' test scores is statistically significant.*

Better (for a lay audience): "On a mathematics test given to fourth graders recently, students in School B achieved a higher average score than students in School A (62.7% and 72.0% correct, respectively). The chances of observing a difference this big in our study if there were no real difference between groups was less than one in a thousand." *This description reports the two scores and suggests that they represented different levels of achievement. Because it is for a lay audience, statistical significance is worded without reference to technical concepts such as* p-values *or test statistics.*

If, contrary to previous evidence, the difference is not statistically significant, write:

"In 2001, Schools A and B achieved similar average math scores on a standardized mathematics test given to fourth graders (71.7% and 72.0% correct, respectively). These results run counter to findings from 1997, which showed appreciably poorer performance in School A than in School B. The difference in the schools' current scores could easily have occurred by chance alone." *This version explains that in 2001 the two schools' scores were very close, and that the recent pattern differs from what was previously observed. Statistical significance is implied in the statement about "appreciably poorer scores"* in the earlier study, and lack of statistical significance in the new study with the phrase *"chance alone."*

Scientific Audiences

Statistically proficient readers expect a description of statistical results, but statistical significance is discussed differently in different parts of scientific papers. A typical scientific paper is organized into an introduction, data and methods section, results section, and discussion and conclusions (see chapters 10 and 11 for additional examples).

Results sections. In the results section of a quantitative piece, report the findings of statistical tests along with descriptors of the size and shape of relationships, following the guidelines in chapters 9 and 11. Indicators of statistical significance are expected features, whether in tables, text, or charts. Report exact *p*-values to two decimal places, writing "$p < 0.01$" for smaller values (see "Choosing a Fitting Number of Digits and Decimal Places" in chapter 4). Standard errors can be reported in a table.

In the prose description, emphasize findings for the key variables in your research question, then limit description of other variables to those that were statistically significant, or follow the discussion of statistically significant findings with a simple list of those that were not.

"On a mathematics test given to fourth graders in fall 2001, students in School B achieved a higher average score than students in School A (62.7% and 72.0% correct, respectively; $p < 0.001$)."
This description explicitly mentions the result of the statistical test (in this case, the p-value*), along with the average scores.*

Alternatively, express statistical significance using a confidence interval:

"On a mathematics test given to fourth graders in fall 2001, school B's average scores were statistically significantly lower than those in School A[, as demonstrated by the fact that the respective confidence intervals do not overlap]. Students in School B scored on average 62.7% of questions correct (95% confidence interval [CI]: 58.5% to 66.9%), as against an average of 72.0% correct in School A (95% CI: 70.0% to 74.0%).

By reporting the confidence intervals around each estimate, this version gives a range of substantive values for each school's average score, and allows readers to assess how the two schools' ranges compare. Include the phrase in brackets only for readers who are not familiar with how to interpret confidence intervals. Complement the written description with a chart showing the 95% CI around the estimated average scores for each school (see "High/Low/Close Charts" in chapter 7).

For findings that are not statistically significant:

"Math performance did not differ according to race, gender, or class size."
In a results section of a scientific paper, wording such as "did not differ" implies lack of a statistically significant difference. Report the math scores for each group and the associated test statistics in a table or chart, either with the text (for a longer report) or in an appendix.

For borderline cases such as when the *p*-value is slightly above 0.05 and sample sizes are small:

"Math scores for fall 2001 revealed no statistically significant difference between Schools A and B (67.7% and 72.0% correct, respectively; $p = 0.09$). However, only 20 students were tested in each school; hence standard errors were relatively large. With a larger number of cases, the observed effect might have reached conventional levels of statistical significance."
By reporting the p-value, this version shows that the difference in test scores narrowly missed statistical significance, then explains the effect of small sample size on the standard error.

Treat an equivalent interscholastic difference in scores and border-line *p*-value based on a large sample size as a nonsignificant finding, without discussion of effect size or sample size.

Discussion sections. For a quantitative article or report, summarize key findings in the discussion and conclusions section, then relate them back to the research question. Discuss both statistically signifi-cant and nonsignificant results related to your main research ques-tion but don't reiterate nonsignificant findings for less central vari-ables. To express the implications of your results, compare your major findings to theoretical expectations and previous empirical results in terms of size and statistical significance. Differences you discuss will typically be assumed to be statistically significant unless you state otherwise. In the discussion, describe statistical significance (or lack thereof) in terms of concepts and conclusions, using words rather than numeric results of statistical tests.

"An experimental study of the new math curriculum showed marked improvement in average test scores among students in high-income districts. In low-income districts, however, effects of the new curriculum were smaller and not statistically significant. Smaller class sizes were also associated with higher math scores, but did not explain the income difference in the effect of the new curriculum. Racial composition of the schools did not affect math performance."

The wording of this summary for the discussion section of a scientific paper is similar to that for a lay audience, but explicitly mentions statistical significance. Numeric results of statistical tests reported in the results section are not repeated in the discussion. To reiterate the importance of study design, the type of study is mentioned but without the nitty-gritty of sample size, data collection, and so forth from the data and methods section.

In all but the briefest articles, complete the picture by discussing possible reasons for discrepant findings about statistical significance from other studies, such as differences in the date or location of the study, the characteristics of the students involved, or how the data were collected (see "Data and Methods in the Discussion Section" in chapter 10). Similar principles apply to discussion of previous studies: when assessing the state of knowledge on a topic discuss only statistically significant findings as "real."

Executive summaries and issue briefs. In executive summaries, issue briefs, or other very short formats, focus on issues related to your main research question and emphasize only statistically significant differences. Those that are not statistically significant should be described as such or omitted. Provide verbal description rather than numeric results of statistical tests:

- "The new math curriculum raised average test scores by five points in high-income schools."
- "Average test scores in low-income schools were not affected by the new curriculum."
- "Smaller classes performed slightly better than large classes."

- "There was no difference between racial groups in math scores within schools of similar income level."

■ SUBSTANTIVE SIGNIFICANCE

The third aspect of the "importance" of a finding is whether the size of an association is substantively significant, which is just a fancy way of asking "So what?" or "How much does it matter?" Is the improvement in math performance large enough to justify the cost of adopting the new curriculum? Statistical significance alone is not a good basis for evaluating the importance of some difference or change. With a large enough sample size, even truly microscopic differences can be statistically significant. However, tiny differences are unlikely to be meaningful in a practical sense. If every fourth grader in the United States were included in a comparison of two different math curriculums, a difference of even half a point in average test scores might be statistically significant because the sample size was so large. Is it worth incurring the cost of producing and distributing the new materials and training many teachers in the new curriculum for such a small improvement?

To assess the substantive importance of an association, place it in perspective by providing evidence about how that half-point improvement translates into mastery of specific skills, the chances of being promoted to the next grade level, or some other real-world outcome to evaluate whether that change is worthwhile. Report and evaluate both the prevalence and consequences of a problem: preventing a rare but serious health risk factor may be less beneficial than preventing a more common, less serious risk factor. For scientific audiences, consider including attributable risk calculations (see Lilienfeld and Stolley 1994), cost-effectiveness analysis (e.g., Gold et al. 1996), or other methods of quantifying the net impact of proposed health treatments, policies, or other interventions as a final step in the results section. For others, integrate results of those computations into the discussion and conclusions.

Address substantive significance in the discussion section as you consider what your results mean in terms of your original research question.

Poor: "The association between math curriculums and test scores was not very substantively significant."

Most people won't know what "substantively significant" means. In addition, this version omits both the direction and size of the association, and doesn't help readers assess whether the change is big enough to matter.

Better (for a lay audience): "Is the new math curriculum worth the investment? Probably not: the half-point average improvement in test scores translates into only a small (5%) increase in the number of students who pass the test or who master important fourth-grade math skills such as multiplication or division. Implementing the new curriculum would cost an estimated $40 million, which could otherwise be spent on items such as reducing class sizes, which would yield larger educational gains."

This version gets straight to the point: is the improvement under the new curriculum big enough to make a meaningful difference? A rhetorical question is an effective way to make this kind of argument, particularly in spoken formats.

Better (for a scientific audience): "Although the improvement in math test scores associated with the new math curriculum is highly statistically significant, the change is substantively inconsequential, especially when the costs are considered: the half-point average increase in math scores corresponds to very few additional students achieving a passing score, or mastering important fourth-grade math skills such as multiplication or division. Spending the estimated $40 million needed to implement the new curriculum on reducing class sizes would likely yield greater improvements."

Like the lay version, this description puts the results back in the context of the original research question. Both substantive and statistical significance are explicitly mentioned; causality is implicitly addressed using words such as "change" and "increase."

■ RELATIONS AMONG CAUSALITY, STATISTICAL SIGNIFICANCE, AND SUBSTANTIVE SIGNIFICANCE

The consequence of a numeric association depends on whether that association is causal, statistically significant, and substantively meaningful. All three conditions are often necessary, and none alone may be sufficient to guarantee the importance of the association. Avoid a long discussion of how much something matters substantively if the association is not causal or the difference between groups is not statistically significant. In scientific papers, review the evidence for statistical and substantive significance and explain that those two perspectives have distinctly different purposes and interpretations, devoting a separate sentence or paragraph to each.

As you evaluate these criteria for the associations you are writing about, remember that even if one condition is satisfied, the others may not be.

- In nonexperimental studies, a statistically significant association does not necessarily mean causation: white hair and high mortality could be correlated .99 with $p < 0.001$, but that does not make white hair a cause of high mortality.
- Conversely, a causal relationship does not necessarily guarantee statistical significance: random error or bias can obscure effects of the curriculum change on math performance.
- Statistical significance does not necessarily translate into substantive importance: the new math curriculum effect could be statistically significant at $p < 0.05$, but the increment to math scores might be very small.
- Conversely, substantive importance does not ensure statistical significance: a large effect might not be statistically significant due to wide variation in the data or a small sample size.
- Causality does not automatically mean substantive importance: the new curriculum may improve math scores, but that change may be so slight as to be unworthy of investment.
- Substantive importance (a "big effect") does not automatically translate into causality, as in the white hair example.

■ CHECKLIST FOR CAUSALITY, STATISTICAL SIGNIFICANCE, AND SUBSTANTIVE SIGNIFICANCE

As you write about associations, discuss each of the following criteria as they pertain to your research question:

- Causality

    Explain the mechanisms linking the hypothesized cause with the presumed effect.

    Describe and weigh the merits of other, noncausal explanations, identifying sources of bias, confounding, or reverse causation.

- Statistical significance

    For a scientific audience,

    –report statistical significance in the results section (see chapters 9 and 11 for illustrative wording), mentioning p-values or confidence intervals in the text and reporting other types of statistical test results in a table;

    –return to statistical significance in the discussion, especially if findings are new or run counter to theory or previous studies. Restate findings in words, not numeric test results or p-values.

    For a nontechnical audience, use the results of statistical tests to decide which results to emphasize, but don't report the numeric details of the test results.

- Substantive significance

    Evaluate the substantive importance of a finding by translating it into familiar concepts such as overall cost (or cost savings) or improvements in specific skills.

    For a technical audience, consider quantifying the difference using z-scores.

- Integration of the three elements

    In your discussion or closing section, relate the findings back to the main research question, considering statistical significance, causality, and substantive significance together.

    For an observed numeric association to be used as the basis for a policy or intervention to improve the outcome under study, all three criteria should be satisfied.

Technical but Important
Five More Basic Principles

In addition to the principles covered in the previous two chapters, there are a handful of more technical issues to keep in mind as you write about numbers: understanding the types of variables you're working with, specifying units, examining the distributions of your variables, and finding standards against which to compare your data. These are important background steps before you decide which kinds of calculations, tables, and charts are appropriate, or select suitable values to contrast with one another. The final principle — choosing how many digits and decimal places to include — may seem trivial or merely cosmetic. However, measurement issues and ease of communication dictate that you select a level of numeric detail that fits your data and your audience.

■ UNDERSTAND TYPES OF VARIABLES

Information about types of variables affects your choice of comparisons. Some calculations make sense only for variables measured in continuous units, others only for those classified into categories. You cannot calculate the mean price for computers if those data were collected in categories of "less than $1,000" versus "$1,000 or more." Some variables allow only one response for each case, others permit more than one response. You cannot analyze patterns of multiple computer ownership if each person reported only which brand of computer they used most often.

Choice of tools for presenting numbers also is affected by type of variable and number of responses. In chapter 7, I explain why line or scatter charts are suitable for some types of variables, and bar or pie charts for others, and why some charts accommodate multiple responses per case while others work for only single-response variables. In chapter 9, I show how to describe distributions for different types of variables. For now, I introduce the vocabulary and properties of variable types.

There are two main characteristics of each variable to consider. Was it measured in continuous or categorical fashion? And, was each case allowed only one response or several responses?

Continuous versus Categorical Variables

Continuous Variables

Continuous variables are measured in units such as years (e.g., age or date), inches (e.g., height or distance), or dollars (e.g., income or price), including those with decimal or fractional values. Continuous variables are one of two types: *interval* and *ratio* — technical terms that I introduce to help you relate the concepts with those you may have encountered in statistics classes (Chambliss and Schutt 2003).

Interval variables can be compared using subtraction (calculating the interval between values; also known as the "absolute difference"; see chapter 5) but not division (calculating the ratio of two values; also known as "relative difference"). Temperature as we conventionally measure it (whether Fahrenheit or Celsius)[1] is an interval variable: if it was 30°F yesterday and 60°F today, it makes sense to say that it is 30 degrees hotter today, but not that it is twice as hot (Wolke 2000). And using a ratio to compare temperatures above and below zero (e.g., −20°F versus +20°F) would be truly misleading.

Ratio variables can be compared using either subtraction or division because a value of zero can be interpreted as the lowest possible value. Distance is an example of a ratio variable: if it is two miles from your house to the mini-mart but four miles to the supermarket, you could either say the supermarket is "two miles farther than" or "twice as far as" the mini-mart.

Categorical Variables

Categorical variables classify information into categories such as gender, race, or income group. They come in two flavors: *ordinal* and *nominal*. Ordinal ("ordered") variables have categories that can be ranked according to the values of those categories. A classic example is letter grades (A, B+, etc.). Nominal ("named") variables include gender, race, or religion, for which the categories have no inherent order.[2]

Continuous and categorical variables are not completely different animals. Continuous variables can be classified into categories. You can create a variable "age group" out of a variable measuring age in years: a nine-year-old would be classified as a child. However you can't create a detailed continuous age variable from a categorical variable that encompasses several values in each age group: knowing that someone is a child does not tell you whether he is one or nine or eleven years old. Categorical versions of continuous variables are useful for simplifying information (by grouping age into five- or ten-year age groups, for example), or for indicating whether values of a continuous variable fall above or below a cutoff like retirement age.

Defining Sensible Categories

Creating good categorical variables takes careful thought. If each case can have exactly one valid value, then every case should fall into exactly one group — no more, no less. Each person is either male or female, and has only one age and one total income at a time. In addition, every person has a gender, age, and income (even if it is $0.00 or negative). In the jargon of set theory, which you might remember from middle school math, classifications such as these are known as *mutually exclusive* (nonoverlapping) and *exhaustive* (encompassing all possible responses). "Under 18 years," "18–64," and "65 and older" are mutually exclusive and exhaustive age groups because the youngest age group starts at zero and the oldest has no upper age limit, covering the full range of possible answers.

Although mutually exclusive and exhaustive seem like straightforward concepts, they can be difficult to implement. Through 1990, the U.S. Census question on race allowed each person to mark only one answer. For people who considered themselves to be multiracial, however, marking one race was not sufficient — the race categories weren't mutually exclusive. To resolve this issue, the 2000 census permitted each person to classify themselves as more than one race, and tabulations of race include both single- and multiple-race categories. These new categories allowed each person to be counted once and only once. According to the new tabulations, multiple-race individuals accounted for about 2.4% of the total population (U.S. Census Bureau 2002a).

A second problem arose for people of Hispanic origin: the Census Bureau treats Hispanic origin and race as separate characteristics covered in separate questions. According to Census Bureau definitions, Hispanic persons can be of any race, and persons of any race can be of Hispanic origin. However, many people of Hispanic origin consider their race to be "Hispanic," not "white," "black," "Asian," or "Native American," so they often left the race question blank or checked "other" (Navarro 2003). For them, the list of categories was incomplete — in other words, it was not exhaustive.

"Other." A common practice is to create a category for "other" responses, allowing for answers researchers didn't anticipate. A survey of favorite ice cream flavors might list chocolate, vanilla, and strawberry, but overlook bubblegum blowout or marshmallow mint. An "other" category also permits uncommon responses to be combined instead of creating separate categories for flavors that are mentioned by only one or two people. Everyone's response fits somewhere, but there aren't dozens of tiny categories to record and present in every table or chart.

If "other" encompasses a large share of cases, however, it can obscure important information, as when many Hispanics mark "other" for race on the census. Sometimes the response "none of the above" is used to indicate "other," but that approach misses the opportunity to find out what answer does apply. To avoid this problem, often questionnaires include a blank for respondents to specify what "other" means in their case. If many respondents list similar answers, they can be grouped into a new category for analysis or future data collection.

Missing values. If you've ever collected data, you know that people sometimes skip questions, refuse to respond, write something illegible or inappropriate, or mark more answers than are allowed. To account for all cases, an "unknown" or "missing" category is used to tabulate the frequency of missing information — an important fact when assessing whether your data are representative of the population under study (see chapter 10 or Chambliss and Schutt 2003). In some studies, detailed reasons for missing data are retained.

Not applicable. Some questions pertain only to some cases. In a survey asking whether someone has changed residences recently and if so when, the "when" question does not apply to those who did not move. To make sure every case is accounted for, such cases are classified "not applicable." Differentiating "not applicable" from "missing" makes it easier for cases to be omitted from calculations that don't pertain to them, leaving out those who didn't move from an analysis of timing of moves rather than incorrectly lumping them in with people who did move but neglected to report when.

Single- versus Multiple-Response Questions

For characteristics like gender or age, each case has only one value. Other situations call for more than one answer per respondent. A school board election asks each voter to select three candidates, or a survey asks respondents to list all types of health insurance coverage within their families, for example. The number of possible responses does not determine the type of variable — both single- and multiple-response items can be either continuous or categorical.

For many multiple-response questions, some people mark no responses, others mark several, and a few mark all possible answers. In some families, everyone has the same kind of health insurance, such as employer-sponsored, or Medicaid. For those families, one response characterizes their insurance coverage. Some families have several kinds of health insurance, such as both employer-sponsored and Medicare, or both Medicaid and Medicare. Two or three responses are needed to characterize their coverage. Families that lack health insurance do not fit any categories. (On some surveys, "uninsured" might be listed as an option, in which case every family would have at least one response.)

Why does it matter that the number of answers to a question can vary from none to many? Because the principle of "mutually exclusive" does not apply to variables created from those questions. Having employer-sponsored health insurance does not preclude a family from also having Medicare for its elderly or disabled members, for example. If you tally up the total number of responses in all categories, they will exceed the number of families surveyed. For cases where none of the responses apply, the total of all responses can be less than the total number of families surveyed. Consequently, the kinds of mathematical consistency checks used to evaluate the distribution of a single-response variable cannot be used for multiple-response questions. For single-response questions, the frequencies of all responses will add up to 100% of the cases. For multiple-response questions, that total could range from 0% (if no one marked any of the categories) to several hundred percent (if many cases marked several categories).

Before you include numbers in your writing, familiarize yourself with how the data were collected, to ensure that you make sensible choices about calculations, consistency checks, and ways of presenting the information.

■ SPECIFY UNITS

To interpret and compare your numbers, specify the units of observation and the units of measurement and systems of measurement. Make a note of the units for any numeric facts you collect from other sources so you can use and interpret them correctly.

Dimensions of Units

Unit of Analysis

The unit of analysis (also known as the "level of aggregation") identifies the level at which numbers are reported. If you measure poverty in number of persons with income below some threshold, your unit of analysis is a person. If you count families with income below a threshold, your unit of analysis is a family. Poverty can also be calculated at the census tract, county, state, or national level. Each approach is valid, but values with different levels of aggregation cannot be compared with one another. In 2001, there were 32.9 million poor *people* but 6.8 million poor *families* in the United States (Proctor and Dalaker 2002). When collecting information to compare against your data, look for a consistent level of aggregation.

Level of aggregation pertains to most quantitative topics. For instance, cancer penetration can be measured by the number of cells affected within a particular organ, cancerous organs in a patient, people afflicted within a family or town, or the number of towns with cases. Avoid confusion by stating the level of aggregation along with the numbers:

> "Mr. Jones's cancer had metastasized, affecting three major organ systems."

> "Breast cancer is widespread in the area, with at least five towns having prevalence rates well above the national average."

Units of Measurement

There are two aspects of units of measurement: scale and system of measurement.

Scale. Scale, or order of magnitude, refers to multiples of units.[3] Are you reporting number of people, number of *thousands* of people, *millions* of people? Consider the following error of omission, which had data analysts scratching their heads: a utility company observed a sudden and substantial drop-off in demand for electricity at the end

Electricity demand, Industrytown, 1978–1979

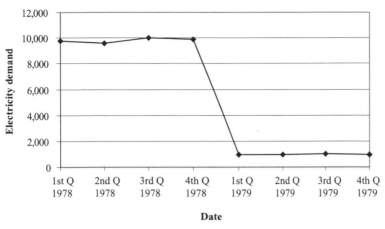

Figure 4.1. Effect of a change in scale of reported data on apparent trends

of 1978 between periods of fairly steady demand (figure 4.1). At first, researchers looked for a real, causal explanation. The region had several major industrial clients. Had one of them closed? Had a competing electricity provider opened up shop? In fact, the apparent drop was due to a change in the scale of units used to report electricity demand, from hundreds of megawatt-hours to thousands of megawatt-hours. The actual amount of electricity used was fairly stable.

System of measurement. There is plenty of room for confusion in a world where metric, British, and other systems of measurement coexist. Virtually every dimension of our experience that is quantified — distance (feet or meters), mass (pounds or kilograms), velocity (miles per hour or kilometers per hour), volume (quarts or liters), money (dollars or euros or pesos or yen), dates (Christian or Jewish or other calendar), and time (standard time, daylight saving time, military time) — can be measured using any of several systems.

The embarrassing experience of the Mars Climate Orbiter in 1999 is a classic illustration of what can happen if units are not specified. Engineers who built the spacecraft specified its thrust in pounds, which are British units. NASA scientists thought the information was in newtons, which are metric units. The miscalculation was overlooked through years of design, building, and launch, and the spacecraft missed its target by roughly 60 miles (Pollack 1999). Even rocket scientists make basic, easily avoidable mistakes about units. Don't emulate them.

Writing about Units

Incorporate units of observation and measurement into the sentence with the pertinent numbers.

"In 1998, per capita income in the United States was $20,120 (U.S. Census Bureau 1999a)."
This sentence includes information on units of measurement (dollars), units of observation (per capita means "for each person") and the W's (what, when, where).

Definitions of Units

Familiar units such as dollars, numbers of people, and degrees Fahrenheit can be used without defining them first. Define unfamiliar or specialized measures such as constant dollars, age-standardized death rates, or seasonally adjusted rates before you use them, and provide a standard citation to explain the calculation. Remember that what is familiar to a group of experts might be completely Greek to another audience; adjust your explanations accordingly.

Inexperienced writers often fail to explain their units precisely or completely, particularly for common but tricky numbers that express relationships between two quantities such as parts of a whole, the relative size of two groups, or rates. For variables that are measured in percentages, proportions, rates, or other types of ratios, include phrases such as "of ____," "per ____," or "compared to ____" so your figures can be interpreted.

Ratios. Ratios are simply one number divided by another. They measure the relative size of two quantities. Sometimes the quantities in the numerator and denominator are mutually exclusive subsets of the same whole. For instance, the sex ratio is defined as number of males per 100 females. Some ratios divide unrelated quantities. For example, population density is number of people per land area (e.g., per square mile).

Proportions, percentages, and fractions. Proportions (and their cousins, percentages) are a special type of ratio in which a subset is divided by the whole, such as males divided by total population. Percentages are simply proportions multiplied by 100. If the proportion

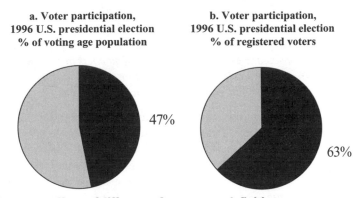

a. Voter participation,
1996 U.S. presidential election
% of voting age population

b. Voter participation,
1996 U.S. presidential election
% of registered voters

47%

63%

**Figure 4.2. Effects of different referent group definitions
on percentage calculations.**
Source: Institute for Democracy and Electoral Assistance 1999.

male is 0.50, then 50% of the population is male. Do not make the all-too-common mistake of treating proportions and percentages interchangeably; they differ by a factor of 100.

For measures such as proportions, percentages, and fractions that compare parts to a whole, make it clear what "the whole" comprises. In technical terms, what does the denominator include? If I had a nickel for every time I have written "percentage of what?" in the margins of a paper, I would be rich. Consider the following statistics on voter turnout from figure 4.2:

Poor: "In 1996, the voter turnout for the presidential election
was 63%."
*Is voter turnout measured as a percentage of the voting age population
(figure 4.2a), or as a percentage of all registered voters (figure 4.2b)?
Because some people of voting age are not registered to vote, the two
measures cannot be directly compared, but to avoid that mistake,
readers need to know which measure is reported.*

Better: "In 1996, 63% of the 146 million registered voters
participated in the U.S. presidential election."
*Here, number of registered voters is identified as the basis of
comparison, so this number can be compared with equivalently
defined voter participation rates for other years or places.*

Best: "In 1996, 63% of the 146 million registered voters participated
in the U.S. presidential election. As a percentage of the voting
age population (197 million people), however, voter turnout was

only 47%, revealing a large pool of potential voters who did not participate."

By specifying the denominator for each statistic, this version gives the information needed to assess comparability of numbers from other sources. The description is enhanced by contrasting the two measures of voter participation and explaining how they are different.

When relationships involve two or more variables, such as the association between poverty and age group, "percentage of what?" is more complicated. In cross-tabulations like table 4.1, there are several possible definitions of the whole against which some part is being compared. Depending on the question you are asking, you might report the percentage *of the total population* that is in each of the six possible poverty/age group combinations (table 4.1a), the percentage *of each poverty category* that falls into each age group (table 4.1b), or the percentage *of each age group* that is poor (table 4.1c).

Approximately one-third of the poor are children (<18 years old; table 4.1b), but one-sixth of children are poor (table 4.1c).[4] These values have completely different meanings, so specify what subgroup is being compared to what whole entity.

Poor: "In 2002, there were a lot of poor children in the United States (16.7%)."
Does 16.7% refer to poor children out of all people, *poor children out of* all poor people *(both incorrect in this case), or poor children out of* all children *(correct)?*

Better: "In 2002, 16.7% of children in the United States were poor."
The referent group (children) for the percentage is stated, clarifying interpretation of the statistic.

Best: "In 2002, 16.7% of children were poor, compared to 10.6% of people aged 18 to 64, and 10.4% of those aged 65 or older."
This sentence makes it clear that the observed poverty rate among children is higher than that for other age groups. Both the units of observation (persons) and measurement (percentage of the age group) are specified and are consistent with one another, hence the comparison is correctly done.

Rates. Rates are a type of ratio with the added element of time. For example, velocity is often measured in miles per hour, death rates as number of deaths per 100,000 people within a specified period of time (Lilienfeld and Stolley 1994). Report the time interval to which

Table 4.1. Three tables based on the same cross-tabulation: (a) Joint distribution, (b) Composition within subgroups, (c) Rates of occurrence within subgroups

a. Poverty by age group, United States, 2002

Age group (years)	Thousands of persons (% of total population)		
	Poor	Non-poor	Total
<18	12,133 (4.3%)	60,520 (21.2%)	72,653 (25.5%)
18–64	18,861 (6.6%)	159,073 (55.8%)	177,934 (62.4%)
65+	3,576 (1.3%)	30,809 (10.8%)	34,385 (12.1%)
Total	34,570 (12.2%)	250,402 (87.8%)	284,972 (100.0%)

b. Age distribution (%) by poverty status, United States, 2002

Age group (years)	Poor		Non-poor		Total	
	Number (1,000s)	% of all poor	Number (1,000s)	% of all non-poor	Number (1,000s)	% of total pop.
<18	12,133	35.1	60,520	24.2	72,653	25.5
18–64	18,861	54.6	159,073	63.5	177,934	62.4
65+	3,576	10.3	30,809	12.3	34,385	12.1
Total	34,570	100.0	250,402	100.0	284,972	100.0

c. Poverty rates (%) by age group, United States, 2002

Age group (years)	# Poor (1,000s)	Total pop. (1,000s)	% Poor within age group
<18	12,133	72,653	16.7
18–64	18,861	177,934	10.6
65+	3,576	34,385	10.4
Total	34,570	284,972	12.1

Source: Proctor and Dalaker 2003

the rate pertains along with the units and concepts in both the numerator and denominator.

A common error is to confuse a death rate for a particular subgroup with deaths in that group as a proportion of all (total) deaths, as in the following example.

Poor: "In the United States in 1999, one-third died from heart disease."

One-third of what? Deaths (correct, in this case)? People? By failing to specify one-third of what, the author leaves this sentence open to misinterpretation: the fraction of all deaths that occurred due to heart disease is not the same as the death rate (per population) from heart disease.

Poor (version 2): "One-third of people died from heart disease in the United States in 1999."

This version is even worse because it implies that one out of every three living people died of heart disease in 1999 — a figure that would translate into roughly 84 million heart disease deaths in the United States that year. In fact, the actual death toll from all causes combined was only 2.3 million. Don't make the mistake of thinking that "one-third is one-third," without specifying the "of what?" part of the fraction.

Best: "In 1999, the number of people who died of heart disease in the United States was 725,000, accounting for roughly one out of every three deaths that year. The death rate from heart disease was 265.9 deaths per 100,000 people (Anderson 2001)."

This version conveys that heart disease accounted for approximately one-third of deaths that year. Mentioning the death rate clarifies the other perspective on heart disease — the annual risk of dying from that cause.

■ EXAMINE THE DISTRIBUTION OF YOUR VARIABLES

As you write about numbers, you will use a variety of examples or contrasts. Depending on the point you want to make, you may need

- a typical value, such as the average height or math score in a sample;
- an expected change or contrast, such as a proposed increase in the minimum wage;
- the extremes; for example, to illustrate the maximum possible change in test scores.

To tell whether a given value is typical or atypical or a change is large or modest, you need to see how it fits in the distribution of values for that variable *in your data and research context*. For instance, the range of math scores will be smaller (and the average higher) in a group of "gifted and talented" students than among all students in an entire school district; which you would use depends on your research question and the available data. Before you select values for calculations or as case examples, use exploratory data analytic techniques such as frequency distributions, graphs, and simple descriptive statistics to familiarize yourself with the distributions of the variables in question. See Moore (1997) or Agresti and Finlay (1997) for more background on descriptive statistics.

Minimum, Maximum, and Range

The first aspects of a distribution to consider are the minimum and maximum observed values and the range — the difference between them. Examine the actual range of values taken on by your variables, not just the theoretically possible range. For example, the Center for Epidemiological Studies of Depression (CESD) scale is an index composed of 20 questions about frequency of certain symptoms, each scaled from 0 to 3. Although in theory the CESD scale could range from 0 to 60, in the general population the mean is between 8 and 10 and scores above 20 are rarely observed (Radloff and Locke 1986). Thus using a change of 25 points as an illustrative example would be unrealistic. See chapter 8 for more discussion of out-of-range values and contrasts.

Measures of Central Tendency

The second aspect of distribution to consider is central tendency — the mean, median, and/or modal values, depending on the type of variable in question. The mean is calculated by adding together all values and dividing that sum by the number of cases. The median is the middle value (at the 50th percentile) when all values are ranked in order from lowest to highest. The mode is the most common value — the value observed the most frequently of all values in the sample. Any of the measures of central tendency can be used for continuous variables, but neither the mean nor the median makes sense for categorical (nominal or ordinal) variables.[5]

Although the mean is the most widely used of the three measures of central tendency for continuous variables, before you rely on it to characterize your data, observe the distribution of values around the mean. It does not always represent the distribution well. In figures 4.3a, b and c, the mean value (6.0) would be an appropriate

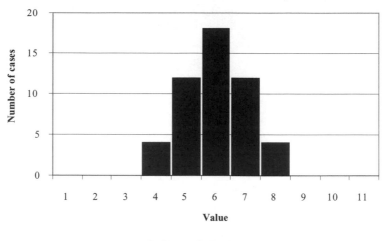

a. Normal distribution
mean = 6.0; SD = 1.07

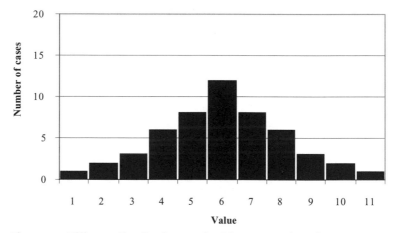

b. Normal distribution
mean = 6.0; SD = 2.18

Figure 4.3. Different distributions each with a mean value of 6.0.
(a) Normal distribution; (b) Normal distribution, same mean, higher SD;
(c) Uniform distribution; (d) Polarized bimodal distribution; (e) Skewed
distribution

c. Uniform distribution
mean = 6.0; SD = 1.43

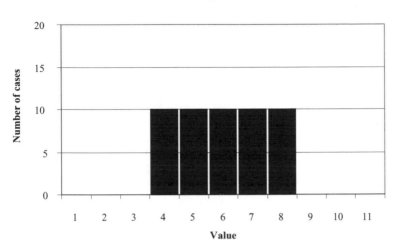

d. Polarized bimodal
mean = 6.0; SD = 4.71

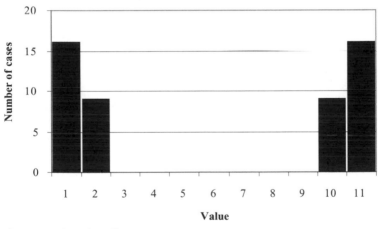

Figure 4.3. (*continued*)

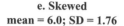

e. Skewed
mean = 6.0; SD = 1.76

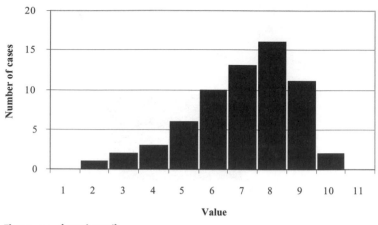

Figure 4.3. (*continued*)

example, although in figure 4.3c it is no more typical than any of the other observed values. (See "Variability" below for an explanation of "SD.")

In figure 4.3d, however, the mean (still 6.0) is not observed for any cases in the sample and hence is not a representative value. Likewise, in figure 4.3e, the mean (again 6.0) is atypical. If such a pattern characterizes your data, the mode would be a better choice of a typical value.

Another caution: the mean can be biased if your sample has one or two outliers — values that are much higher or much lower than those in the rest of the sample. Use Tukey's box-and-whisker or stem-and-leaf techniques to display deviation from the mean or identify the presence of outliers (see chapter 7 or Hoaglin et al. 2000). See also chapter 10 for a discussion of how to describe your treatment of outliers.

Variability

Another important consideration is the variability in your data, the extent to which values are spread around the mean. It is usually summarized by the variance or standard deviation (SD). For example, an absolute difference of 5 points is "bigger" or more meaningful in a distribution that is tightly clustered around the mean (e.g., SD = 3.0; figure 4.3a) than in one with more spread (e.g., SD = 5.0; figure 4.3b). In the first instance, 5 points is 1.66 standard deviations from the mean, placing it farther out in the distribution than in the second instance, where 5 points is 1.00 standard deviations. To convey the position of a given value in the overall distribution, report its rank, percentile, or z-score.

Alternatively, use the "five number summary" (Moore 1997)—the minimum value, first quartile value (Q1), median, third quartile (Q3), and maximum value—to illustrate the spread. The minimum and maximum values encompass the range, while the interquartile range (Q1 to Q3) shows how the middle half of all values are distributed within the full span of the data. These numbers can be reported in tabular form or a box-and-whisker chart.

■ DEFINE STANDARD CUTOFFS AND PATTERNS

Comparison against a standard is a useful way of assessing whether a particular value is commonplace or exceptional, or an observed pattern typical or unusual for the topic under study.

What Is a Standard?

Standards include cutoffs, patterns, and records that define the highest and lowest observed values. Some cutoffs are based on physical principles: the properties of water change below 32°F. Other cutoffs are based on social or legal convention: 21 as the minimum drinking age in most states, 50% as the definition of a simple majority. Commonly used standard patterns include the J-shaped age pattern of mortality (higher in infancy than in childhood, then steadily increasing through middle age before accelerating into old age), the seasonal pattern of temperature variation for a given location, and growth charts for height and weight of children from birth to adulthood.

Some standard patterns are empirically derived, like the mean temperature for New York City on January 1 calculated from several decades of data, or the median height for 12-month-old girls computed from a national sample. Other standards are conventions agreed upon by experts in the field. The Bureau of Labor Statistics calculates the Consumer Price Index (CPI) with 1982–1984 as the base period when CPI = 100 (U.S. Bureau of Labor Statistics 2002b). Demographers and epidemiologists at the Census Bureau and Centers for Disease Control recently replaced the 1940 age structure with that for 2000 as the basis for their "standard million" for all age adjustments (Anderson and Rosenberg 1998; CDC 1999).

Often the initial choice of a standard is somewhat arbitrary — it doesn't really matter which year or population is chosen. However, the same convention must be used to generate all numbers to be compared because the results of an age adjustment or a constant dollar calculation vary depending which standard was used. As always, read for and specify the context (W's), units, and methods used to apply the standard to ensure comparability.

Although the term "standard" implies uniformity of definition, there is a striking variety and malleability of standards. As of January 1, 2002, the National Weather Service began using the average conditions from 1971 through 2000 to assess temperatures, replacing the relatively cool decade of the 1960s with the relatively warm decade of the 1990s. Thus a temperature that would have been interpreted as unusually warm if it had occurred on December 31, 2001, when the old standard was in use could have been considered normal or even cool if it had occurred one day later, when the new standard was in place. Periodically, the standard referent year for constant dollars, the standard population for age adjustment of death rates, and human growth standards are also updated.

Standards also vary by location. What constitutes a normal daytime high temperature in Los Angeles in January is quite different from the normal daytime high for that month in Chicago or San Paolo. A different age pattern of mortality is observed in the United States and other developed countries today (where chronic diseases account for most deaths) than in Afghanistan and other less developed countries (where infectious and accidental causes of death predominate; Omran 1971, Preston 1976). In addition, standards or thresholds may differ according to other characteristics. For instance, poverty thresholds vary by family size and age composition: the threshold for a single elderly person is lower than for a family with two adults and two children.

Why Use Standards?

Standards are used to assess a given value or pattern of values by comparing them against information about pertinent physical or social phenomena. Such comparisons factor out some underlying pattern to help ascertain whether a given value is high, low, or average.

- Does a particular value exceed or fall below some cutoff that has important substantive meaning? For instance, alcohol consumption is illegal only below a certain age.
- Is an observed trend consistent with other concurrent changes? Did college tuition rise faster than the general rate of inflation, for example?
- Is the pattern for a given case typical or unusual? For instance, is a child growing at the expected rate? Is he significantly above or below the average size for his age? If so, is that gap increasing, decreasing, or stable as he gets older?
- Is a particular change expected based on cyclical patterns or due to some other factor? Did a new law reduce traffic fatalities, or is such a decline expected at the time of the year the law took effect, for example?

In addition to some measure of average value, standards frequently include information on range or other aspects of distribution. Weather standards mention record high and low temperatures as well as averages. Growth charts for children typically show the 10th, 25th, 50th, 75th, and 90th percentiles for age and sex.

Selecting an Appropriate Standard

For many nontechnical topics, cutoffs and patterns are part of cultural literacy. Most Americans grow up knowing they'll have the right to vote when they turn 18 and can retire at 65. The freezing point of water, the concept of 50% or more as a democratic majority, and that it is warmer in summer than winter are also generally known. For more technical issues or if precise values are needed, read the related literature to become familiar with standard cutoffs, patterns, or standardization calculations. See chapter 5 for additional discussion of how to use standards in numeric contrasts.

Where and How to Discuss Standards

For lay audiences, use of standards is a behind-the-scenes activity. Report the conclusions but not the process. Do children from low-income families grow normally? Did this year's employment follow the typical cyclical pattern? Because standards vary, mention the time, place, and other attributes of the standard you are using: "in constant 1990 dollars," "compared to the normal daily high for November in Chicago," or "below the 2002 poverty threshold for a family of two adults and one child."

For a scientific audience, specify which standard has been applied. If the approach is new or unusual, include the formula and a description in the methods section, a footnote, or an appendix. If the calculations and explanation are lengthy, cite a published source where readers can find the details. Explain cutoffs, standard patterns, or standardization processes that are unfamiliar to your audience, and consider using diagrams (see "Reference Lines" in chapter 7) or analogies (chapter 8) to illustrate.

■ CHOOSE A FITTING NUMBER OF DIGITS AND DECIMAL PLACES

How many digits and decimal places should you include as you write about numbers? Too many are cumbersome and uninformative and may overstate the precision with which the data were originally measured. Too few may not meet your readers' objectives.

Precision of Measurement
The precision of measurement limits the level of detail that can be reported. If a ruler is marked with increments for each millimeter (tenth of a centimeter or 0.1 cm), one can "eyeball" to approximate halfway between those marks, or to the nearest 0.05 cm. All values measured with that ruler and all calculations based on those data should be reported with no more than two decimal places (Logan 1995; NIST 2000).

It is surprising how often calculators and computers seem to magically enhance the implied level of detail and precision of numeric information: just because your calculator or computer output displays eight or more digits or decimal places does not mean that information is accurate. If the original measurement was measured to the nearest ounce, up to one additional level of detail can be reported. Additional decimal places are misleading. Likewise, if you are averaging income (reported in thousands of dollars) across several counties, you can report one level down (e.g., hundreds of dollars), but not single dollars and cents. Make sure the number of decimal places in reported calculations is consistent with the precision of the original measurement. See Logan (1995) for a comprehensive discussion of how measurement and calculations affect the correct number of "significant digits."[6]

Number of Digits

Precision of measurement sets an upper limit on the appropriate number of digits and decimal places for your data. Rarely, however, are all those digits needed to make your point. For most purposes, "approximately six billion persons" is an adequate description of the world's population at the turn of the millennium. The number "6,049,689,552 persons" is more detail than all but the most persnickety demographer could want to know, and almost certainly exaggerates the precision of the estimate. To provide a bit more detail, write "6.0 billion" or "6.05 billion" persons. Information about the last few hundred persons is not very informative when the overall scale is in the billions. Often, the main point is the similarity of two or more numbers; if so, don't display extra digits merely to reveal tiny differences. And you don't want your readers pausing to count commas to figure out the scale of the number: "Let's see. Three commas . . . that's billions."

In most prose, two to four digits are enough to illustrate your point without too much detail. Consider these three ways of reporting results of a very close election:

Poor: "In the recent election, Candidate A received 2,333,201 votes while Candidate B received 2,333,422 votes."
To figure out who won and by how much, readers must wade through a lot of digits and then do the math themselves.

Better: "Candidate B won the recent election over Candidate A, with 2,333,422 votes and 2,333,201 votes, respectively."
This version conveys who won, but readers must still calculate the margin of victory.

Best: "In an extremely close election, Candidate B eked out a victory over Candidate A, receiving only 221 more votes out of more than 4.6 million votes tallied — a margin of less than 100th of 1% of the total votes."
By presenting the calculations, the key point is far more accessible than in the previous two versions. Who won and by how much? Phrases such as "extremely close" and "eked" communicate how narrow the victory was much more effectively than just reporting the numbers, and none of the numbers presented include more than three digits. If the exact number of votes is needed, accompany the description with a simple table reporting the tallies.

Number of Decimal Places

In general, include the smallest number of decimal places that suit the scale of your numbers — in many cases, none. If most of the variation is in the thousands, millions, or billions, detail in the second decimal place won't add much to the main point: do we really need to know the federal budget down to the penny? On the other hand, for numbers less than 1.0, a couple of decimal places are needed for the variation to be visible: because of rounding, differences between tax assessment rates of 0.072% and 0.068% won't be evident unless you show three decimal places. And p-values can't be evaluated if they are rounded to the nearest whole number.

Having chosen an appropriately modest number of digits and decimal places for the text, do not turn around and report a zillion digits in your accompanying tables. Yes, tables are good for detail, but there is a limit to what is useful. Don't overwhelm your readers (let alone the poor typist) with a table of six columns and 20 rows, each cell of which contains eight digits and six decimal places, particularly if your associated narrative discusses each of those numbers rounded to the nearest two digits.

Use the recommendations in table 4.2 to decide what level of detail is suitable for the types of numbers you report, then design your tables and prose accordingly. On occasion, you might exceed the recommended number of digits or decimal places, but do so only if fewer will not accomplish your purpose. For some types of numbers, there are well-established conventions about how many decimal places to include:

- Monetary denominations include two decimal places to show value to the nearest cent, except for values of $1 million or greater, when decimal places are usually superfluous. Even on my bank statement (with a balance far below a million dollars), I rarely look at how many pennies I have.
- Proportions include three decimal places if several values presented are less than .10 or would be rounded to the same value; otherwise, two will suffice.
- Percentages often don't need any decimal places unless the values are very similar to one another (e.g., 5.9 and 6.1, or 66.79 and 67.83). In such cases, include one or two decimal places, as shown.
- Test statistics (e.g., t-statistic or χ^2), require two decimal places to compare them against critical values.

- p-values conventionally include two decimal places, although three may be shown if $p < 0.01$.

In general, I recommend choosing the numbers of digits and decimal places depending on the scale of the numbers, aiming for no more than four total digits in prose and no more than six (ideally fewer) in tables. Possible exceptions include tables in reports intended as standard data sources for public use, and "dazzle" statistics to catch your audience's attention with a single showy number. In the latter case, you might report the federal budget down to the last cent, then remind them that such detail may be fun but is probably unwarranted. Report fewer digits for general background statistics than for detailed quantitative analyses, and use a consistent scale and number of decimal places within a series of numbers to be compared.

Changing Scale, Rounding, and Scientific Notation

One way to reduce the number of digits you report is to change the scale of the numbers, rounding to the nearest million or thousandth, for example. To decide on an appropriate scale, consider the highest and lowest values you report and choose a scale that gracefully captures most values using three to four numerals. In 1999, the populations of the fifty United States ranged from approximately 480 thousand people in Wyoming to 33.1 million people in California (U.S. Census Bureau 1999b). Because most states' populations exceed one million, round the figures to the nearest million with one or two decimal places to capture both small and large states' populations: 0.5 million people in Wyoming, 33.1 million in California.

Changing scale also can help reduce the number of digits for proportions or other statistics that have several leading zeros without losing any meaningful information.[7] Convert proportions to percentages to save two decimal places, sparing readers the chore of counting zeros to assess scale. For instance, a proportion of 0.0007 becomes 0.07% or could be rounded to 0.1%. This averts the common mistake of calling proportions percentages and makes the scale of the numbers easier to grasp. Or, for a chemical sample weighing 0.0000023 grams, report it as 2.3 micrograms; in a nonscientific piece, include a note that one microgram equals one millionth of a gram. In a lab report or other document for a biological or physical science audience, use scientific notation — another convention for succinctly presenting only the meaningful digits of a number; write 2.3×10^{-6} grams.

Table 4.2. Guidelines on number of digits and decimal places for text, charts, and tables, by type of statistic

Type of Statistic	Text or Chart			Table		
	Total digits[a]	Decimal places	Examples	Total digits	Decimal places	Examples
Integer[b]	3 to 4	Not applicable	7 million 388	Up to 6	Not applicable	7,123 thousand[c] 388
Rational number	3 to 4	1 to 2	32.1 −0.71	Up to 6	Up to 3; enough to show 2 significant digits	32.1 −0.71 0.0043
Percentage	3 to 4	1 if several #s would round to same value; otherwise none	72% 6.1%	3 to 4	2 if several #s would round to same value; otherwise 1	72.1% 6.12%
Proportion	Up to 3	3 if several #s would round to same value; otherwise 2	.36 .002	Up to 3	3 if several #s would round to same value; otherwise 2	.36 .002

Monetary value	3 to 4	None for large denominations; 2 for small	$2 million $12·34	3 to 4	None for large denominations; 2 for small	$2 million $12·34
Ratio	3 to 4	1 to 2	12.7 0.8	3 to 4	2 if one or more ratios <1.0; otherwise 1	12.7 0.83
Test statistic (e.g., t-statistic; chi-square)	3 to 4	2	$\chi^2 = 12.19$ $t = 1.78$	3 to 4	2	$\chi^2 = 12.19$ $t = 1.78$
p-value	Up to 3	2	$p < 0.01$ $p = 0.06$	Up to 3	2 for values ≥ 0.01 3 for values <0.01	$p = 0.06$ $p < 0.001$

Note: See Logan (1995) for considerations on appropriate number of digits for calculations, and Miller (forthcoming) for guidelines on digits and decimal places for results of multivariate statistical models.

[a] Including decimal places. If number of digits exceeds this value, round or change scale.

[b] Integers include the positive and negative counting numbers and zero (Kornegay 1999). By definition, they have no decimal places.

[c] The word "thousand" (or other unit) would appear only in the column head, not in the table cells; see table 4.1b for an example.

Numbers versus Numerals

A few more technical points: some editors require that numbers under 10 and units (e.g., "percent," "million") be spelled out rather than reported in numeral form. These guidelines vary across disciplines, so consult a manual of style for your field. Spell out numbers at the beginning of a sentence: "Thirty percent of all deaths were from heart disease," rather than "30 percent of all deaths were from heart disease." Or, rephrase the sentence to put the number later in the sentence. "Heart disease accounted for 30% of all deaths." Whenever possible, separate distinct numeric values with more than a comma, using symbols or names for units (e.g., %, grams) or adverbs (e.g., "approximately," "nearly") to help readers distinguish where one number ends and the next begins. For instance, replace "100, 320, and 799 grams, respectively" with "100 grams, 320 grams, and 799 grams, respectively." See University of Chicago Press (2003) or Alred et al. (2000) for additional technical writing guidelines.

■ CHECKLIST FOR FIVE MORE BASIC PRINCIPLES

- Familiarize yourself with each of your variables. Are they:
  Categorical or continuous?
    - —If categorical, are they nominal or ordinal?
    - —If continuous, are they ratio or interval?
  Single or multiple response?
- Know the units of measurement for each variable.
  Check units:
    - —Level of aggregation or unit of analysis.
    - —Scale or order of magnitude.
    - —System of measurement, such as British, metric or other.
  Check comparability within your work and that of others.
- Examine the distribution of your variables: range, central tendency, variance, and symmetry in order to identify typical and atypical values or contrasts.
- Consider standard cutoffs, distributions, or historic records.
  Find out which are used for your topic.
  Cite references for standards.
  Put details in appendixes or footnotes.
- Pick an appropriate number of digits and decimal places, taking into account
  Precision with which the data were originally measured, and
  Objectives of your work.
    - —Aim for four digits with up to one decimal place in the text and charts, up to one to two more in tables (see table 4.2 for guidelines).
    - —Round or change the scale to reduce number of digits, or leading or trailing zeros.

Tools

PART II

In this section, I introduce some basic tools for calculating and comparing numbers, designing tables and charts, and choosing quantitative examples and analogies. Used in concert with the principles described in the previous few chapters, these tools will help you develop effective ways to present quantitative information.

To explain the purpose and application of the tools, I have written these chapters in a "teaching" style. In general, this is *not* how you will write about numbers. For example, your readers don't need a detailed description of how you approached writing up $p = 0.08$, the steps to calculate percentage change, why you right-justified the numbers in your table, or why you chose a stacked bar chart rather than a pie chart. Make those decisions, do those calculations, and create your charts or tables to function well, but don't write about how or why you did so. Instead, present the fruits of those labors, following the examples and guidelines throughout this book.

An important exception is when you are writing about numbers for a problem set or course paper for a research methods or statistics course. In those instances you may be asked to show your calculations and explain your thought process to demonstrate that you have mastered the corresponding concepts and skills. Check with your professor to find out whether to include this information in your course assignments. If you later revise a course paper for publication or presentation to another audience, remove most of the "teaching statistics" material and focus instead on the products of that behind-the-scenes work.

Types of Quantitative Comparisons

One of the most fundamental skills in writing about numbers is describing the direction and magnitude of differences among two or more values. You may need to quantify the size of a difference — whether an election was close or a landslide, for example. You may want to assess the pace of change over time — whether inflation was slow or rapid in recent years, for instance. Or, you may want to show whether a value exceeds or falls short of some important cutoff, such as whether a family's income is below the poverty line and if so by how much.

There are several commonly used ways to compare numeric values: rank, absolute difference, relative difference, percentage difference, and z-score.[1] With the exception of z-scores, which require some basic statistical knowledge, these calculations involve no more than elementary arithmetic skills — subtraction, division, or a combination of the two. For most authors, the difficult part of quantitative comparison is deciding which aspects are best suited to the question at hand and then explaining the results and their interpretation clearly and correctly. In the sections below, I describe how to choose among, calculate, and describe these measures.

As with the tools described in the next few chapters, an important aspect of working with quantitative comparisons is to coordinate them with the associated narrative. Think about how you prefer to word your comparisons, then perform the corresponding calculations accordingly. Doing so will spare your readers the confusion of interpreting ratios that you have accidentally described "upside down" or subtraction you have inadvertently explained "backward" (see examples below).

■ CHOICE OF A REFERENCE VALUE

The first step in comparing numbers is to decide which values to compare. Often you will contrast a figure from your own data against numbers or distributions from other sources. For instance, you might compare average children's height for one country against international growth standards, or today's scorching temperature against historic records for the same date and location. In addition, you might contrast several values from within your own data, such as average heights of children from several different countries, or the daily high temperatures over the past week.

Use of Standards and Conventions

As discussed in chapter 4, standards and conventions exist in many fields. A few examples:

- As of early 2003, the year 1984 was used as the baseline or reference value for the Consumer Price Index when calculating inflation (U.S. Bureau of Labor Statistics 2002b).
- National norms for exam scores and physical growth patterns are standard distributions used to evaluate individual test scores or height measurements.
- The federal poverty thresholds (Proctor and Dalaker 2003) are reference values that are commonly used to assess family income data.

If conventions or standards are commonly applied in your field and topic, use them as the reference values in your calculations.

Comparisons within Your Own Data

If external standards don't exist or you want to provide additional contrasts, pick salient reference values within your own data. Some guidelines about deciding on a reference value or group:

- The value for all groups combined is a good reference value as long as none of the subgroups comprises too large a share of that whole. None of the 50 states is so large that its value dominates the total population of the United States, so the United States is a fine basis of comparison for each of the individual states. However, comparing values for males against those both sexes combined is a poor choice because males make up half the population, strongly influencing the value for the whole population. Instead, compare males to another subgroup (in this case the only other subgroup) — females.

- Social norms and considerations of statistical power often suggest comparison against the modal (most common) category. In an assessment of market share, comparison with the industry leader makes sense.
- Pick a reference group to suit your audience. For a report to your state's Department of Human Services, that state is the logical point of reference. For a presentation to a construction workers' union, compare their benefits, salary, and occupational safety figures against those for other industries and occupations.
- If there is no standard benchmark date for a temporal comparison, changes are often calculated relative to the earliest value under consideration, sometimes against the most recent value.
- Choice of a reference value may depend on data availability.
  The U.S. Census is conducted at 10-year intervals and surveys are conducted periodically, so you may have to compare against the closest census or survey date even if it doesn't exactly match the date of interest.
  Information on small groups or unusual cases may have to be approximated using data on related groups or similar cases.

The initial choice of a reference group or value may be arbitrary: it might not matter which group or place or date you choose as the basis of comparison. However, once you have selected your reference, be consistent, using it for all calculations used to address a particular question. If you have decided on the Midwest as the reference region, calculate and report values for each of the other regions compared to the Midwest, not the South versus the Midwest and the Northeast versus the West.

If you compare against a standard threshold or other value from outside your data, report its value in the text, table, or chart. For comparisons against standard distributions involving many numbers (e.g., national norms for test scores or physical growth) provide descriptive statistics or a summary chart, then refer to a published source for more detailed information.

Wording for Comparisons

Name the reference group or value in your description of all numeric contrasts so the comparison can be interpreted. "The sex ratio was 75" doesn't convey whether that is 75 males per 100 females or 75 females per 100 males. The two meanings are not interchangeable.

Before you choose a reference value within your own data, anticipate how you will word the description. If you naturally want to compare all the other regions to the Midwest, make it the reference, then calculate and describe accordingly: "The Northeast is [measure of difference] larger (or smaller) *than the Midwest.*" Without the phrase "than the Midwest," it isn't clear whether the comparison is relative to the past (in other words, the region grew), to other concurrent estimates of the Northeast's population, or to some other unspecified region.

■ TYPES OF QUANTITATIVE COMPARISONS

There are several types of numeric contrast, each of which provides a different perspective on the direction and magnitude of differences between numbers. In addition to reporting the values themselves, we use rank, absolute difference, relative difference, percentage difference, or z-score to help interpret the meaning of those values in the context of a research question. In this chapter, I use those terms for convenience of discussion and to relate them to mathematical and statistical concepts used elsewhere. For most audiences, however, you should avoid the technical jargon, substituting phrases such as those shown in the illustrative sentences throughout this chapter.

Value

The value is the amount or level of the measure for one case or time point: Ian Thorpe's time in the 400-meter freestyle at the 2000 Olympics; the population of the United States in 1950; the current cost of a gallon of gasoline. Always report the value, its context, and its units. However, reporting the value alone leaves its purpose and meaning unclear. Is gasoline more expensive than last year? By how much? Is that a lot? To answer such questions, include one or more of the following numeric comparisons.

Rank

Rank is the position of the value for one case compared to other values observed in the same time or place, to a well-established standard, or against a historic high or low value. How did Thorpe's time in the 400 freestyle compare to those of other swimmers in the race? To his previous times? To the world record in that event? "First place," "lowest ever," and "middle of the pack" are examples of rankings. Two identical values share the same rank just as two identical race times constitute a tie. For instance, the values of X for cases 4 and 5 in table 5.1 are both 50, so they share the rank of 1.

Percentile

When many cases are being compared, use percentiles to convey rank. Your SAT score report included your percentile score to show how well you performed relative to all students who took the test. Percentiles are calculated by ranking all of the values and categorizing them into 100 groups each containing an equal share (1/100th) of the distribution (Utts 1999). Values that are lower than 99% of all other values are in the first (or bottom) percentile, while those that exceed 99% of all other values are in the 99th (or top) percentile. The 50th percentile, or middle value, is the median; half of all values are lower and half are higher than the median. Because percentiles encompass all the values in a distribution, they are bounded between 0 and 99: it is impossible to be below the lowest value or above the highest value.

To describe rank in somewhat less detail, report deciles (ranges of 10 percentiles), quintiles (one-fifth of the distribution, encompassing 20 percentiles), quartiles (ranges of 25 percentiles), or terciles (the bottom, middle, and top thirds of the distribution).

Wording for Rank

To report rank, select words that describe both relative position and the concept being compared: "fastest," "least expensive," "second most dense," make it clear that the descriptions pertain to velocity, price, and density, respectively. If you use the words "rank" or "percentile," also mention what is being compared: "Kate's math SAT score placed her in the second highest quartile of students nationwide," or "Product Z ranked third overall in terms of consumer satisfaction."

Rank and percentile do not involve units of their own but are based on the units of the values being compared. If you have already reported the values and their units elsewhere, omit them from your description of rank. If not, rank and value can often be incorporated into the same sentence.

Table 5.1. Formulas and case examples for different types of quantitative comparisons

Formula	Reference value X	Rank based on X	Number of interest Y	Rank based on Y	Absolute difference Y − X	Relative difference (ratio) Y/X	Percentage difference or percentage change [(Y − X)/X] × 100
Case 1	1	3	2	5	1	2.00	100
Case 2	1	3	26	3	25	26.00	2,500
Case 3	25	2	50	2	25	2.00	100
Case 4	50	1	25	4	−25	0.50	−50
Case 5	50	1	51	1	1	1.02	2

Note: Ranks based on X and Y are from highest (1) to lowest.

Poor: "Joe's rank for height is 1."
   Although this statement may be correct, it can be restated in a more straightforward and informative way.
Better: "Standing 6' 3", Joe is the tallest person in his class."
   This version conveys the value, rank, and reference group in easily understood terms.

Advantages and Disadvantages of Rank

Rank is useful when all that matters is the order of values, not the distance between them. In elections, the critical issue is who came in first. Rank in class or quartiles of standard test scores are often used as admission criteria by colleges.

Although rank and percentile both provide information about relative position (higher or lower, faster or slower), they do not indicate *by how much* one value differed from others. In the 2000 U.S. presidential election, rank in electoral votes identified the winner but was not the only salient information. Bush's small margin of victory over Gore caused much debate and recounting of the popular vote — demands that would not have surfaced had the difference been larger. And some might argue that students at the bottom of the highest quartile and at the top of the second quartile are so similar that they should receive similar college admission offers.

To quantify size of difference between two or more values, use absolute difference, relative difference, percentage difference, or z-score. Their formulas (except z-scores) are presented in table 5.1, along with some numeric examples. Throughout table 5.1, X represents the reference value and Y represents another number of interest.

Absolute Difference (or Absolute Change)

Absolute difference subtracts the reference value (X) from the number of interest (Y), or Y minus X. For case 1 in table 5.1, the absolute difference is 1 unit ($Y - X = 2 - 1 = 1$). The absolute difference for case 5 is also 1 unit ($51 - 50 = 1$), although both X and Y are much higher. Absolute difference can be used for either interval or ratio data.

Wording for Absolute Difference

An absolute difference is computed by subtracting one value from another, so describe it in terms of a *difference* or *margin.* Mention the units, which are the same as those for the values being compared.

Table 5.2. Application of absolute difference, relative difference, and percentage change to United States population data

Region	(1) Population (millions) 1990	(2) Ratio 1990 (relative to Midwest)	(3) % Difference 1990 (rel. to Midwest)	(4) Population (millions) 1999	(5) Absolute change (millions) 1990–1999	(6) % Change 1990–1999
United States	248.8	NA	NA	272.7	23.9	9.6
Northeast	50.8	0.85	−14.9	51.8	1.0	2.0
Midwest	59.7	1.00	0.0	63.2	3.5	5.9
South	85.5	1.43	43.2	96.5	11.0	12.9
West	52.8	0.88	−11.6	61.2	8.4	15.9

Source: U.S. Census Bureau 1999b.

Poor: "The absolute change was 23.9 million (table 5.2)."
This sentence reports the magnitude but not the direction of the change, does not explain what concept or cases are being compared, and uses unnecessary jargon.

Better: "In late 1999, the Census Bureau estimated a total U.S. population of 272.7 million persons — an increase of 23.9 million over the 1990 population (column 5 of table 5.2)."
This version specifies the two cases being compared (their years), mentions the pertinent concept (population) and units (millions of people), and reports the direction and size of the change.

Advantages and Disadvantages of Absolute Difference

The absolute difference is useful when the difference itself is of interest. How much more will something cost and is that amount within your budget? How many more people live in South Florida now than 10 years ago and will that additional population overtax water supplies?

However, the absolute difference does not address all questions well. Is a $0.50 price increase large? It depends on the initial price. For a candy bar costing less than a dollar, a $0.50 increase is substantial. For a car costing $20,000 the same $0.50 increase is trivial. To illustrate that point, use a measure of difference relative to the initial value.

Relative Difference or Change

The relative difference is the *ratio* of two numbers, the number of interest (Y) divided by the reference value (X). If the quantity in numerator (Y) is larger than that in the denominator (X), the ratio is greater than 1.0, as in cases 1, 2, 3, and 5 in table 5.1. If the numerator is smaller than the denominator, the ratio is below 1.0, as in case 4 ($25/50 = 0.50$).

By dividing one value by the other, the relative difference adjusts for the fact that a one-unit absolute difference has very different interpretations if both values are very small than if both values are very large. In both cases 2 and 3, the absolute difference is 25 units. However, the relative difference is much larger in case 2 (ratio = 26.0) because the reference value is very small ($X = 1$). In case 3, the reference value is much higher ($X = 25$), yielding a much smaller ratio (2.0). Relative difference can be used for ratio variables but not interval variables: it makes no sense to say that it is 1.25 times as hot today as yesterday, for example.

Table 5.3. Phrases for describing ratios and percentage difference

Type of ratio	Ratio example	Rule of thumb	Writing suggestion[a]
< 1.0 (e.g., 0.x) *Percentage difference* = ratio × 100	0.80	[Group] is only x% as ____[b] as the reference value.	"Males were only 80% as likely as females to graduate from the program."
Close to 1.0	1.02	Use phrasing to express similarity between the two groups.	"Average test scores were similar for males and females (ratio = 1.02 for males compared to females)."
> 1.0 (e.g., 1.y) *Percentage difference* = (ratio − 1) × 100.	1.20	[Group] is 1.y times as ____ as the reference value. OR [Group] is y% ____er than the reference value.	"On average, males were 1.20 times as tall as females." OR "Males were on average 20% taller than females."
	2.34	[Group] is (2.34 − 1) × 100, or 134% more ____ than the reference value.	"Males' incomes were 134% higher than those of females."
Close to a multiple of 1.0 (e.g., z.00)	2.96	[Group] is (about) z times as ____.	"Males were nearly three times as likely to commit a crime as their female peers."

[a] Females are the reference group (denominator) for all ratios in table 5.3.

[b] Fill in an adjective, verb, or phrase in each "____" to convey the aspect being compared, e.g., "taller," "likely to graduate."

Wording for Relative Difference

Describe a relative difference in terms of *multiples:* the value in the numerator is some multiple of the value in the denominator (without using that jargon . . . see table 5.3).Do not just report the ratio in the text without accompanying explanation:

Poor: "In 1990, the Southern numerator was 1.43 times the Midwestern denominator (column 2 of table 5.2)"
The terms "numerator" and "denominator" indicate that the comparison involves division, but the sentence doesn't express what aspect of the regions is being compared.
Poor (version 2): "In 1990, the ratio between the South and the Midwest was 1.43 (column 2, table 5.2)."
This version doesn't convey what is being measured or which region has the higher value.
Better: "In 1990, the South was 1.43 times as populous as the Midwest (column 2, table 5.2)."
In this version, it is immediately evident what is being compared, which region is bigger, and by how much.

If the ratio is close to 1.0, use wording to convey that the two values are very similar. For ratios below 1.0, explain that the value is smaller than the reference value. For ratios above 1.0, convey that the value is larger than the reference value. Table 5.3 gives examples of ways to explain ratios without using phrases such as "ratio," "relative difference," "numerator," or "denominator."

Common Errors When Describing Ratios

Some cautions: word your explanation to conform to the kind of calculation you performed. I have seen people subtract to find a 2-unit difference between scores of 73 and 71, and then state that the score for the second group was twice as high as for the first. Likewise, if you divide to find a ratio of 1.03, do not explain it as a "1.03 unit difference" between the quantities being compared.

Explain ratios in terms of multiples *of the reference value,* not multiples *of the original units.* For example, although the 1990 populations of the South and Midwest were originally measured in millions of persons (column 1 of table 5.2), the ratio of 1.43 does not mean there were 1.43 *million* times as many people in the South as in the Midwest. During the division calculation the millions "cancel," as they say in fourth-grade math class, so there were 1.43 times as many people in the South as in the Midwest in 1990.

Avoid calculating the ratio with one group as the denominator and then explaining it "backward" or "upside down": for example, do not report the relative size of the southern and midwestern populations in a table as ratio = 1.43 and then describe the comparison as Midwest versus South ("The population of the Midwest was 0.70 times that of the South.").[2] Decide in advance which way you want to phrase the comparison, then compute accordingly.

Percentage Difference and Percentage Change

Percentage *difference* is a ratio that expresses the difference between two values in relation to the reference value. Percentage *change* is a ratio that expresses the amount of change in relation to the original quantity. A one-unit absolute difference yields a much larger percentage difference with an initial level of 1 (case 1 in table 5.1) than for an initial level of 50 (case 5). To compute percentage difference, divide the absolute difference by the reference value, then multiply the result by 100 to put it in percentage terms: $[(Y - X)/X] \times 100$. If you do *not* multiply by 100, you have a *proportionate* difference or change.

Percentage difference is typically calculated by subtracting the smaller from the larger value, hence such comparisons often yield positive percentage differences. Negative percentage differences usually occur only when several values are being compared against the same reference value, with some falling below and some above that value. For example, in 1990 the Northeast was 14.9% smaller than the Midwest ($[(50.8 \text{ million} - 59.7 \text{ million})/59.7 \text{ million}] \times 100 = -14.9\%$), whereas the South was 43% larger than the Midwest ($[(85.5 \text{ million} - 59.7 \text{ million})/59.7 \text{ million}] \times 100 = 43.2\%$; column 3, table 5.2).

A percentage *change* compares values for two different points in time. Conventionally, a percentage change subtracts the earlier (V_1) from the later value (V_2), then divides that difference by the initial value and multiplies by 100: $[(V_2 - V_1)/V_1] \times 100$.

- If the quantity increased over time, the percentage change will be positive. For the West region: $(V_{1999} - V_{1990})/V_{1990} \times 100 = (61.2 \text{ million} - 52.8 \text{ million})/52.8 \text{ million} \times 100 = 8.4 \text{ million}/52.8 \text{ million} \times 100 = 15.9\%$, reflecting a 15.9% increase in population between 1990 and 1999 (column 6 of table 5.2).
- If the quantity decreased over time, the percentage change will be negative. Between 1990 and mid-1999, the District of Columbia lost 14.5% of its population, decreasing from 607,000 persons to 519,000 in 1999 (U.S. Census Bureau 1999b): $(519 - 607)/607 \times 100 = -88/607 \times 100 = -14.5\%$.

If the time interval is very wide (e.g., several decades or centuries), sometimes the average of the values for the two times is used as the denominator: $(V_2 - V_1)/[(V_1 + V_2)/2] \times 100$. When you report a percentage change, indicate which date or dates were used as the base for the calculation.

A percentage difference is one variant of relative difference: if you know either the ratio or percentage difference between two values, you can calculate the other measure of relative difference:

- For ratios that are greater than 1.0, percentage difference = (ratio −1) × 100. Conversely, ratio = (percentage difference/100) + 1. A recent article in the American Journal of Public Health reported that ready-to-eat cookies being sold in some popular fast-food or family restaurants have 700% more calories than the standard USDA portion size (Young and Nestle 2002) — a ratio of eight times the calories of a "standard" cookie.
- For ratios less than 1.0, percentage difference = ratio × 100. If there are 0.85 northeasterners per midwesterner, then the population of the Northeast is 85% as large as that of the Midwest (column 2, table 5.2).

Wording for Percentage Change or Difference

To describe percentage change or difference, identify the cases being compared and the direction of the difference or change. A percentage difference is expressed as a *percentage of the reference value,* replacing the units in which the original values were measured.

Poor: "The Western population percentage change was 15.9."
This sentence is awkwardly worded and does not convey which dates are being compared.

Better: "During the 1990s, the population of the West region grew from 52.8 million to 61.2 million persons — an increase of 15.9% (column 6, table 5.2)."
This version reports both value (population in each time period) and percentage change, including direction, magnitude, concepts, and units.

To report a negative value of percentage change or percentage difference, select words to convey direction:

Poor: "In 1990, the populations of the West and Midwest were 52.8 million and 59.7 million persons, respectively, so the percentage difference between the West and the Midwest is negative (−11.6%; column 3, table 5.2)."

Although this sentence reports the correct calculation, wording with negative percentage differences is unwieldy.

Better: "In 1990, the West had 11.6% fewer inhabitants than the Midwest (52.8 million persons and 59.7 million persons, respectively; table 5.2)."

The phrase "fewer inhabitants than the Midwest" clearly explains the direction of the difference in population between regions.

Common Errors for Wording of Percentage Difference

Do not confuse the phrases "*Y* is 60% *as high as X*" and "*Y* is 60% *higher than X*." The first phrase suggests that *Y* is lower than *X* (i.e., that the ratio $Y/X = 0.60$), the second that *Y* is higher than *X* (i.e., $Y/X = 1.60$). After you calculate a ratio or percentage difference, explain both the direction and the size of the difference, then check your description against the original numbers to make sure you have correctly communicated which is bigger — the value in the numerator or that in the denominator. See also table 5.3 for example sentences.

Watch your math and reporting of units to avoid mixing or mislabeling percentages and proportions. A proportion of 0.01 equals 1%, *not* 0.01%.

Other Related Types of Quantitative Comparisons

Annual Rates

Many annual rates such as interest rates or population growth rates are measures of change over time that are reported in percentage form. However, an annual growth rate cannot be calculated simply by dividing a percentage change over an *n* year period by *n*. For example, the annual growth rate in the West between 1990 and 1999 is *not* 15.9%/9 years. The explanation lies in the process of compounding. Box 5.1 illustrates the effect of annual compounding in a savings account over a 10-year period, in which interest is added to the principal each year, so the interest rate is applied to a successively larger principal each year. The same logic applies to population growth: each year there are more people to whom the annual growth rate applies, so even if that growth rate is constant, the absolute number of additional people rises each year.[3] Between 1990 and 1999, the West region grew at an average annual rate of 1.65%.[4]

Percentage versus Percentile versus Percentage Change

A common source of confusion involves "percentage difference," "difference in percentage points" and "difference in percentiles." Just

---

Box 5.1. Compounding of an Annual Interest Rate

If you deposit $1,000 in a savings account at 3% interest compounded annually, the first year you will earn $30 interest. The next year, the 3% interest rate will apply to the new balance of $1,030, yielding $30.90 interest. In the tenth year, that same 3% interest rate will generate $39.14 interest, because the accrued interest over the previous nine years raised the principal to $1,343.91 (assuming no withdrawals or additional deposits). Over the entire 10-year period, the balance will increase 34%.

---

because they all have "percent-" in their names does not mean they are equivalent measures. If X and Y are expressed as percentages, their units of measurement are percentage points; hence the absolute difference between their values is reported as a *difference in percentage points*. A rise in the unemployment rate from 4.2% to 5.3% corresponds to an increase of 1.1 percentage points, *not* a 1.1% difference. The *percentage difference* in those unemployment rates is (5.3% −4.2%)/4.2% × 100, which is a 26% increase relative to the initial value.

Percentages and percentiles calculate the share of a whole and the rank within a distribution, respectively. By definition, neither can be less than zero or greater than 100: no case can have less than none of the whole, or more than all of it. In contrast, percentage change and percentage difference measure relative size against some reference value and are not constrained to fall between 0 and 100. If a value is more than twice the size of the reference value, the percentage difference will be greater than 100%, as in case 2 in table 5.1. Similarly, if the quantity more than doubles, the corresponding percentage change will exceed 100%. If a quantity shrinks over time, as with the population of Washington D.C. in the 1990s, the corresponding percentage change will be less than 0% (negative).

To illustrate how percentage, percentile, and percentage change interrelate, Box 5.2 and table 5.4 apply those measures to SAT scores for a fictitious student. The description also illustrates how to integrate several different types of quantitative comparisons into a coherent discussion to make different points about the numbers.

Box 5.2. Relations among Percentage,
Percentile, and Percentage Change

The following description is annotated to indicate whether the numbers are value (denoted "V"), percentage correct (P), rank (R), absolute difference (A), or percentage change (C). Those annotations and the material in brackets are intended to illustrate how the different statistics relate to one another and would be omitted from the description for most audiences.

"The first time he took the SATs, Casey Smith correctly answered 27 out of 43 (V) questions (63%) (P; see table 5.4). Compared to all other students who took the test nationwide, he placed in the 58th percentile (R). The next year, he improved his score by 9 percentage points (A) [from 63% of questions correct (P) to 72% correct (P)], placing him in the 70th percentile (R). That change was equivalent to a 14.3% improvement in his score (C) [a 9 percentage-point improvement (A), compared to his initial score of 63% correct (V)]. His rank improved by 12 percentiles (A) [relative to his first-year rank of 58th percentile (R)]."

Table 5.4. Examples of raw scores, percentage,
percentile, and percentage change

Comparison of standardized test scores, Casey Smith 1999 and 2000

Year	(V) Questions correct (#)	Total # of questions	(P) Questions correct (%)	(A) Absolute difference in % correct[a]	(R) Percentile	(C) % Change in % correct
1999	27	43	63	NA	58	NA
2000	31	43	72	9%	70	14.3

[a] Difference in percentage points.

Standardized Score, or Z-Score

Standardized scores, or z-scores, are a way of quantifying how a particular value compares to the average, taking into account the spread in the sample or a reference population. A Z-score is computed by subtracting the mean from the value for each case, then dividing that difference by the standard deviation (Utts 1999). A positive z-score corresponds to a value above the mean, a negative z-score to a lower-than-average value. For instance, on a test with a mean of 42 points and a standard deviation of 3 points, a raw score of 45 points corresponds to a z-score of 1.0, indicating that the individual scored one standard deviation above the mean. Z-scores are best used when the distribution is approximately normal (bell-shaped).

In addition to correcting for level by subtracting the mean value, z-scores adjust for the fact that a given absolute difference is interpreted differently depending on the extent of variation in the data. Among 6-month-old male infants, mean height is 66.99 centimeters (cm) with a standard deviation (SD) of 2.49 cm. (Centers for Disease Control 2002). Hence a baby boy who is 2.54 cm shorter than average would have a z-score of -1.02, indicating height roughly one standard deviation below the mean. Among 6-year-old boys, however, there is wider variation around mean height (115.39 cm.; SD = 5.05 cm), so a boy 2.54 cm. shorter than average (the same absolute difference as for the infant) would be only about half a standard deviation below the norm for his age ($z = -0.50$).

Sometimes the mean and standard deviation used to calculate z-scores are from within your sample, other times from a standard population. For example, international growth standards for children's height-for-age and weight-for-height are used to provide a consistent basis for evaluating prevalence of underweight, overweight, and long-term growth stunting in different populations (Kuczmarski et al. 2000; World Health Organization 1995).

Report the mean and standard deviation of the distribution used to derive the z-scores and whether those figures were derived from within your own data or from an external standard. If an external standard was used, name it, explain why it was chosen, and provide a citation. If you report z-scores for only a few selected cases, also report the unstandardized value for those cases in the text or a table; for more cases, create a graph comparing your sample to the reference distribution.

The units of a z-score are *multiples of standard deviations,* not the original units in which the variable was measured: "With a raw score of 47, Mia scored one standard deviation below the national average."

■ CHOOSING TYPES OF QUANTITATIVE COMPARISONS FOR YOUR WRITING

The types of variables you are working with constrain which types of quantitative comparisons are appropriate (Chambliss and Schutt 2003).

- Ratio variables: rank, absolute, and relative difference all make sense.
- Interval variables: rank and absolute difference work, but relative difference does not.
- Ordinal variables: only rank can be calculated.
- Nominal variables: the only pertinent comparison is whether different cases have the same or different values, but differences cannot be quantified or ranked.

For variables where several of these contrasts are possible, different types of quantitative comparisons provide distinct perspectives about the same pair of numbers. Always report the value of a variable to set the context and provide data for other calculations, then present one or two types to give a more complete sense of the relationship. To help readers interpret both value and absolute difference, mention the highest and lowest possible values and the observed range in the data. A one-point increase on a five-point Likert scale[5] is substantial — equal to one-fourth of the theoretically possible variation. A one-point increase in the Dow Jones Industrial Average is minuscule — equivalent to a 0.01% change compared to its level of roughly 10,000 points.

The value is also important for putting a relative difference in context: suppose a study reports that a pollutant is three times as concentrated in one river as in another. A very low concentration in both locations (e.g., 1 part per million (ppm) versus 3 ppm) has very different environmental implications than a high concentration in both (e.g., 1% versus 3%). Likewise, reporting the percentage difference or percentage change without the value can be misleading. A 100% increase (doubling) in the number of scooter-related injuries over a three-month period might be considered alarming if the injury rate in the baseline period was already high, but not if there were initially few injuries because scooters were not in widespread use.

The choice of which calculations to include depends on your

topic and discipline. Read materials from your field to learn which types of quantitative comparisons are customary in your field. Use those calculations, then consider whether other types of comparisons would add valuable perspective.

- Report results of a race, election, or marketing study in terms of rank and absolute difference.
- Describe time trends in terms of percentage change and absolute difference, substituting ratios to express large changes such as doubling, tripling, or halving.
- Describe variations in risk or probability in terms of ratios. Because the ratio and percentage change are simply mathematical transformations of one another (table 5.3), present only one of those statistics to avoid repetition. Likewise, report only one measure of rank (e.g., position, percentile, decile, or quartile) along with information on the number of cases involved in the ranking.

■ CHECKLIST FOR TYPES OF QUANTITATIVE COMPARISONS

- Always report the values of the numbers being compared, either in the text itself or in a table or chart.
- Select one or two additional types of quantitative comparisons.
- Report the values and units of the numbers being compared, and specify which value or group is the reference value.
- Interpret your calculations to convey whether the values are typical or unusual, high or low. For trends, explain whether the values are stable or changing, and in what direction.
- Describe results of each quantitative comparison to match its calculation:
  "Difference" or "margin" of the original units for subtraction
  Multiples of the reference value for ratios
- Explain standard definitions, constants, or reference data, and provide citations.

Creating Effective Tables

Good tables complement your text, presenting numbers in a concise, well-organized way to support your description. Make it easy for your audience to find and understand numbers within your tables. Design table layout and labeling that are straightforward and unobtrusive so the attention remains on the substantive points to be conveyed by your data rather than on the structure of the table. In this chapter, I explain the following:

- How to create tables so readers can identify the purpose of each table and interpret the data simply by reading the titles and labels
- How to make tables self-contained, including units, context, source of the data, and definitions of abbreviations
- How to design a layout that contributes to the understanding of the patterns in the table and coordinates with your written description

The first section gives principles for planning effective tables. The second explains the "anatomy of a table" — the names and features of each table component. The third describes common types of tables, and the fourth gives guidelines on how to organize tables to suit your audience and objectives. The final section offers advice about how to draft a table and create it on a computer.

■ PRINCIPLES FOR PLANNING EFFECTIVE TABLES

Creating Focused Tables

Many reports and papers include several tables, each of which addresses one aspect of the overall research question — one major topic or a set of closely related subtopics, or one type of statistical analysis, for instance. A consultant's report on different options for a new commuter rail system might present information on projected ridership under different fare pricing scenarios (one table), estimated costs of land acquisition for right-of-way, commuter parking, and other related needs (a second table), and annual financing costs under several different assumptions about interest rates and term of the loan (a third table).

Creating Self-Contained Tables

Often tables are used separately from the rest of the document, either by readers in a hurry to extract information or as data sources that become detached from their origins. Label each table so your audience can understand the information without reference to the text. Using the title, row and column headings, and notes, they should be able to discern the following:

- The purpose of the table
- The context of the data (the W's)
- The location of specific variables within the table
- Coding or units of measurement for every number in the table
- Data sources
- Definitions of pertinent terms and abbreviations

The units and sources of data can be specified in any of several places in the table depending on space considerations and whether the same information applies to all data in the table.

▪ ANATOMY OF A TABLE

Title

Write a title for each table to convey the specific topics or questions addressed in that table. In documents that include several tables or charts, create individualized titles to differentiate them from one another and to convey where each fits in the overall scheme of your analysis.

Topic

In the title, name each of the major components of the relationships illustrated in that table. To avoid overly long titles, use summary phrases or name broad conceptual categories such as "demographic characteristics," "physical properties," or "academic performance measures" rather than itemizing every variable in the table. (The individual items will be labeled in the rows or columns; see below). The title to table 6.1 mentions both the outcome (number of households) and the comparison variables (household type, race, and Hispanic/non-Hispanic origin).

Table 6.1. Anatomy of a table

Households by type, race and Hispanic origin (thousands), United States, 1997

Characteristic	All households	Family households					Nonfamily household		
		Total	Married couple	Other families			Total	Female house-holder	Male house-holder
				Female house-holder	Male house-holder				
Race/ethnicity									
White	86,106	59,511	48,066	8,308	3,137		26,596	14,871	11,725
Non-Hispanic White	77,936	52,871	43,423	6,826	2,622		25,065	14,164	10,901
Black	12,474	8,408	3,921	3,926	562		4,066	2,190	1,876
All other[a]	3,948	2,961	2,330	418	212		986	455	532
Origin									
Non-Hispanic	93,938	63,919	49,513	11,040	3,366		30,018	16,762	13,258
Hispanic[b]	8,590	6,961	4,804	1,612	545		1,630	754	875
Total	102,528	70,880	54,317	12,652	3,911		31,648	17,516	14,133

Source: U.S. Census Bureau 1998.

[a] "All other" races includes Asians, Pacific Islanders, Native Americans, and those of unspecified race.

[b] People of Hispanic origin may be of any race.

Context

Specify the context of the data by listing the W's in the table title: where and when the data were collected, and if pertinent, restrictions on who is included in the data (e.g., certain age groups). If the data are from a specific study (such as the National Survey of America's Families or the Human Genome Project) or institution (e.g., one college or hospital), include its name in the title or in a general note below the table. Minimize abbreviations in the title. If you must abbreviate, spell out the full wording in a note.

Units

State the units of measurement, level of aggregation, and system of measurement for every variable in the table. This seemingly lengthy list of items can usually be expressed in a few words such as "price ($) per dozen," or "distance in light-years." Whenever possible, generalize units for the table rather than repeating them for each row and column. If the same units apply to most numbers in the table, specify them in the title. If there isn't enough space in the title, or if the units vary, mention units in the column or row headings. In table 6.1, the title states that all numbers are reported in thousands of households.

The following examples illustrate these principles for writing good titles:

Poor: "Descriptive statistics on the sample."
This title is truly uninformative. What kinds of descriptive statistics? On what variables? For what sample?

Better: "Means and standard deviations for soil components"
This title makes it clear what topics and statistics the table includes, but omits the context.

Best: "Means and standard deviations for soil components, 100 study sites, Smith County, 1990."
In addition to mentioning the topic, this title mentions the date and place the data were collected, as well as sample size.

Row Labels

Name the concept for each row and column in its associated label so readers can interpret the numbers in the interior cells of the table. The identity and meaning of the number in the shaded cell of table 6.1 is households of all types (known from the column header) that include black persons (row label), with population measured in thousands of households (title).

If the units of measurement differ across rows or columns of a table, mention the units in the pertinent row or column label. A table of descriptive statistics for a study of infant health might include mean age (in days), weight (in grams), length (in centimeters), and gestational age (in weeks). With different units for each variable, the units cannot be summarized for the table as a whole. Do not assume that the units of measurement will be self-evident once the concepts are named: without labels, readers might erroneously presume that age was measured in months or years, or weight and length reported in British rather than metric units.

Minimize use of abbreviations or acronyms in headings. If space is tight, use single words or short phrases. Explain the concepts measured by each variable as you describe the table so the brief monikers will become familiar. If readers need to see a long or complex wording, refer them to an appendix that contains that part of the original data collection instrument. Do not use eight-character variable names from statistical packages — your audience will not know what they mean.

Poor:

Table X. Descriptive statistics on sample

Variable	Mean	Standard deviation
YNDSR	##	##
Q201a	##	##

Short, cryptic acronyms such as "YNDSR" might be required by your statistics software but rarely are sufficient to convey the meaning of the variable. A variable name based on question number (such as "Q201a") can help you remember which questionnaire item was the original source of the data, but obscures the variable's identity. Feel free to use such shorthand in your data sets and in initial drafts of your tables, but replace them with meaningful phrases in the version your audience will see.

Better:

Table X. Means and standard deviations on socioeconomic and attitudinal variables

Variable	Mean	Standard deviation
Income-to-needs ratio	##	##
Extent of agreement with current welfare system	##	##

These labels clearly identify the concepts in each row. In a scientific article, define the income-to-needs ratio and attitudinal measures in the data and methods section or note to the table. For a lay audience, replace technical labels with everyday synonyms.

Indenting

When organizing rows in a table, place categories of a nominal or ordinal variable in consecutive rows under a single major row header with the subcategories indented. Counts and percentages for groups that are indented equally can be added together to give the total. In table 6.1, for example, "White," "Black" and "All other" together comprise all households. Row labels that are indented farther indicate subgroups and should not be added with the larger groups to avoid double counting. "Non-Hispanic white" is indented in the row below "White," showing that the former is a subgroup of the latter. In the terminology of chapter 4, "white" and "non-Hispanic white" are not mutually exclusive, so they should not be treated as distinct groups when calculating totals or frequency distributions.[1] To indicate that Hispanics should not be added to the other racial groups within the table, the origin contrast is given a separate left-justified row label with rows for Hispanics and non-Hispanics below. Finally, a footnote explains that Hispanics can be of any race, indicating that they should not be added to the racial categories.

Panels

Use panels — blocks of consecutive rows within a table separated by horizontal lines ("rules") or an extra blank row — to organize material within tables. Arrange them one above another with column headings shared by all panels. Panels can introduce another dimension to a table, show different measures of the relationship in the table, or organize rows into conceptually related blocks.

Adding a dimension to a table. Examples of tables that use panels to introduce an additional dimension to a table:
- Separate panels for different years. For example, the relationship between race, ethnic origin, and household structure (table 6.1) might be shown at 10-year intervals from 1960 through 2000 with each year in a separate panel, labeled accordingly. The panels introduce a third variable to a two-way (bivariate) table, in this case adding year to a cross-tabulation of household structure and race or origin. The

panels would share the column headings (household structure), but repeat the row headings (for race and ethnic origin) in each panel.
- Separate panels by other characteristics. For instance, the relationship between household structure and race and ethnic origin might be shown for each of several regions or income levels.

Different measures for the same relationship. Also use panels to organize a table that presents different measures of the same concept, such as number of cases or events, along with measures of distribution or rate of occurrence:
- Table 6.1 could be modified to include a second panel reporting the *percentage* of households in each category to supplement the first panel showing the *number* of households.
- A table might present *number of deaths* according to cause or other characteristics in one panel and *death rates* in another, as in many Centers for Disease Control reports.

For these types of applications, repeat the row headings within each panel and specify the units separately in a header for each panel.

Organizing conceptually related blocks. When a table contains many related variables in the rows, use panels to organize them into blocks of similar items. In table 6.2 rather than lumping all 11 questions on AIDS transmission into one section, the table is arranged into two panels — the top panel on knowledge of ways AIDS is likely to be transmitted, the bottom panel on ways it is unlikely to be transmitted — each labeled accordingly. Within each panel, results are shown separately for each specific question, followed by a summary statistic on that broad knowledge area.

If two small, simple tables have the same column headers and address similar topics, you can combine them into a single table with panels, one panel for the set of rows from each of the smaller tables. Although Table 6.2 could have been constructed as two separate tables — one on likely modes of AIDS transmission and the other on unlikely modes, creating a single table facilitates comparison across topics, such as pointing out that the likely modes are all better understood than the unlikely modes.

For tables that you describe in your text, avoid using more than two or three panels per table, and try to fit each table onto one page or on facing pages. Refer to each panel in your written description to direct readers to specific concepts and numbers as you mention them. Appendix tables that organize data for reference use can include more panels and spill onto several pages. For multipage tables, repeat the table title and column headings on each page, and label the panels (topics, units) so that your readers can follow them without written guidance.

Column Headings

Each column heading identifies the variable or measure (e.g., mean, standard deviation) in that column. The guidelines listed above for labeling abbreviations, notes, and units in rows also apply to columns. If most numbers in a large table are measured in the same unit, use a spanner across columns to generalize with a phrase such as "percentage unless otherwise specified," then name the units for variables measured differently (e.g., in years of age or price in dollars) in the labels for the appropriate columns.

Column Spanners

Column spanners (also known as "straddle rules") show that a set of columns is related, much as indenting shows how a set of rows is related. In table 6.1, households fall into two broad categories — family households and nonfamily households — each of which is demarcated with a column spanner. Beneath the spanners are the associated household subtypes: "Family households" comprise "Married couple" and "Other families," with "Other families" further subdivided into "Female householder" and "Male householder." Nonfamily households include those headed by a "Female householder" and those headed by a "Male householder." Each column spanner also encompasses a column for the total number of households of that type: the "Total" column under the "Family households" spanner is the sum of the "Married couple" and the two "Other families" columns.

Interior Cells

Report your numbers in the interior cells of the table, following the guidelines in table 4.2 for number of digits and decimal places. Many disciplines omit numeric estimates based on only a few cases, either because of the substantial uncertainty associated with those estimates or to protect confidentiality of human subjects (appendix 1 in Benson and Marano 1998; NCHS 2002). Conventions about minimum sample sizes vary by discipline, so follow the standards in your field. If there is an insufficient number of cases to report data for one or

Table 6.2. Use of panels to organize conceptually related sets of variables

Knowledge about AIDS transmission, by language spoken at home and ability to speak English, New Jersey, 1998

Mode of transmission	English ($N = 408$)	Spanish/ English ques. ($N = 32$)	Spanish/ Spanish ques. ($N = 20$)	Chi-square	(*p*-value)
		Language spoken at home/ language used on questionnaire			
Likely modes of transmission					
Sexual intercourse with an infected person[a]	93.6	87.5	95.0	1.9	(.39)
Shared needles for IV drug use[a]	92.4	90.6	65.0	17.6	(.000)
Pregnant mother to baby[a]	89.5	75.0	80.0	7.2	(.03)
Blood transfusion from infected person[a]	87.5	81.3	60.0	12.5	(.002)
Mean percentage of "likely" questions correct	91.7	83.6	75.0	8.3[b]	(.000)

Unlikely modes of transmission

Working near someone with the AIDS virus[a]	81.6	75.0	35.0	25.4	(.000)
Using public toilets[a]	66.4	53.1	30.0	12.7	(.002)
Eating in a restaurant where the cook has AIDS[a]	61.3	50.0	35.0	3.7	(.04)
Being coughed or sneezed on[a]	57.8	50.0	25.0	8.8	(.01)
Sharing plates, cups or utensils[a]	56.4	46.9	25.0	8.3	(.02)
Visiting an infected medical provider[a]	35.0	34.4	25.0	0.8	(.65)
Mean percentage of "unlikely" questions correct	59.8	51.6	29.2	8.2[b]	(.000)
Mean percentage of all questions correct	72.1	64.4	47.5	11.7[b]	(.000)

Source: Miller 2000a.

[a] Percentage of respondents answering AIDS transmission questions correctly

[b] Test for difference based on ANOVA. Reported statistic is the F-statistic with 2 degrees of freedom.

more cells in your table, type a symbol in place of the numeric estimate and include a footnote that specifies the minimum size criterion and a pertinent citation.

Notes to Tables

Put information that does not fit easily in the title, row, or column labels in notes to the table. Spell out abbreviations, give brief definitions, and provide citations for data sources or other background information. To keep tables concise and tidy, limit notes to a simple sentence or two, referring to longer descriptions in the text or appendixes if more detail is needed. If a table requires more than one note, label them with different symbols or letters, rather than numbers, which could be confused with exponents, then list the notes in that order at the bottom of the table following the conventions for your intended publisher. (Letters also allow the reader to distinguish table notes from text notes.)

If you are using secondary data, provide a source note to each table, citing the name and date of the data set or a reference to a publication that describes it. If all tables in your article, report, or presentation use data from the same source, you might not need to cite it for every table. Some journals or publishers require the data source to be specified in every chart or table, however, so check the applicable guidelines.

■ COMMON TYPES OF TABLES

This section describes common variants of univariate, bivariate, and three-way tables. See also Nicol and Pexman (1999) for guidance on tables to present specific types of statistics, or Miller (forthcoming) regarding tables of multivariate regression results.

Univariate Tables

Univariate tables show information on each variable alone rather than associations among variables. Common types of univariate tables include those that present the distribution of a variable or composition of a sample (e.g., table 6.3) or descriptive statistics on a series of related outcomes, such as categories of consumer expenditures (table 6.4).

A univariate table can include more than one type of numeric information for each variable. Table 6.3 includes separate columns for the number and percentage of cases with each attribute, labeled ac-

Table 6.3. Univariate table: Sample composition

Demographic characteristics of study sample,
United States, 2002

Demographic characteristic	Number of cases	Percentage of sample
Gender		
Male	1,000	48.6
Female	1,058	51.4
Age group (years)		
18–39	777	37.8
40–64	852	41.4
65+	429	20.8
Educational attainment		
<High school	358	17.4
=High school	1,254	60.9
>High school	446	21.7
Race/ethnicity		
Non-Hispanic white	1,144	55.6
Non-Hispanic black	455	22.1
Hispanic	328	15.9
Asian	86	4.2
Other race	45	2.2
Overall sample	2,058	100.0

cordingly. Table 6.4 presents the mean and the standard deviation for levels of expenditures on different categories of goods and services among the uninsured.

Bivariate Tables

Bivariate, or two-way, tables show the relationship between two variables. Common types of bivariate tables are cross-tabulations, those that present differences in means or other statistics for one variable according to values of a second variable, and correlations. The nature of your variables — categorical or continuous — will determine which type of table applies to your topic.

Table 6.4. Univariate table: Descriptive statistics

Means and standard deviations of selected categories
of consumer expenditures ($) among people without
health insurance, United States, 1994–1998

Real expenditures	Mean	Std. dev.
Housing	1,125	862
Transportation	956	1,616
Food eaten at home	751	513
Utilities	473	347
Food eaten away from home	249	312
Education	186	638
All other	1,099	NA
Total	4,839	2,875

Source: Levy and DeLeire 2002.
Note: Unweighted $N = 5,324$

**Table 6.5. Bivariate table: Rates of occurrence based
on a cross-tabulation**

Poverty rates (%) by age group, United States, 2000

	Age group (years)			
	<18	18–64	65+	Total
Population (1,000s)	72,653	177,934	34,385	34,570
% Poor	16.7	10.6	10.4	12.1

Source: Proctor and Dalaker 2003

Cross-Tabulations

A cross-tabulation shows the joint distribution of two categorical
variables — how the overall sample is divided among all possible
combinations of those two variables. Table 6.5 shows how poverty
rates differ according to age group, calculated from a cross-tabulation
of two variables: age group and poverty status. Readers could calculate the number of persons in each poverty category from the total

Table 6.6. Comparison of sample with target population

Birth weight, socioeconomic characteristics, and smoking behavior,
NHANES III sample, 1988–1994, and all U.S. births, 1997

	NHANES III sample [abc]	All U.S. births, 1997 [d]
Birth weight		
Median (grams)	3,402	3,350
% Low birth weight (<2,500 grams)	6.8	7.5
Mother's age		
Median (years)	26.0	26.7
% Teen mother	12.5	12.7
Mother's educational attainment		
Median (years)	12.0	12.8
% <High school	21.6	22.1
% =High school	35.0	32.4
Mother smoked while pregnant (%)	24.5	13.2
Number of cases	9,813	3,880,894

[a]Weighted to population level using weights provided with the NHANES III
(Westat 1996); sample size is unweighted.
[b]Information for NHANES III is calculated from data extracted from National
Center for Health Statistics (U.S. DHHS 1997).
[c]Includes non-Hispanic white, non-Hispanic black, and Mexican American
infants with complete information on family income, birth weight, maternal
age, and education.
[d]Information for all U.S. births is from Ventura et al. (1999) except median
mother's age (Mathews and Hamilton 2002).

number of persons and the percentage poor in each age group[2] (see
"Which Numbers to Include" below).

Tables can also be used to compare composition of a sample and
population, as in table 6.6, where characteristics of a survey sample
used to study birth weight are compared against those among all
births that occurred nationally in the same time period. Or, they can
present information on alternative measures of a concept, such as rat-
ings of items at several points in time or from each of several sources
(not shown).

Table 6.7. Bivariate table: Pairwise correlations

Correlations among county-level demographic and economic characteristics, New Jersey 1999–2001

Characteristics	Demographic characteristics					Economic characteristics		
	Black pop.	Black ID[a]	Pop. density	Total pop.	Non-English speakers (%)	Unemp. rate (%)	Income inequality[b]	Child pov. rate (%)
Demographic								
Black population	1.00							
Black ID[a]	0.15	1.00						
Pop. density (persons/sq. mi.)	0.39	0.12	1.00					
Total population	0.31	0.12	0.58[d]	1.00				
Non-English speakers (%)	0.39	0.05	0.91[d]	0.49[c]	1.00			
Economic								
Unemployment rate (%)	0.31	−0.17	0.22	−0.16	0.33	1.00		
Income inequality[b]	0.10	0.94[d]	0.10	0.09	−0.02	−0.15	1.00	
Child poverty rate (%)	0.69[d]	−0.07	0.53[c]	0.12	0.61[d]	0.75[d]	−0.06	1.00

Source: Quality Resource Systems 2001.

Note: N = 21 counties.

[a] ID = Index of dissimilarity, a measure of residential segregation.

[b] Gini coefficient.

[c] $p < 0.05$.

[d] $p < 0.01$.

Differences in Means

Bivariate tables are also used to present statistics for one or more continuous variables according to some categorical variable. Table 6.2 shows how AIDS knowledge varies by language group, presenting mean scores for two topic areas for each of three language groups.

Correlations

A bivariate table can present correlations among continuous variables. In table 6.7, each interior cell holds the pairwise correlation between the variables named in the associated row and column. For instance, in the late 1990s, the correlation between the child poverty rate and the unemployment rate in New Jersey's 21 counties was 0.75.

To present more detailed information about the joint distribution of two continuous variables, use a line graph or scatter chart (see chapter 7).

Three-Way Tables

Three-way tables present information on associations among three variables or sets of related variables, such as the joint distribution of three categorical variables. One way to show a three-way relationship is to use column spanners. In table 6.8, the columns contain two variables — gender and type of drug — with rows for selected major cities in the United States. The spanner divides the table into sections for males and females. Within each of those spanners is a column for each of three types of drugs and for all drugs combined. This structure facilitates comparison across types of drugs within each gender because the drugs are in adjacent columns. If you want to emphasize comparison of drug use for males against that for females, place type of drug in the column spanner (there would be four such spanners) with columns for each gender arranged underneath.

This type of design works only if the two variables used in the column spanners and the columns below have no more than a few categories apiece. For variables with more categories, use panels or a chart to present three-way relationships.

■ ORGANIZING TABLES TO COORDINATE WITH YOUR WRITING

As you write about the patterns shown in your tables, proceed systematically, comparing numbers either across the columns or down the rows of your table. To describe both types of patterns, create

Table 6.8. Three-way table with nested column spanners

Drug use by arrestees in selected major United States cities by type of drug and sex, 1999

| | Percentage testing positive[a] | | | | | | | |
| | Male | | | | Female | | | |
City	Any drug[b]	Marijuana	Cocaine	Heroin	Any drug	Marijuana	Cocaine	Heroin
Atlanta, GA	76.7	44.4	51.3	4.3	77.2	33.5	62.0	4.5
Chicago, IL	74.4	44.6	41.7	20.1	76.9	26.5	64.3	32.4
Los Angeles, CA	62.4	32.3	35.6	5.5	61.6	21.0	36.7	8.2
Miami, FL	66.0	36.2	49.2	3.4	NA	NA	NA	NA
New York, NY	74.7	40.8	44.2	15.2	81.3	26.2	65.1	21.1
Washington, DC	68.9	34.9	37.7	16.0	NA	NA	NA	NA

Source: U.S. Census Bureau, 2002b.

[a]Based on data from the Arrestee Drug Abuse Monitoring Program: U.S. National Institute of Justice, *2000 Arrestee Drug Abuse Monitoring: Annual Report*, available at http://www.ncjrs.org/txtfiles1/nij/193013.txt.

[b]Includes other drugs not shown separately.

separate paragraphs for the "down the rows" and "across the columns" comparisons (see appendix A).

Decide on the main point you want to make about the data using one or more of the principles described below. Arrange the rows and columns accordingly, then describe the numbers in the same order they appear in the table. If possible, use the same organizing principles in all the tables within a document, such as tables reporting descriptive statistics and mean outcomes on the same set of variables.

For ordinal variables, the sequence of items in rows or columns will be obvious. List the possible response categories in their ranked order: from "Excellent" to "Poor" or from "Agree strongly" to "Disagree strongly," for example, either in ascending or descending order, depending on how you prefer to discuss them. Arrange information for several dates or time periods in chronological order.

For nominal variables (such as religion or race) or for tables that encompass several different variables (such as AIDS knowledge topics), the values of the categories or items do not have an inherent order. In those instances, use one or more of the following principles to organize them.

Theoretical Grouping

Arranging items into theoretically related sets can be very effective. Using panels to separate likely and unlikely modes of AIDS transmission in table 6.2 reveals important distinctions between the items that would be obscured if they were listed in one undifferentiated block. The accompanying discussion can then emphasize that the former topics were much better understood than the latter without asking readers to zigzag through the table to find the pertinent numbers.

Empirical Ordering

An important objective of many numeric tabulations is to show which items have the highest and the lowest values and where other items fall relative to those extremes. If this is your key point, organize the table in ascending or descending order of numeric values or frequency as in table 6.4.[3] If the ranking varies for different measures shown within one table, decide which you will emphasize, then use it as the basis for organizing the rows.

Order of Importance in Your Analysis

Most research questions concern relationships among two or three variables, with other variables playing a less important role. Logically, you will discuss the key variables first, so put them at the top of your table. For instance, a table of descriptive statistics for a study of how educational attainment and work experience affect wages might put the outcome variable (wages) in the top row, followed by the other main variable or variables (work experience and educational attainment), and then other factors considered in the study (e.g., gender, age).

Alphabetical Ordering

Few substantively meaningful patterns happen to occur alphabetically, hence alphabetical order is usually a poor principle for arranging items within tables to be discussed in the text. On the other hand, alphabetical order is often the best way to organize data in appendix tables or other large data tabulations that are not accompanied by written guidance. In such cases, using a familiar convention helps readers find specific information quickly. The daily stock market report of opening, closing, high, and low price of thousands of stocks is such an example.

Order of Items from a Questionnaire

Unless your analysis is mainly concerned with evaluating the effects of questionnaire design on response patterns, do not list items in the order they appeared on the questionnaire. Again, this order is unlikely to correspond to underlying empirical or theoretical patterns, so your table and description will not match.

Multiple Criteria for Organizing Tables

For tables with more than a few rows of data, a combination of approaches may be useful: you might group items according to their characteristics, then arrange them *within* those groups in order of descending frequency or other empirical consideration. In table 6.2, knowledge of AIDS transmission is first grouped into likely and unlikely modes of transmission, then in descending order of knowledge within each of those classifications.

Sometimes it makes sense to apply the same criterion sequentially, such as identifying major theoretical groupings and then minor topic groupings within them. Political opinion topics could be classified into domestic and foreign policy, for example, each with a major row heading. Within domestic policy would be several items apiece on education, environment, health, transportation, and so forth, yielding corresponding subcategories and sets of rows. Foreign policy would also encompass several topics.

If you have organized your table into several theoretically or empirically similar groups of items, alphabetical order can be a logical way to sequence items *within* those groups. For example, data on the 50 United States are often grouped by major census region, then presented in alphabetical order within each region. Alphabetical order within conceptual or empirical groupings also works well if several items have the same value of the statistics reported in the table (e.g., mean or frequency). Conventions about placement of "total" rows vary, with some publications placing them at the top of the table or panel, others at the bottom. Consult your publisher's instructions to decide where to place your total row.

■ TECHNICAL CONSIDERATIONS

Which Numbers to Include

A table is a tool for presenting numeric evidence, not a database for storing data or a spreadsheet for doing calculations. Except for a data appendix or a laboratory report, omit the raw data for each case: readers don't need to wade through values of every variable for every case in a large data set. Generally you will also leave out numbers that represent intermediate steps in calculating your final statistics. Like a carpenter, do the messy work (data collection and calculations) correctly, then present a clean, polished final product. Decide which numbers are needed to make the table's substantive points, then keep the other data out of the table, where your readers don't trip over it on their way to the important stuff.

The output from a statistical program is usually a poor prototype of a table for publication: such output often includes information that isn't directly relevant to your research question and thus should be omitted from your table. For example, output from a cross-tabulation usually shows the count (number of cases), row percentage, column percentage, and percentage of the overall (grand) total for every cell. Determine which of those statistics answer the question at hand — usually *one* of the percentages and possibly the number of cases for each cell — and report only those numbers in your table. In most instances, report the number of cases only for the margins of a cross-tabulation, because the counts for interior cells can be calculated from the marginals (the row and column subtotals found at the edges ("margins") of the cross-tabulation) and the interior percentages, as in table 6.5.

Cross-tabulations of dichotomous (2-category) variables in particular include a lot of redundant information. If you report the percentage of cases that are male, the percentage female is unnecessary because by definition, it is 100% minus the percentage male. Likewise for variables coded true/false, those that indicate whether some event (e.g., high school graduation, a political coup) did or did not happen, whether a threshold was or wasn't crossed (e.g., obesity, the speed of sound), or other variants of yes/no.[4] Hence a tabulation of approval of legal abortion (a yes/no variable) by a six-category religion variable will yield 12 interior cells, 8 marginals, and the grand total, each of which contains counts and one or more percentages. In your final table, only seven of those numbers are needed to compare abortion attitudes across groups: the share of each religious group that believes abortion should be legal and the approval rate for all religions combined.

Number of Decimal Places and Scale of Numbers

Within each column, use a consistent scale and number of decimal places. For instance, do not switch from nanometers in one row to micrometers in other rows of a column reporting the size of viruses and bacteria. Likewise, keep the scale and number of decimal places the same for all columns reporting numbers measured in similar units: if all your columns show death rates, use a uniform scale (e.g., deaths per 100,000 persons across the board, not per 1,000 in some columns).

Follow the guidelines in chapter 4 regarding the following:
- Number of digits and decimal places that inform but do not overwhelm your readers. Change the scale or use scientific notation to avoid presenting overly long numbers or those with many zeros as placeholders.
- Conventions about decimal places for certain kinds of numbers: two decimal places for small monetary denominations, none for integers.
- Precision of measurement that is consistent with the original data collection.

Alignment

There are certain standard or sensible ways to align the contents of different table components:

- Left justify row labels, then use indenting to show subgroups.
- Use decimal alignment in the interior cells to line up the numbers properly within each column, especially when symbols are used in some but not all rows (e.g., to denote statistical significance). Right alignment works too, assuming you have used a consistent number of decimal places for all numbers in the column and no symbols are needed.
- Center column titles over the pertinent column and column spanners over the range of columns to which they apply.

Portrait versus Landscape Layout

Tables can be laid out in one of two ways: *portrait* (with the long dimension of the page vertical, like table 6.3), or *landscape* (with the long dimension horizontal, like table 6.1). For print documents and web pages, start with a portrait layout, because the accompanying text pages are usually vertical. For slides or chartbooks, start with a landscape layout to match the rest of the document.

These general considerations aside, pick a layout that will accommodate the number of rows and columns needed to hold your information. If you have more than a dozen rows, use a portrait layout or create a multipanel landscape table that will flow onto more than one page. Unless your column labels and the numbers in the corresponding interior cells are very narrow, four to five columns are the most that can fit in a portrait layout, up to 12 narrow columns in a landscape layout.

Consider alternative arrangements of variables in the rows and columns. If you are cross-tabulating two variables, there is no law that decrees which variable must go in the rows. Take, for example, a table comparing characteristics of geographic entities: the 50 United States are virtually always listed in the rows because a 50-column table would be ungainly. On the other hand, the six populated continents easily fit in the columns of a landscape table. Which variable to put in the rows is determined by the number of categories (countries or continents), not the concept being measured. A long, skinny table can be revised by bringing the bottom half up alongside the top half. Repeat the column heads side by side and separate the two halves by a vertical rule.

Type Size

For your tables, use a type size consistent with that in your text — no more than one or two points smaller. With the possible exception of reference tables, tiny scrunched labels with lots of abbreviations and microscopically printed numbers are usually a sign that you are trying to put too much into one table. Redesign it into several tables, each of which encompasses a conceptually related subset of the original table. Arrange a large appendix table into a few panels per page using one or more of the criteria explained above to divide and organize the variables so readers can find information of interest easily.

Table and Cell Borders

Many word processing programs initially create tables with gridlines delineating the borders between cells. However, once you have typed in the row and column labels, most of those lines are no longer needed to guide readers through your table. Places where it *is* useful to retain lines within a table include borders between panels, and lines to designate a column spanner.

Word processing programs offer table templates or auto formatting — predesigned formats complete with fancy colors, fonts, shading, and lines of different thickness. While some lines and other features can make it easier to read a table, others simply add what Edward Tufte (2001) refers to as "nondata ink": aspects of the design that distract readers rather than adding to the function of the table. Design your tables to emphasize the substantive questions and pertinent data, not the superfluous eye candy.

Formatting for Different Publications

Table formatting varies by discipline and publisher. Some require titles to be left-justified, others centered. Some require all capital letters, others mixed upper- and lowercase. Many journals also have specific guidelines for labeling footnotes to tables and use of other symbols within tables. Requirements for types of punctuation and use of lines within the table also vary. Consult a manual of style for your intended publisher before you design your tables. Even if you aren't required to follow specific guidelines, be consistent as you format your tables: do not left justify one table title, then center the title for the next table, or label footnotes to the first table with letters but use symbols to denote footnotes in the second.

■ DRAFTING YOUR TABLES

Conceptualize the contents and layout of a table early in the writing process, certainly before you start typing the information into a word processor and possibly even before you collect or analyze the data. Identifying the main question to be addressed by each table helps you anticipate the statistics to be calculated. Thinking ahead about the specific points you will make about patterns in the table helps you design a layout that coordinates with the description.

Drafting Your Table with Pencil and Paper

To create an effective table, plan before you type. Separating these steps helps you think about a layout and labels that emphasize the substantive concepts to be conveyed before you get caught up in the point-and-click task of creating the table on a computer. By not planning ahead, you are more likely to write incomplete titles or labels, create too few columns or rows, overlook important features like column spanners or footnotes, and to arrange these elements poorly. You must then go back and reconstruct the table on the screen — quite a hassle if the numbers have already been typed in — increasing the risk that numbers end up in the wrong cells of the table.

To test possible layouts for your tables, use scrap paper, a pencil, and an eraser. Don't skimp on paper by trying to squeeze drafts of all four (or however many) tables you need to plan onto one page. Use a full page for each table. Expect to have to start over a couple of times, especially if you are new to planning tables or are working with unfamiliar concepts, variables, or types of statistical analyses.

Aim for a fairly complete draft of each table, showing the shape, number of rows and columns, and complete titles, labels, and notes. Make it enough like your desired final product that someone else could type it without having to consult you, more as a check of clarity and completeness than actual preparation for a typist.

Determining the Shape and Size of Your Table

Create one column for each set of numbers to be displayed vertically, then add a column for row labels. Make the column for row labels wide enough to accommodate a short, intelligible phrase that identifies the contents (and sometimes units) in each row. Most numeric columns can be narrower (see below).

Count how many variables you will be displaying in the rows, then add rows to accommodate the table title and column headings. Depending on the content and organization of your table, you may need additional rows to fit column spanners, labels for panels, information on the overall sample (e.g., total sample size), results of statistical tests, or simply white space to increase ease of reading.

Once you know how many rows and columns you need, assess whether a landscape or portrait layout will work better. For tables with approximately equal numbers of rows and columns, try it both ways to see which fits the information better and is easier to read. Orient your scrap paper accordingly, then draw in gridlines to delineate the rows and columns. Erase gridlines to show column spanners and draw in horizontal lines to differentiate panels. The idea is to have a grid within which you can test out the labels and other components of the table. You will probably redesign and redraw it a couple of times before you are satisfied, so don't bother to measure exact spacing or draw perfect, straight lines in your rough drafts. The software will that do for you, once you have decided what the table should look like.

Interior Cells
The interior cells of the table are where your numbers will live. When planning column widths, consider the following questions:
- What is the maximum number of digits you will need in each column?
- Do you need to include units' indicators (e.g., $, %), thousands' separators (e.g., the comma in "1,000"), or other characters that will widen your column?
- Will you be using symbols within the table cells, to key them to a footnote or to indicate statistical significance, for example?

Evaluating Your Table Layout
Before you type your table into a word processor, evaluate it for completeness and ease of understanding. To test whether your table can stand alone, pick several cells within the table and see whether you can write a complete sentence describing the identity and meaning of those numbers using only the information provided in the table. Better yet, have someone unfamiliar with your project do so.

Creating Your Table in a Word Processor
Word processing software can be a real boon for creating a table: simply tell your computer to make a 7-column by 12-row table on a landscape page and voila! However, some word processors think they know what you want better than you do, and will automatically format aspects of your table such as page layout, alignment, type size, and whether text wraps to the next line. After you have created the basic table structure on the computer, save it, then check carefully

that each part of the table looks the way you showed it on your rough draft. Occasionally, the computer's ideas will improve upon yours, however, so consider them as well.

A few hints:

- *Before* you begin to create the table, inform the word processor whether you want a portrait or landscape page layout, then save the document. Then when you specify the desired number of columns, their width will be calculated based on the full available width (usually 6.5" for portrait, 9.5" for landscape, assuming 1" margins all around). Much easier than manually resizing columns from portrait to landscape after the fact . . .

- Specify alignment for each part of the table after creating the initial grid. An alternative in some software programs is to impose a selected, preformatted design for your table (see your software manual or Help menu for more information).

- Alter appearance of table and cell borders:

  Once titles and labels are in place, omit many cell borders for a cleaner look.

  Resize column widths to accommodate row labels and numbers.

  Delineate panels within the table. If you have omitted most row borders, use a single, thin line or a blank row to separate panels; if you have retained borders between all rows, use a thicker line, a double line, or a blank row between panels.

As you transfer your design into the word processor, you may discover that a different layout will work better, so learn from what appears on the screen and then revise it to suit.

■ CHECKLIST FOR CREATING EFFECTIVE TABLES

- Title: write an individualized title for each table:
  State the purpose or topic of that table.
  Include the context of the data (the W's).
  Identify units, if the same for all or most variables in the table.
- Other labeling
  Label each row and column:
    −Briefly identify its contents.
    −Specify units or coding if not summarized in table title.
  Use footnotes:
    −Identify the data source (if not in table title).
    −Define all abbreviations and symbols used within the table.
- Structure and organization
  Use indenting or column spanners to show how adjacent rows or columns relate.
  Apply theoretical and empirical principles to organize rows and columns.
    −For text tables, coordinate row and column sequence with order of discussion.
    −For appendix tables, use alphabetical order or another widely known principle for the topic so tables are self-guiding.
  Report the fewest number of digits and decimal places needed for your topic, data, and types of statistics.
  Use consistent formatting, alignment, and symbols in all tables in a document.
- Check that table can be understood without reference to the text.

Creating Effective Charts

Well-conceived charts provide a good general sense of pattern, complementing a prose description by graphically depicting the shape and size of differences between numbers. Design your charts to emphasize the evidence related to your research question rather than drawing undue attention to the structure of the chart itself. Edward Tufte (2001) stresses minimizing "nondata ink" and "ducks"—his terms for excessive labeling and garish features that distract readers from the numeric information itself. Many of the principles for designing effective tables apply equally to charts:

- Label charts so readers can identify the purpose of each chart and interpret the data from the titles and labels alone.
- Make charts self-contained, including units, context, and source of the data, and definitions of abbreviations.
- Design each chart to promote understanding of the patterns in that chart and to coordinate with your written description.

I begin this chapter with a quick tour of the anatomy of a chart, with general guidelines about features shared by several types of charts. Using examples of pie, bar, line, and scatter charts and their variants, I then show how to choose among those types for different topics and types of variables. Finally, I discuss additional design considerations and common pitfalls in chart creation. For other resources on chart design, see Tufte (1990, 1997, 2001) and Zelazny (2001).

■ ANATOMY OF A CHART

All charts need good titles, labels, and notes.

Chart Titles

The same principles that guide creation of table titles also work for charts. Briefly:

- Specify the topic and W's in each chart title. A short restatement of the research question or relationships shown in the chart often works well.
- Use the title to differentiate the topic of each chart from other charts and tables in the same document.

Axis titles, labels, and legends identify the concepts and units of the variables in charts, much as row and column labels do in tables.

Axis Titles and Axis Labels

Charts that illustrate the relations between two or more variables usually have an *x* (horizontal) axis and a *y* (vertical) axis. Give each axis a title that identifies its contents and units of measurement, and include labels for categories or values along that axis. Write brief but informative axis titles and labels, using short phrases or single words instead of acronyms whenever possible. In the axis *title* name the overall concept ("Year" for the *x* axis title in figure 7.1), then assign axis *labels* to identify values (1980, 1985 . . . in figure 7.1) or names of categories (Saudi Arabia, Russia . . . ; figure 7.4) along the axis.

For continuous variables, minimize clutter by marking major increments of the units, aiming for 5 to 10 value labels on each axis. Remember, charts are best used when precise values aren't important, so your axis labels need only show approximate values. To choose an appropriate increment for the axis scale, consider the range, scale, precision of measurement, and how the data were collected. To present census data for 1950 through 2000, for example, make those dates the

Median sales price of new single-family homes, by region, United States, 1980–2000

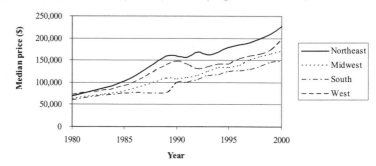

Figure 7.1. Anatomy of a chart: Multiple line chart.
Source: U.S. Census Bureau 2001a.

limits of the axis values and label 10-year increments to match the data collection years.

As with tables, try to fit units of measurement into the title of each chart. If there isn't room, name the general concept or dimension in the table title ("Median sales price" in figure 7.1), then give specific units for that dimension ($) in the axis title. For pie charts, which don't have axes, identify units in the title, footnote, or data labels.

Legend

Use a legend to identify the series or categories of variables that are not labeled elsewhere in the chart. In figure 7.1, the legend specifies which line style corresponds to each of the four regions. See below for how to use legends in other types of charts.

Data Labels

Data labels are typed numeric values adjacent to the pertinent slice, point, or bar in a chart (e.g., the reported percentages in figure 7.2b). To keep charts simple and readable, use data labels sparingly. Again, the main advantage of a chart is that it can illustrate general levels or patterns, which will be evident without data labels if your chart has adequate titles. Complement the general depiction in the chart with your text description, reporting exact values of selected numbers to document the patterns (see "Generalization, Example, Exception" in chapter 2, and appendix A for guidelines). If your audience requires exact values for all numbers in the chart, replace the chart with a table or include an appendix table rather than putting data labels on each point.

Reserve data labels for

- reference points; and
- reporting absolute level associated with a pie or stacked bar chart, such as total number of cases or total value of the contents of the pie (e.g., total dollar value of annual outlays in figure 7.2).

■ CHART TYPES AND THEIR FEATURES

Charts to Illustrate Univariate Distributions

Univariate charts present data for only one variable apiece, showing how cases are distributed across categories (for nominal or ordinal variables) or numeric values (for interval or ratio variables).

Pie Charts

Most people are familiar with pie charts from elementary school. A pie chart is a circle divided into slices like a pizza, with each slice representing a different category of a variable, such as expenditure categories in the federal budget (figure 7.2). The size of each slice illustrates the relative size or frequency of the corresponding category. Identify each slice either in a legend (figures 7.2a and b) or in a value label adjacent to each slice (figure 7.2c). Although you can also label each slice with the absolute amount or percentage of the whole that it contributes (figure 7.2b) the basic story in the chart is often adequately illustrated without reporting specific numeric values: is one slice much larger (or smaller) than the others, or are they all about equal?

To compare two or three pie charts that differ in the total size they represent, you can make them proportionate to that total. For instance, if the total budget in one year was twice as large as in another, create the former pie with twice the area of the latter.

Use pie charts to present composition or distribution — how the parts add up to the whole. Each pie chart shows distribution of a single variable, such as favorite ice cream flavors from a survey or the organic and mineral composition of a soil sample. Because they illustrate composition, pie charts can be used only for variables whose values are mutually exclusive — after all, the slices of a single pizza don't overlap one another in the pan.

- Display only one variable per pie chart: either age or gender distribution — not both.[1]
- Don't use pie charts to compare averages or rates across groups or time periods. Those dimensions don't have to add up to any specifiable total, so a pie chart, which shows composition, doesn't fit the topic:

  High school graduation rates for boys and for girls *don't* add up to the graduation rate for the two genders combined.

  Average temperatures in each of the 12 months of the year are *not* summed to obtain the average temperature for the year. Such logic would yield an average annual temperature of 664°F for the New York City area.
- Don't use a pie chart to contrast dimensions of quantitative comparison such as rates, ratios, percentage change, or average values of some outcome; instead use a bar or line chart.
- Don't use a pie chart to present multiple-response variables, such as which reasons influenced buyers' choice of a car

a. U.S. federal outlays by function, 2000

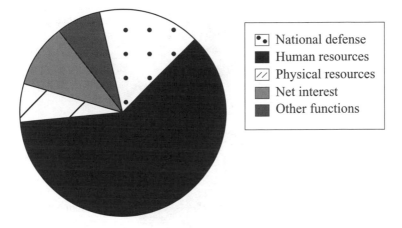

Total outlays: $1.8 trillion

b. U.S. federal outlays by function, 2000

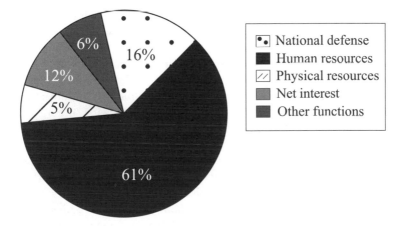

Total outlays: $1.8 trillion

Figure 7.2. Pie charts to illustrate composition, (a) without data labels, (b) with data (numeric value) labels, (c) with value labels.
Source: U.S. Office of Management and Budget 2002.

c. U.S. federal outlays by function, 2000

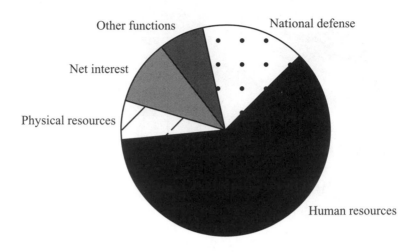

Total outlays: $1.8 trillion

Figure 7.2. (*continued*)

model. Instead, create a different pie chart for each possible response, or use a bar chart to show frequency of each response.

- Avoid pies with many skinny slices. Consider combining rare categories unless one or more of them is of particular interest to your research question. Or, create one pie that includes the most common responses with a summary slice for "other," then a second pie that shows a detailed breakdown of values within the "other" category.

In addition to the above pie-chart no-nos, some aspects of composition are more effectively conveyed with a different type of chart.

- Use a histogram to present the distribution of values of an ordinal variable, especially one with many categories. Histograms show the order and relative frequency of those values more clearly than a pie.
- To compare composition across more than three groups (e.g., distribution of educational attainment in each of 10 countries), use stacked bar charts, because they are easier to align and compare than several pie charts. Or, create a multipanel histogram.

Histograms

Histograms are a form of simple bar chart used to show distribution of variables with values that can be ranked along the x axis. Use them to present distribution of:

- an ordinal variable, such as the share of adults who fall into each of several age groups (figure 7.3); or
- an interval (continuous) variable with 20 or fewer values. For ratio variables or interval variables with more than 20 values such as IQ score, use a line chart to present distribution.

Array the values of the variable across the x axis and create a bar to show the frequency of occurrence of each value, either number of cases or percentage of total cases, measured on the y axis. To accurately portray distribution of a continuous variable, don't leave horizontal space between bars for adjacent x values. Bars in a histogram should touch one another (as in figure 7.3) unless there are intervening x values for which there are no cases. For example, in figure 4.3d, no cases have any of the values 3 through 9, so there is a gap above the labels for those values, between the bars showing frequency of the x values 2 and 10.

Line charts and box-and-whisker plots can also be used to illustrate distribution of a single variable (see respective sections below).

Don't use histograms to display distribution of nominal variables such as religion or race, because their values do not have an inher-

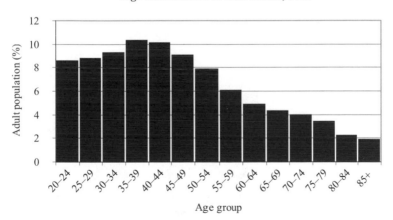

Age distribution of U.S. adults, 2000

Figure 7.3. Histogram to illustrate distribution of an ordinal variable.
Source: U.S. Census Bureau 2002d.

ent order in which to arrange them on the *x* axis. Instead, use a pie chart.

A histogram can be used to display distribution of an ordinal variable with unequal width categories; see cautions under "Line Chart for Unequally Spaced Ordinal Categories" in the section on "Common Errors in Chart Creation" below.

Charts to Present Relationships among Variables
Bar Charts

Simple bar chart. A simple bar chart illustrates the relationship between two variables — a categorical predictor variable on the *x* axis, and a continuous outcome variable on the *y* axis. Most dimensions of quantitative comparison — number, absolute difference, ratio, or percentage change — can be shown in a bar chart, making it an effective tool for comparing values of one variable across groups defined by a second variable. Create one bar for each group with the height of the bar indicating the value of the outcome variable for that group, such as mean crude oil production (*y* axis) for each of five countries (*x* axis, figure 7.4).

To format a simple bar chart, place the continuous variable on the *y* axis and label with its units. The variable on the *x* axis is usually

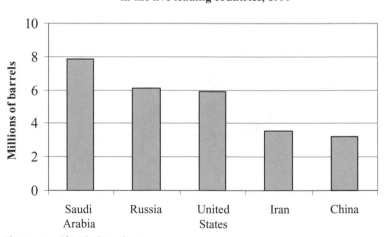

**Daily crude oil production
in the five leading countries, 1999**

Figure 7.4. Simple bar chart.
Source: U.S. National Energy Information Center 2003.

nominal or ordinal. Arrange the categories of nominal variables such as race or country of residence in meaningful sequence, using theoretical or empirical criteria. Display the categories of ordinal variables or values of a continuous variable in their logical order (e.g., income group, letter grades). Simple bar charts don't need a legend because the two variables being compared are defined by the axis titles and labels, hence the same color is used for all the bars.

Clustered bar chart. Use a clustered bar chart to introduce a third dimension to a simple bar chart, illustrating relationships among three variables — a continuous outcome variable by two categorical predictor variables. For example, figure 7.5a shows how emergency room (ER) use for asthma varies according to race and income level simultaneously. One predictor (income group) is shown on the *x* axis, the other predictor (race) in the legend, and the outcome (relative odds of ER use for asthma) on the *y* axis.

Clustered bar charts also work well to show patterns for multiple-response items (how votes for the top three candidates for school board varied according to voter's party affiliation) or a series of related questions. Figure 7.6 includes one cluster for each of 10 AIDS knowledge topics, with one bar for each language group. The height of each bar shows the percentage of the pertinent language group that answered that question correctly.

Finally, clustered bar charts can be used to show distribution of one variable for each of two or three groups, with the histogram for each group comprising one cluster within the chart.

To format a clustered bar chart, place one categorical variable on the *x* axis, the other in the legend, and the continuous variable on the *y* axis. Label each cluster on the *x* axis for the corresponding category of the first predictor variable, then include a legend to identify values of the second predictor.

To decide which variable to show on the *x* axis and which to put in the legend, anticipate which contrast you want to emphasize in your description. Although the description of either version of figure 7.5 will include both the income pattern of ER use and the racial pattern of ER use (see appendix A), each arrangement highlights a different contrast. Figure 7.5a underscores the pattern of emergency room use for asthma across income groups (on the *x* axis). Figure 7.5b presents the same data but reverses the variables in the legend (income group) and the *x* axis (race), highlighting the comparisons across racial groups.

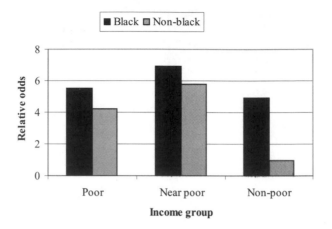

a. Relative odds of emergency room visits for asthma, by race and income, United States, 1991

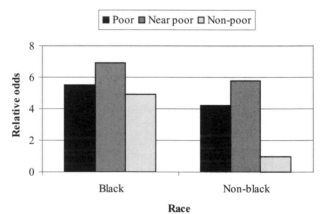

b. Relative odds of emergency room visits for asthma, by race and income, United States, 1991

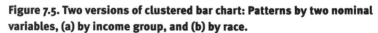

Figure 7.5. Two versions of clustered bar chart: Patterns by two nominal variables, (a) by income group, and (b) by race.

Source: Miller 2000b; data are from U.S. DHHS 1991.

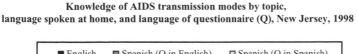

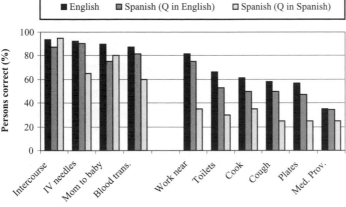

Figure 7.6. Clustered bar chart: Series of related outcomes by a nominal variable.

Source: Miller 2000a.

Note: See table 6.2 for detailed wording.

Stacked bar chart. Create a stacked bar chart to show how the distribution of a variable varies according to another characteristic, such as how age composition varies by race, or how different causes of death add up to the respective overall death rates for males and for females. Because they illustrate the contribution of parts to a whole (composition), stacked bar charts can be used only for variables with mutually exclusive categories, just like pie charts. For multiple-response variables or series of related items, use a clustered bar chart.

There are two major variants of stacked bar charts: those that show variation in level, and those that show only composition. To emphasize differences in level while also presenting composition, construct a stacked bar chart that allows the height of the bar to reflect the level of the outcome variable. Figure 7.7a shows how total federal outlays were divided among major functions with data at 10-year intervals. For each year, the dollar value of outlays in each category is conveyed by the thickness of the respective slice (defined in the legend), and the value of total outlays for all functions combined by the overall height of the stack.

a. U.S. federal outlays by function, 1950–2000

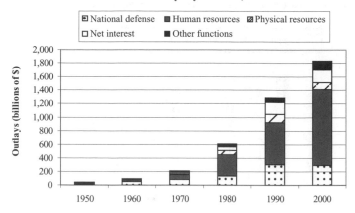

b. U.S. federal outlays by function, 1950–2000

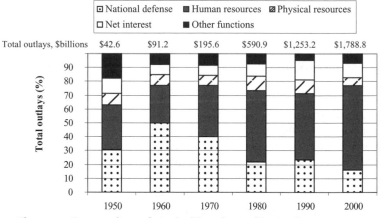

Figure 7.7. Two versions of stacked bar charts, illustrating (a) variation in level, (b) percentage distribution.
Source: U.S. Office of Management and Budget 2002.
Note: Human resources include education, training, employment, and social services; health; Medicare; income security; Social Security; and veterans benefits and services. Physical resources include energy; natural resources and environment; commerce and housing credit; transportation; and community and regional development. Other functions include international affairs; general science, space and technology; agriculture; administration of justice; general government; and allowances.

If there is wide variation in the level of the outcome variable, however, this type of stacked bar chart can obscure important intergroup differences in the distribution of those components. For example, with more than a forty-fold increase in total outlays between 1950 and 2000, it is virtually impossible to assess the relative contribution of each category in the early years based on figure 7.7a.

To compare composition when there is more than a three-fold difference between the lowest and highest Y values across groups or periods, create a stacked bar chart with bars of equal height, and show percentage distribution in the stacked bar. This variant of a stacked bar chart highlights differences in composition rather than level. Figure 7.7b shows that the share of outlays going to defense dropped from roughly 50% in 1960 to 16% in 2000.

Because this version of a stacked bar chart does not present information on absolute level (e.g., outlays in billions of dollars) for each stack, report that information in a separate table, at the top of each stack (e.g. Figure 7.7b), or in a footnote to the chart.

In formatting stacked bar charts, the variables on the x axis and in the slices (legend) must be categorical; the variable on the y axis is continuous. For stacked bar charts in which the height of the bar reflects the level of the outcome variable, the units on the y axis are those in which the variable was originally measured. In figure 7.7a, for example, the y axis shows federal outlays in billions of dollars. For stacked bar charts that emphasize composition (e.g., figure 7.7b), the y axis units are percentage of the overall value for that stack, and by definition, the height of all the bars is the same, since each bar reflects 100% of that year's outlays.

To decide which variable goes on the x axis and which goes in the slices, think about the causal sequence of the variables to be displayed. On the x axis, put the variable that is first in the causal chain, then show how the legend variable differs within those categories.

Line Charts
Single line charts. Use single-line charts to illustrate the relationship between two continuous variables, such as how housing costs change across time (figure 7.8) or how mortality rates vary by year of age. Single line charts can also be used to show distribution of a continuous variable, like the familiar "bell curve" of the IQ distribution.

As in the other types of *XY* charts described above, typically the predictor variable is shown on the x axis and the outcome variable on the y axis, along with their associated units. If you plot smoothed data

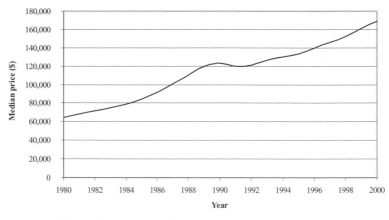

Median sales price of new single-family homes, United States, 1980–2000

Figure 7.8. Single line chart.
Source: U.S. Census Bureau 2001a

(such as moving averages of temporal data, or seasonally adjusted patterns), or other transformations of the original variable, report those transformations in a footnote and refer to the text for a more detailed explanation. No legend is needed because the two variables are identified in the respective axis labels.

Multiple line charts. Create a multiple-line chart to add a third dimension to a single line chart, presenting trends in housing costs by region, for instance (figure 7.1).

Place the continuous outcome variable on the *y* axis, the continuous predictor on the *x* axis, and the categorical predictor in the legend. Use a different line style for each category, with the line styles identified in the legend.

Multiple line charts with two different y-scales. Line charts can also show relations between a continuous variable (on the *x* axis) and each of two closely related continuous outcomes that are measured in different units (on the *y* axes). Figure 7.9 shows trends in the number and percentage poor in the United States. Because the units differ for the two outcome variables, one is presented and identified by the title on the left-hand *y* axis (in this case the percentage of the population that is poor), the other on the right-hand *y* axis (millions of people in poverty). Use the legend to convey which set of units pertains to each line: the dotted line shows poverty rate and is read from the left-hand *y* axis (sometimes called the *Y*1 axis), while the solid line shows the number of poor persons in the same year, on the right-hand (*Y*2) axis.

Charts that use two different *y* axes are complicated to explain and read, so reserve them for relatively savvy audiences and only for variables that are closely related, such as different measures of the same concept. Explicitly refer to the respective *y* axes' locations and units as you describe the patterns.

XYZ line charts. To illustrate the relationship among three continuous variables, such as temperature, pressure and volume, create a three-dimensional line chart, sometimes called an *XYZ* chart after the three axes it contains. Label each axis with the name and units of the pertinent variable.

High/Low/Close Charts

High/low/close charts present three *Y* values for each *X* value. They are probably most familiar as ways to present stock values. The different stocks are arrayed across the *x* axis, with the value on the *y* axis. Alternatively, to show a trend in the price of a single stock, put

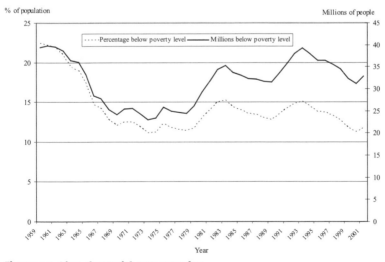

Number and percentage poor, United States, 1959–2001

Figure 7.9. Line chart with two *y*-scales.
Source: Proctor and Dalaker 2002.

**Median and interquartile range, socioeconomic index (SEI),
by race/ethnicity, 1993 U.S. General Social Survey**

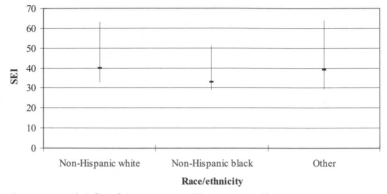

**Figure 7.10. High/low/close chart to illustrate median
and interquartile range.**
Source: Davis, Smith, and Marsden 2003.

dates on the *x* axis. The closing price is shown as a single dot above
the pertinent stock label, with a vertical line connecting it to the high
and low values.

Comparing distribution. Use a high/low/close chart to compare
the distribution of a continuous variable across categories of an ordinal or nominal variable. Figure 7.10 shows the interquartile range of
a socioeconomic index (SEI) according to race: the median SEI for
each racial group is plotted above its label, along with bars showing
the first and third quartiles (the interquartile range).

Alternatively, mean values for each group can be presented with
the upper and lower bars showing the standard deviation, coefficient
of variation, or confidence interval. Error bars also can be added to
bar or line charts.

Tukey box-and-whisker plots. Statistician John Tukey developed
another variant of this type of chart, now widely known as "box-and-
whisker" plots (Tukey 1977; Hoaglin, Mosteller, and Tukey 2000).
The "box" portion of the graph shows the distance between the first
and third quartiles, with the median shown as a dot inside the box.
"Whiskers" (vertical lines) extend upward and downward from those
points to illustrate the highest and lowest values in the distribution.

Outliers — highest or lowest values that are distant from the next closest values — are graphed with asterisks.

Use box-and-whisker techniques to become acquainted with your data, assess how well measures of central tendency (e.g., mean or median) represent the distribution, and identify outliers. Such exploratory graphs are rarely shown in final written documents, but can be invaluable background work to inform your analyses.

In formatting high/low/close charts or error bars, different values to be plotted for each X value must be measured in consistent units — all in dollars, for example. The x variable should be either nominal or ordinal; for a continuous x variable, create a line chart with confidence bands. Identify the meaning of the vertical bars either in the title (as in figure 7.9) or a legend.

Scatter Charts

Use scatter charts to depict the relationship between two continuous variables when there is more than one Y value for each X value, such as several observations for each year. A point is plotted for each X/Y combination in the data, creating a "scatter" rather than a single line. In figure 7.11, each point represents the price plotted against miles per gallon for a particular make and model of car from 2000.

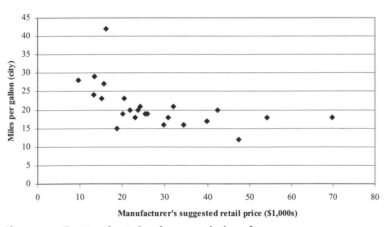

Miles per gallon by manufacturer's suggested retail price, selected '00 and '01 motor vehicles

Figure 7.11. Scatter chart showing association of two continuous variables.

Source: Autoweb.com 2000.

Scatter charts can be combined with other formats or features, such as to show points from two different sets on the same scatter chart, using different symbols to plot points from each set. For example, an asterisk could be used to show data for foreign cars, a pound sign for domestic models.

For a simple scatter chart, no legend is needed because the two variables and their units are identified in the axis titles and labels. For a scatter chart showing more than one series, provide a legend to identify the groups associated with different plotting symbols.

Maps of Numeric Data

Maps are superior to tables or other types of charts for showing data with a geographic component because they show the spatial arrangement of different cases. They can display most types of quantitative comparisons, including level, rank, percentage change, rates, or average values for each geographic unit. For example, figure 7.12 displays average annual pay for each of the lower 48 United States in 1999, revealing a cluster of states with pay in the top quartile in the Northeast and a cluster of bottom-quartile states in the northern Rockies and upper Midwest. These patterns would be much more difficult to visualize from tabular presentation of data or other types of charts.

Maps can also convey location, distance, and other geographic attributes, by using concentric circles to display points of varied distances from a marked feature, such as a train station. Include a legend to explain shading or symbols used on the map and a ruler to show scale. Most of the basic principles mentioned above for effective titles and layout also apply to maps. See Monmonier (1993) or Slocum (1998) for in-depth guides to using maps to display numeric data.

■ ADDING DIMENSIONS TO CHARTS

Most of the chart types described above can display relationships among two or at most three variables. Use panels or combine formats to include additional variables.

- To illustrate the age distribution for each of three countries, for instance, create one panel like that in figure 7.3 for each country, then display all the panels on a single page or on facing pages. Use a uniform axis scale and chart size for all

Average annual pay ($1,000s) by state, United States, 1999

Thousands of $

☐	23.3–26.9
☐	27.0–29.9
☐	30.0–34.1
■	34.2–50.9

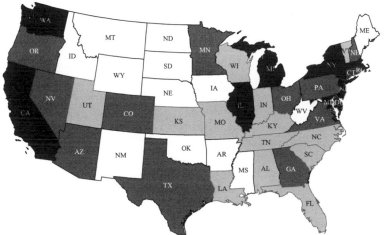

Figure 7.12. Map to illustrate numeric pattern by geographic unit.
Source: U.S. Census 2002d.

panels of the chart to avoid misleading viewers (see "Common Errors in Chart Creation" below).

- To compare changes across time in the distribution of federal outlays for several countries — as in figure 7.7, but with more countries — create a cluster for each year with a stack for each country and slices for each category of outlay.

■ ADVANCED CHART FEATURES

If your analysis involves comparing your data against standard values or patterns or identifying exceptions to a general pattern, consider using reference points, lines, regions, or annotations in your chart. Include these features only if they are vital to illustrating a pattern or contrast, then refer to them in the accompanying narrative. Many charts work fine without these extra bells and whistles, which can distract your readers and clutter the chart.

Annotations

Annotations include labels to guide readers to specific data values or to provide information to help interpret the chart. On a graph showing a skewed distribution you might report and indicate the median or mean with arrows and a short note or label, for instance. Reserve such annotations for when they convey information that is otherwise not evident from the chart. If the distribution is a symmetric bell curve, keep the graph simple and report median and mean in the text or a table.

Annotations can also be used to show outliers or values you use as illustrative examples. In that case, omit data labels from all other values on the chart, naming only those to which you refer in the text.

Reference Points, Lines, and Regions

Include reference points, lines, or regions in your chart to call attention to one or more important values against which other numbers are to be evaluated.

Reference Points

Reference points are probably most familiar from spatial maps. A famous example of the analytic importance of a reference point is the spot map created by John Snow (1936) in his investigation of the London cholera epidemic of 1854. By mapping the location of water pumps where many residents obtained their drinking and cooking water along with the residence of each cholera case, he was able to demonstrate a link between water source and cholera.

Reference Lines

Use reference lines to show a threshold level or other reference value against which to compare data on individual cases or groups. Standard patterns such as the age pattern of mortality for all causes may be curvilinear.

Horizontal reference lines. On an *XY* chart, a horizontal reference line identifies a value of the outcome variable that has some important substantive interpretation.

- On a scatter chart of blood alcohol levels, cases above a line showing the legal limit would be classified as legally drunk.
- On a bar chart showing relative difference, a line at $Y = 1.0$ differentiates cases above and below the reference value (ratios >1.0 and <1.0, respectively).

Vertical reference lines. To identify pertinent values of a continuous predictor variable, include a reference line emanating upward from the x axis. For example, show the date of a change in legislation on a trend chart.

Reference Regions

Use a reference region to locate a range of values on the x axis (a vertical region) or y axis (horizontal band) that are relevant to your analysis. In figure 7.13, shading periods of recession facilitates comparison of how the number of poor persons increased and decreased during and between those periods.

Reference regions can also enhance spatial maps: analyses of effects of nuclear accidents like Chernobyl included maps with con-

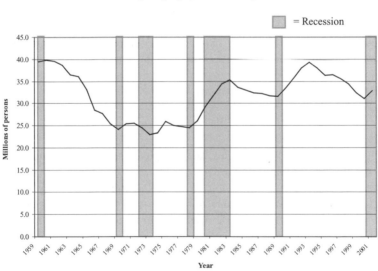

Number of poor people, United States, 1959–2001

Figure 7.13. Line chart with reference regions.
Source: Proctor and Dalaker 2002.

centric circles to show geographic extent of different levels of exposure. In a study of whether to merge local emergency services, you might show which locations can be reached within five minutes by a local police or fire company, which you also plot on the map.

■ CHOOSING AN APPROPRIATE CHART TYPE

To choose among the many types of charts to present your numbers, first figure out how many and what types of variables you are working with, then consider your audience.

Number and Types of Variables in a Chart

Table 7.1 summarizes the different types of charts for presenting distribution of a single variable, relationships between two variables, and relationships among three variables. Within each of those broad categories, chart types are organized according to whether they involve categorical (nominal or ordinal) or continuous variables, or a mixture of the two types. Start by finding the row that matches the type of task and the number and types of variables for your chart (leftmost column), then read across to find suggested chart types with examples of topics and comments on chart design and application.

Unless otherwise noted in the column for example topics, the chart type can accommodate only single-response items; for multiple-response items, a separate chart of that type must be created for each category of response. Accompany charts that present multiple-response items with a footnote explaining that each respondent could have given more than one answer, hence the sum of frequencies across all categories can exceed the number of respondents.

Audience

For nonscientific audiences, keep graphs as simple and familiar as possible. Most people understand pie charts, line charts, and simple bar charts. Reserve complicated three-dimensional charts, high/low/close charts, logarithmic scales, and charts with two different Y-scales for audiences that have worked with them before. For speeches, design most slides with simple, focused charts even for scientific audiences; complicated charts are often hard to read from slides and take longer to explain well.

■ OTHER CONSIDERATIONS

Designing Charts to Coordinate with Your Writing

Design charts so the order in which you mention variables or values in the text matches the order in which they appear in the chart, following the principles for coordinating with your writing described in chapter 6. For nominal variables, identify the main point you want to make about the data, then arrange the values on the axes or in the legend accordingly. For ordinal, interval, or ratio variables, retain the natural order of values on your axes.

Use of Color

Graphics software often automatically uses different colors for each line or bar in the chart. Although slides and some publications permit use of color, in many instances you will need to replace color with different patterns or shades of gray.

- Most documents are printed in grayscale, meaning that the only colors available are black, white, and shades of gray.
- Even if your original will be printed in color, it may be photocopied into black and white.
- Handouts printed from slides are often distributed in black and white.

What appear as different primary hues or pastel tints on a computer screen can become virtually indistinguishable tones in a black and white rendition. Choose a color or shading scheme that will remain evident and interpretable regardless of how your chart is reproduced. For color documents or slides, select colors with maximum contrast such as yellow, red, and blue, then make a second version in black and white for other uses For black-and-white documents, replace colors with one of the following:

- For line charts, pick a different style (solid, dashed, dotted) for each line. If data points are plotted, also vary the plotting symbol, using a circle for one group, a diamond for another, etc.
- For pie charts, bar charts, or maps that include shaded regions, use a different type of shading for each group.
  If there are only two or three groups (slices or bar colors), use white for one, black for the second, and gray for a third. Avoid using color alone to contrast more than three categories in grayscale, as it is difficult to discriminate among light, medium, and dark gray,

Table 7.1. Choice of chart type for specific tasks and types of variables

Task	Type of chart	Example of topic	Comments
Distribution of one variable			
Nominal with ≤5 categories	Pie	Religious affiliation, major religions	Arrange categories by theoretical criteria or in order of frequency.
Nominal with >5 categories	Simple bar	Religious affiliation, major and minor religious groups	
Ordinal	Histogram	Distribution of letter grades	Arrange categories in numeric order.
Continuous with <20 values	Histogram or line	Age distribution in 10-year age groups	Arrange values in numeric order.
Continuous with ≥20 values	Line	Distribution of height in inches	Arrange values in numeric order.
Continuous with summary measures of range or variance	Box-and-whisker	Distribution of height in inches	Use to illustrate minimum, maximum, interquartile range, or other summary measures of variance.

Relationships between two variables

Both categorical		
Simple bar	Percentage low birth weight (LBW) by race	For a dichotomous (two-category) outcome, use bar height to show frequency of one value (e.g., % LBW) for each categorical predictor.
Clustered bar or clustered histogram	Political party affiliation for young, middle-aged, and elderly adults	For distribution of one variable within each of two or three groups, use a clustered bar to create a histogram for each group.
Stacked bar	Political party affiliation by 10-year age groups	To compare distribution of a variable across more than three groups of a second variable, use a stacked bar.
One categorical, one continuous		
Simple bar	Average math scores by school district	Illustrate one Y value for each X value.
High/low/close	Distribution of math scores within each of several districts	Illustrate distribution of Y values for each X value (e.g., district). *See* Box-and-whisker.

Table 7.1. (*continued*)

Task	Type of chart	Example of topic	Comments
One categorical, one continuous (*continued*)		Multiple response: distribution of scores in various subjects within one school district	Illustrate distribution of *Y* values for each *X* value (e.g., academic subject area). *See* Box-and-whisker.
Both continuous	Single line	Trend in monthly unemployment rate	Use a line chart if there is only one *Y* value for each *X* value or to show a summary (e.g., regression line).
	Scatter	Heights and weights of children in an elementary school	Use a scatter chart to show individual points or if there is more than one *Y* value for each *X* value.
Relationships among three variables			
All categorical	Two-panel stacked bar	Political party by age group by gender	Use one panel for each value of one categorical predictor, one bar for each category of other predictor, and slices for each category of outcome variable.

Two categorical, one continuous	Clustered bar	Average math scores by school district and type of school	
		Multiple response: average scores for different subject areas by type of school	To compare multiple-response variables across groups, create a separate cluster for each item (e.g., subject area) with bars for each group.
Two continuous, one categorical	Multiple line	Trend in annual income by age group	Include a separate line for each group.
		Multiple response: trend in income components by age group	To compare multiple-response continuous variables across groups, create a separate line for each response.
	Scatter	Heights and weights of children in schools with and without school breakfast	Use different symbols to plot values from the different series.
All continuous	Three-dimensional line (XYZ)	Height, weight, and age of children	

particularly if the graph has been photocopied from an original.

For four or more slices or bar colors, use different shading schemes (e.g., vertical, horizontal, or diagonal hatching, dots) in combination with solid black, white, and gray to differentiate among the groups to be compared.

- For scatter charts, use a different plotting symbol to plot values for each different group. For more than two or three groups create separate panels of a scatter plot for each group, as patterns for more than three types of symbols become difficult to distinguish on one graph.

Once you have created your chart, print it out to evaluate the color or shading scheme: check that line styles can be differentiated from one another, that different slices or bars don't appear to be the same shade, and that your shading combinations aren't too dizzying.

Three-Dimensional Effects

Many graphing software programs offer the option of making bars or pie slices appear "3-D." Steer clear of these features, which tend to disguise rather than enhance presentation of the data. Your objective is to convey the relative values for different groups or cases in the chart — a task accomplished perfectly well by a flat (two-dimensional) bar or slice. By adding volume to a two-dimensional image, 3-D effects can distort the relative sizes of values by artificially inflating the apparent size of some components. Also avoid tilted or other angled perspectives on pie or bar charts, which can misrepresent proportions. See Tufte (2001) for more details and examples.

Number of Series

For legibility, limit the number of series, particularly if your chart will be printed small. On a multiple-line chart, aim for no more than eight categories (corresponding to eight lines on the chart) — fewer if the lines are close together or cross one another. In a clustered bar chart, consider the total number of bars to be displayed, which equals the number of clusters multiplied by the number of groups in the legend. To avoid overwhelming your readers with too many comparisons, display no more than 20 bars in one chart. An exception: if you will be generalizing a pattern for the entire chart (e.g., "the black bar is higher than the gray bar in every subgroup") with little attention to individual bars, you can get away with more bars.

To display a larger number of comparisons, use theoretical criteria to break them into conceptually related blocks, then make a separate chart or panel for each such block. For example, the questions about knowledge of AIDS transmission shown in figure 7.6 comprise 10 out of 17 AIDS knowledge questions from a survey. A separate chart could present patterns of general AIDS knowledge as measured by the other 7 questions, which dealt with disease characteristics, symptoms, and treatment. Remember, too, that a chart is best used to convey general impressions, not detailed values; if more detail is needed, substitute a table.

Landscape versus Portrait Layout

Some charts work well with a portrait (vertical) layout rather than the traditional landscape (horizontal) chart layout. Revising figure 7.6 into a portrait layout (figure 7.14) leaves more room to label the AIDS

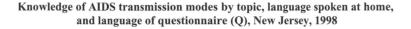

Knowledge of AIDS transmission modes by topic, language spoken at home, and language of questionnaire (Q), New Jersey, 1998

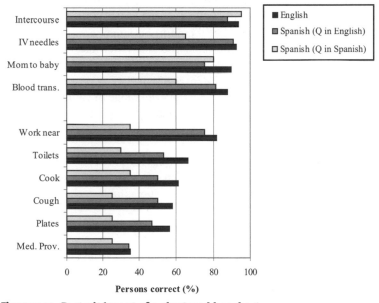

Figure 7.14. Portrait layout of a clustered bar chart.
Source: Miller 2000a.

knowledge topics (now on the vertical axis). Experiment with differ-ent pencil-and-paper drafts of your layout before creating the chart on the computer, sketching in the pertinent number of values or groups and the labels for the respective axes.

Linear versus Logarithmic Scale

If the range of values to be plotted spans more than one or two or-ders of magnitude, consider using a logarithmic scale. On a logarith-mic scale, the distance between adjacent tick marks on the axis cor-responds to a 10-fold *relative* change or multiple: in figure 7.15b, for example, the first three tick marks on the *y* axis are for 1, 10, and 100 deaths per 1,000, instead of the uniform 2,000-unit *absolute* change between tick marks in figure 7.15a.

Because of the very high mortality rates among the elderly, when mortality rates across the life span are plotted on a linear scale (fig-ure 7.15a), mortality differences among persons aged 1 to 55 are al-most imperceptible, although there is a nearly 40-fold difference be-tween the lowest and highest death rates in that age range. Plotted on a logarithmic scale (figure 7.15b), differences among the low-mortality age groups are easily perceived, yet the much higher mortality rates among the oldest age groups still fit on the graph.

A warning: many nonscientific audiences may not be familiar or comfortable with logarithmic scales, so avoid their use for such read-ers. If you must use a log scale in those contexts, mention that differ-ences between some values are larger than they appear and use two or three numeric examples to illustrate the range of values before de-scribing the pattern shown in your data.

Digits and Decimal Places

Charts are best used to illustrate general patterns rather than to present exact data values. Choose a level of aggregation with at most five or six digits to avoid illegible axis labels (table 4.2).

■ COMMON ERRORS IN CHART CREATION

Watch out for some common errors that creep into charts — par-ticularly those produced with computer software. Graphing applica-tions seem to be programmed to visually maximize the difference be-tween displayed values, resulting in misleading axis scales and design that varies across charts. Check your charts for the following design issues before printing your final copy.

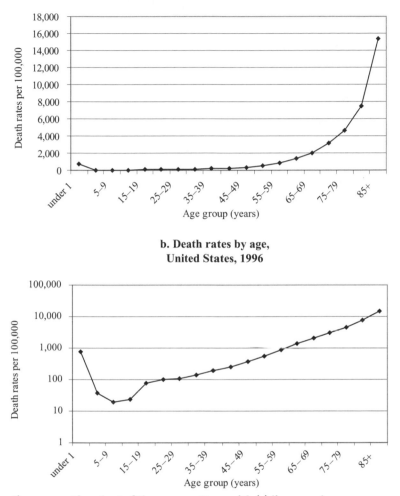

**a. Death rates by age,
United States, 1996**

**b. Death rates by age,
United States, 1996**

**Figure 7.15. Line chart of the same pattern with (a) linear scale,
(b) logarithmic scale.**

Source: Peters et al. 1998, table 2.

Axis Scales

With rare exceptions, include 0 on all axis scales to avoid artificially inflating apparent differences. Even a small change can appear huge if the Y-scale begins at a sufficiently high value. In figure 7.16a, the Y-scale starts at 60%, giving the appearance that the voter participation rate plummeted close to its theoretical minimum, when in fact it was still fully 63% in the latest period shown. When the chart is revised to start the Y-scale at 0, the possible range of the variable is correctly portrayed and the decline in voter participation appears much more modest (figure 7.16b).

This kind of error crops up most often when presenting small differences between large numbers. If this is your objective, plot the difference between values instead of the values themselves, and report the values elsewhere in the document.

Inconsistent Design of Chart Panels

Use uniform scale and design when creating a series of charts or panels to be compared.

Consistent Y- and X-Scales

Show the same range of Y values on each panel: panels a and b of figure 7.17 compare knowledge of unlikely (panel a) and likely (panel b) modes of AIDS transmission. However, the y axis in panel b runs from 0 to 100, while that in panel a runs from 0 to 90. Hence bars that appear the same height in fact represent two very different values. For example, knowledge of "working near someone with AIDS" appears to be as good as knowledge of the four "likely" modes of AIDS transmission, when in fact knowledge of "work near" is lower than all of them. When the scales for the two panels are consistent (figures b and c), the relative knowledge levels are displayed correctly.

Occasionally you will have to use different scales for different panels of a chart to accommodate a much wider range of values in one group than another. If so, point out the difference in scale as you compare the panels in the text.

Other Design Elements to Check

- Consistent sizing of comparable charts. Once you have specified a consistent scale for charts to be compared, ensure that the panels are printed in a uniform size on the page, each occupying a half sheet, for example. If one panel is much smaller, a bar of equivalent numeric value will appear shorter

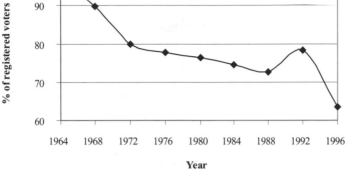

a. Voter participation, U.S.
presidential elections, 1964–1996

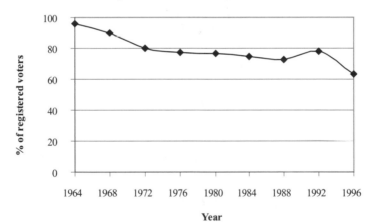

b. Voter participation, U.S.
presidential elections, 1964–1996

**Figure 7.16. Line charts of same pattern with
(a) truncated *y*-scale, (b) full *y*-scale.**
Source: Institute for Democracy and Electoral Assistance 1999.

Knowledge of AIDS transmission modes by topic, language spoken at home, and language of questionnaire (Q), New Jersey, 1998

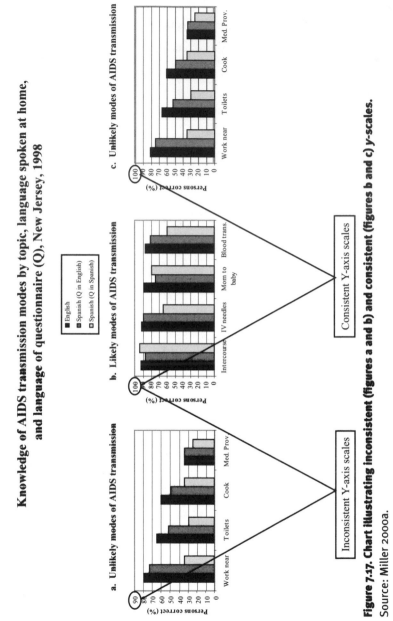

Figure 7.17. Chart illustrating inconsistent (figures a and b) and consistent (figures b and c) y-scales.
Source: Miller 2000a.

than on a larger chart, misleading readers into thinking that the value displayed is lower.

- Consistent ordering of nominal variables, both on the chart axes and within the legend. If panel A sorts countries in descending order of the outcome variable but panel B uses regional groupings, the same country might appear in very different places in the two panels. Or, if you intentionally organize the charts differently to make different points, mention that as you write your description.

- Uniform color or shading scheme (for lines, bars, or slices). Make English-speakers the same color in every panel of a given chart, and if possible, all charts within the same document that compare across language groups.

- Consistent line styles (for line charts). If you use a dotted line for the Northeast in panel A, make sure it is represented with a dotted line in panel B.

- Standardized plotting symbols (for scatter charts involving more than one series). If an asterisk represents foreign cars in a plot comparing foreign and domestic models, use that same symbol in other charts that compare the same two classifications.

- Consistent footnote symbols: if * = $p < 0.01$ on figure X, don't use it to indicate $p < 0.05$ on figure Y.

Use of Line Charts Where Bar Charts Are Appropriate
Line Chart for Nominal Variables

Line charts connect Y values for consecutive values on the x axis. Reserve them for interval or ratio data — in other words, variables that have an inherent numerical order and for which absolute difference can be calculated. Do not connect values for nominal categories such as crude oil production by country (figure 7.18). The countries were organized in descending order of the outcome variable, but could equally well have followed alphabetical order or grouping by geographic region, so the connecting line is misleading. For nominal variables, use a bar chart (figure 7.4).

Line Chart for Unequally Spaced Ordinal Categories

A more insidious problem is the use of line charts to connect values for ordinal variables that are divided into unequally spaced categories, as with the income data shown in figure 7.19a. Equal spacing

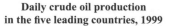

**Daily crude oil production
in the five leading countries, 1999**

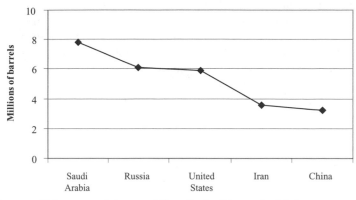

Figure 7.18. Inappropriate use of line chart with nominal data.
Source: U.S. National Energy Information Center 2003.

a. Income distribution, percentage of households, United States, 2000

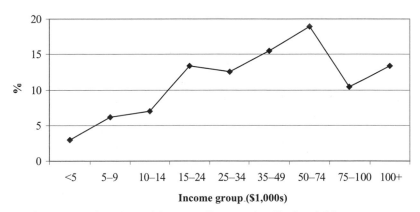

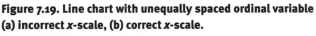

**Figure 7.19. Line chart with unequally spaced ordinal variable
(a) incorrect *x*-scale, (b) correct *x*-scale.**
Source: U.S. Bureau of the Census 2001c.

b. Income distribution, percentage of households, United States, 2000

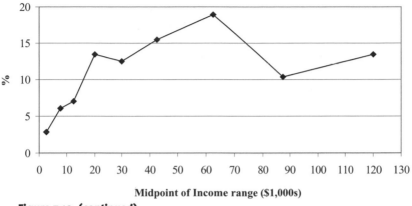

Midpoint of Income range ($1,000s)

Figure 7.19. (*continued*)

of unequal categories misrepresents the true slope of the relationship between the two variables (change in the Y variable per unit change in the X variable). To prevent such distortion treat the X values as interval data by plotting each Y value above the midpoint of the corresponding income range (figure 7.19b).

■ CHECKLIST FOR CREATING EFFECTIVE CHARTS

- To choose an appropriate chart type, compare the attributes of your topic and data to those summarized in table 7.1.

  Consider type of variables.

  Consider number of variables.

  Establish objective of chart, either
  - −composition (univariate); or
  - −comparison of values of some other variable across groups (bivariate or higher order).

- Evaluate your charts for completeness and consistency.

  Does the title differentiate the topic from those of other charts and tables in the same document?

  Is the chart self-contained? Consider
  - −context (W's),
  - −units for each variable,
  - −legend (if needed),
  - −definitions and abbreviations, and
  - −data sources.

  Does organization coordinate with narrative?

  Is design (color, line type, etc.) consistent with similar charts in the same document?

  Are axis scale and printed size consistent with other associated charts?

  Does the axis scale include zero?

  Is the chart readable in black and white?

Choosing Effective Examples and Analogies

Examples, analogies, and metaphors are valuable tools for illustrating quantitative findings and concepts. However, choosing effective ones is more complicated than it might first appear. How do you pick analogies that your audience can relate to? How do you avoid selecting numeric contrasts that are too large or too small, or that don't correspond to likely uses of your calculations?

As noted in chapter 2, an ideal example is simple, plausible, and relevant to both the issue and audience. Simplicity involves length, familiarity, and wording, while relevance entails considering standard cutoffs and patterns in the field and other contextual issues. Empirical issues such as the range of values in your data and how the variables are measured should also inform your choice of example. I begin this chapter by describing ways to use examples and analogies in quantitative writing, then present criteria to help you choose effective examples.

■ WHY USE NUMERIC EXAMPLES?

Every numeric example performs one of several purposes: to generate interest in the topic of your work, quantify differences across cases, groups, or time periods, or illustrate the implications of a statistical finding in broader social or scientific context.

Establish the Importance of Your Topic

Engage your readers' interest by demonstrating the importance of your topic, ideally right at the beginning of the work. Catch their attention with a few choice statistics on the frequency with which some problem occurs or the consequences of that phenomenon. If you show that doing something a new way can save them a lot of money or extend their lives by several years, readers will want to find out more about it. If told that scholastic performance is getting worse in their town or that conditions are better elsewhere, they will be motivated to continue reading.

Compare to Previous Statistics

To establish the context and comparability of your findings, relate new information to what is already known. Contrast this year's stock prices with last year's or compare your findings with results of previous studies. Use quantitative contrasts to assess the extent of similarity or difference between data from different sources. This application of numeric examples is often used in an introduction, a review of the previous literature, or a concluding section of a work.

Illustrate Repercussions of Analytic Results

Use examples to assess substantive significance. Multiply information about proposed property tax changes by the assessed value of a typical home to give residents a sense of how much the new tax will cost them. Combine estimates of reductions in airborne particulates from a new pollution-prevention technology with information on the respiratory effects of particulates to place the new technology in a broader environmental and health perspective. Use this approach in a general article or in the analytic or concluding section of a scientific paper.

■ WHY USE ANALOGIES?

Use analogies to help readers grasp the scale of your numbers, understand the shape of an unfamiliar pattern or a relationship between variables, or follow the logic in a multistep calculation. Metaphors, similes, and other related rhetorical devices can also be used to accomplish these tasks; for simplicity I refer to this family of concepts as "analogies."

Analogies to Illustrate Scale

Explain very large or very small numbers to audiences that are not conversant with that scale by illustrating those numbers with concrete analogies. To convey the enormity of the world population, the Population Reference Bureau (1999) used the following illustrations of "how much is a billion?"

- "If you were a billion seconds old, you would be 31.7 years of age."
- "The circumference of the earth is 25,000 miles. If you circled the earth 40,000 times, you would have traveled 1 billion miles."
- "There are about 44 million words in the Encyclopedia Britannica. You would need more than 136 full sets of the Encyclopedia to get 6 billion words."

Analogies can also express the scale of very small numbers.

- Translate a very low concentration into the equivalent number of drops of the substance in an Olympic-size swimming pool.
- Provide a benchmark for assessing risk by comparing it to the chances of being struck by lightening.

Other dimensions such as weight, volume, or velocity can also be portrayed with analogies. For a nutrition fact sheet or diet guide, relate standard portion sizes to common objects: a standard 4-ounce serving of meat is equivalent to a regulation-size deck of playing cards; a half-cup serving of rice would fill half a tennis ball.

Analogies to Demonstrate Patterns or Relationships

Portray patterns or relationships using descriptors such as "U-shaped" or "bell-shaped." To illustrate a positive association, compare it to how children's height and age move up together. To describe an inverse association, refer to the relationship between higher prices and lower demand. Analogies can also be used to explain more complicated patterns or relationships. In the business section of the *New York Times,* seasonal adjustment of employment rates was related to the mental process many people apply to the way their body weight changes with the seasons (box 8.1). The fact that the analogy was published shortly after the winter holidays probably only increased its effectiveness.

Analogies to Explain Processes or Calculations

To explicate unfamiliar processes or calculations, relate them to well-known ones. If you liken exponentiating and taking logarithms to "doing and undoing" a mathematical calculation and follow with a more elementary example of inverse operations such as multiplication and division, most listeners will quickly grasp the basic idea. Descriptions of more complex calculations can also be clarified by comparison to familiar processes, although they often require longer,

---

Box 8.1. Analogy for Seasonal Adjustment.

From the *New York Times* Job Market section: "Most of us routinely engage in a little seasonal adjustment of our own. Say, for example, you always put on five pounds between Dec. 1 and New Year's Day, and then work it off at the gym over the next six months. When you step on the scale on Jan. 1, you don't say 'Yikes! I'm turning into a blob.' You say 'Here we go again." But what if, one year, there were a sugar-plum shortage, and you gained only two pounds? You'd probably be relieved. But you'd be even happier if you used economics-style seasonal adjustments, because then you could claim that you actually *lost* three pounds. And so you would have, compared with what you usually weigh at that time of year." (Eaton 2002)

---

step-by-step explanations. Consider the following ways to introduce odds ratios to a nonstatistical audience:

Poor: "If the probability of a divorce among people who married as teens is denoted P_t and the probability of a divorce among people who married at older ages is P_o, the odds ratio of divorce for teens compared to older people is the odds for the first group divided by the odds for the second group, or $[P_t/(1 - P_t)]/[P_o/(1 - P_o)]$." *An equation full of symbols and subscripts is likely to scare off most nonstatisticians. Even those hardy enough to tackle it will spend a lot of time wading through the notation instead of understanding the logic. For folks who understand odds and odds ratios, just tell them which is the comparison group (e.g., the denominator); the equation is probably superfluous.*

Not much Better: "Odds ratios are one set of odds divided by another. For example, the odds of a divorce are different depending on age at marriage, so we take the ratio of the odds in one case (e.g., people who married as teens) to the odds in the other case (e.g., people who married at older ages). The ratio of 4/1 to 2/1 equals 2, so the odds ratio is 2." *The basic logic is in place here, but for an audience not used to thinking about odds, the source of the figures is not clear. Where did the 4/1 come from? The 2/1? Most people will remember that a ratio involves division, but wording such as "ratio of __ to __" often confuses nonmath folks.*

Finally, readers are left on their own to interpret what that value of the odds ratio means.

Best (for a lay audience): "Odds ratios are a way of comparing the chances of some event under different circumstances. Many people are familiar with odds from sports. For example, if the Yankees beat the Red Sox in two out of three games so far this season, the odds of another Yankees victory would be projected as 2-to-1 (two wins against one loss). Now suppose that the chances of a win depend on who is pitching. Last year, the Yankees won two out of three games against the Red Sox when Clemens pitched (2-to-1 odds) and two out of four times when Pettite was on the mound (1-to-1 odds). The *odds ratio* of a Yankees win for Clemens compared to Pettite is 2-to-1 divided by 1-to-1, or 2. In other words, this measure suggests that the odds of a Yankees victory are twice as high if Clemens is the starter. The same logic can be used to estimate how the relative chances of other types of events differ according to some characteristic of interest, such as how much odds of divorce vary by age at marriage."

This explanation is longer but every sentence is simple and explains one step in the logic behind calculating and interpreting an odds ratio.

For statistically knowledgeable audiences, you needn't explain the calculation, but a brief analogy is an effective introductory device:

> "An odds ratio measures how the chances of an event change under different conditions, such as the odds of a Yankees victory if Clemens is pitching compared to when Pettite is on the mound."

■ CRITERIA FOR CHOOSING EXAMPLES AND ANALOGIES

In chapter 2, I introduced two criteria for choosing effective examples: simplicity and plausibility. Here, I elaborate on those criteria and offer several others — familiarity, timeliness, relevance, intended use, and comparability.

Simplicity

Simplicity is in the eye of the beholder, to adapt the old expression. To communicate ideas, choose examples and analogies to fit your audience, not yourself. What seems obvious to one person may be hopelessly obscure to another. A necessarily thorough explanation for one group may be overkill for another. If you are writing for several audiences, adapt the content and wording of your analogies to suit each group. For many audiences, the ideal analogy will be as non-quantitative as possible.

Familiarity

Choose analogies that your audience can relate to their own experience. For adults, you might illustrate the penalties associated with missing a deadline by mentioning the consequences of being late for the income tax return filing date. For children, being tardy for school is a better analogy. If your average reader will need to look up a concept or term to grasp your point, find another analogy.

Timeliness increases familiarity. To introduce the field of epidemiology to a group of undergraduates in the mid-1990s, I used the 1976 Legionnaire's disease outbreak at a convention of the Pennsylvania American Legion — the group from which the disease took its name. I subsequently realized most of my students were still in diapers when that outbreak occurred, which is why my example drew a sea of blank stares. A few years later when the movie *Outbreak* was released, students flocked to me to recount scenes from the movie that illustrated various concepts we were learning in class. Now I scan the popular press shortly before I teach to identify fresh examples of the topics I will cover. Especially for a general audience, pick examples that are current or so famous (or infamous) that their salience does not fade with time.

Vocabulary

Don't obscure your message with a poor choice of words. Use terminology with which your audience is comfortable. Your objective is to communicate, not to demonstrate your own sophistication. Many readers will be completely befuddled by "penultimate" or "sigmoid," but even second graders will understand "second to last" or "S-shaped."

Plausibility

Assessing plausibility requires an intimate acquaintance with both your topic and your data. Don't mindlessly apply values gleaned from other studies. For instance, opinions and preferences in a sample of the elderly might not represent those among younger adults or children. Review the literature in your field to learn the theoretical basis of the relationships you are analyzing, then use descriptive statistics and exploratory data analytic techniques to familiarize yourself with the distributions of your key variables and identify unusual values.

Sometimes you will want to use both typical and atypical values, to illustrate upper and lower limits or best-case and worst-case scenarios. If so, identify extreme values as such so your audience can differentiate among utopian, draconian, and moderate estimates. See below for more information on sensitivity analyses that compare estimates based on several sets of values or assumptions.

Relevance

A critical facet of a numeric example or comparison is that it be relevant — that it match its substantive context and likely application.

Substantive Context

Before you select numeric values to contrast, identify conventional standards, cutoffs, or comparison values used in the field.

- Evaluations of children's nutritional status often use measures of the number of standard deviations above or below the mean for a standard reference population (Kuczmarski et al. 2000). If you don't use those measures or the same reference population, your findings cannot easily be compared with those of other studies.
- Eligibility for social programs like Medicaid or food stamps is based on multiples of the Federal Poverty Level. If you use purely empirical groupings such as quartiles or standard deviations of the income distribution, your examples will not be directly applicable.

Intended Use

Before you choose examples, find out how your intended audience is likely to use the information. Suppose you are studying characteristics that affect responsiveness to a drug rehabilitation program. For an academic audience, you might report estimates from a statistical model that controls simultaneously for age, sex, and educational attainment. For program directors or policy makers, describe patterns for specific age or education groups that correspond to program design features instead.

Comparability

Comparability of Context

In background examples, present data from a similar context (who, what, when, and where). For comparisons, choose data from a context that differs in at most one of those dimensions. If you compare women under age 40 from California in 2000 with people of all ages from the entire United States in 1980, it is hard to know whether any observed differences are due to gender, age, location, or date. Which dimension you vary will depend on the point you want to make: are you examining trends over time, or differences by gender, age group, or location? In each case, cite information that differs only in that dimension, keeping the other W's unchanged.

Comparability of Units

Make sure the numbers you compare are in consistent units and that those units are familiar to your readers. If you are combining numbers from different data sources that report different units, do the conversions before you write, then report all numbers in the same type of unit.

Poor: "The 2002 Toyota Prius hybrid (gas/electric) engine requires 4.6 liters of gasoline per 100 kilometers, compared to 33 miles per gallon for a 2002 Toyota Corolla with a gasoline-only engine (www.fueleconomy.gov 2002)."

For some idiosyncratic reason, in the British measurement system fuel economy is reported in terms of distance traveled on a given volume of gasoline (miles per gallon — the higher, the better), but in the metric system the convention is how much gas is required to go a given distance (liters per 100 kilometers — the lower, the better). Hence, this comparison is worse than "apples and oranges." If readers don't pay attention to the units, they will simply compare 4.6 against 33. American and British readers will incorrectly conclude that the gasoline-only engine has better fuel economy, while metric thinkers will conclude that the hybrid is better, but based on incorrect logic.

Better (for those who use British units): "Hybrid (electric/gas) engines improve considerably on fuel economy. For example, the 2002 Toyota Prius hybrid engine gets 52 miles per gallon (mpg) compared with 33 mpg for the 2002 Toyota Corolla with a gasoline-only engine."

Better (for the rest of the world): "Hybrid (electric/gas) engines improve considerably on fuel economy. For example, the 2002 Toyota Prius hybrid engine requires only 4.6 liters of gasoline per

100 kilometers (L/100 km) as against 7.2 L/100 km for the 2002 Toyota Corolla with a gasoline-only engine."
Apples to apples or oranges to oranges, as the case may be. No need for your readers to conduct a four-step conversion calculation . . .

■ SENSITIVITY ANALYSES

Sensitivity analyses show how results or conclusions vary when different definitions, assumptions, or standards are used. Each definition, assumption, and standard constitutes a different example and is chosen using the criteria outlined above. Sensitivity analyses can be used as follows:

- *To compare results of several different scenarios.* When projecting future population, demographers often generate a series of high, medium, and low projections, each of which assumes a different growth rate (U.S. Census Bureau 2000a). Typically, the medium value is chosen to reflect current conditions, such as the population growth rate from the past year, while the high and low values are plausible higher and lower growth rates.
- *To compare a new standard or definition against its current version.* In the mid-1990s, the National Academy of Sciences convened a panel of experts to assess whether the existing definition of poverty thresholds should be changed to reflect new conditions or knowledge (Citro et al. 1996). Their report included a table showing what poverty rates would have been in each of several demographic groups under both the old and new definitions of poverty (table 8.1).

To present detailed results of a sensitivity analysis, create a chart or table like table 8.1. To compare three or more scenarios for a scientific audience, report the assumptions in a column of a table, a footnote, or an appendix. If the assumptions, definitions, or calculations are described in another published source, give a brief description in your document and cite the pertinent source. For audiences that aren't interested in the technical details, conduct the analysis behind the scenes and describe the findings in nonstatistical language:

"Under the current measure, the 1992 poverty rate for the United States as a whole was 14.5%, compared to 18.1% with a new housing cost index and proposed resource definition recommended by an expert panel of the National Academy of Sciences (Citro et al. 1996, 263)."

Table 8.1. Tabular presentation of a sensitivity analysis

Poverty rates (%) by group under current and proposed poverty measures, United States, 1992

	Current measure[b]	Proposed measure[a]		Percentage point change Current vs. proposed	
		Alt. 1	Alt. 2	Alt. 1	Alt. 2
Total population	14.5	18.1	19.0	3.6	4.5
Age					
Children <18	21.9	26.4	26.4	4.5	4.5
Adults 65+	12.9	14.6	18.0	1.7	5.1
Race/ethnicity					
White	11.6	15.3	16.1	3.7	4.5
Black	33.2	35.6	36.8	2.4	3.6
Hispanic	29.4	41.0	40.9	10.6	10.5

Source: Citro et al. 1996
[a] Alternative 1 uses the same income threshold as the current measure, an economy scale factor of 0.75, housing cost index, and a new proposed resource definition. Alternative 2 is the same as alternative 1 but with an economy scale factor of 0.65. See chapter 5 of Citro et al. 1996 for additional information.
[b] "Current measure" is based on the 1992 threshold of $14,800 for a two-adult/two-child family.

■ COMMON PITFALLS IN CHOICE OF NUMERIC EXAMPLES

Failing to examine the distribution of your variables or falling into one of several decimal system biases can create problems with your choice of numeric examples.

Ignoring the Distributions of Your Variables

Overlooking the distributions of your variables can lead to some poor choices of numeric examples and contrasts. Armed with information on range, mean, variability, and skewness of the major variables you discuss, you will be in a better position to pick reasonable values and characterize them as above or below average, typical, or atypical.

Using Atypical Values

Make sure the examples you intend as illustrations of typical values are in fact typical: avoid using the mean to represent highly skewed distributions or other situations where few cases have the mean value. For instance, if Einstein had happened to be one of 10 people randomly chosen to try out a new math aptitude test, the mean score would have vastly overstated the expected performance of an average citizen, so the median or modal value would be a more representative choice. If half the respondents to a public opinion poll strongly agree with a proposed new law and the other half passionately oppose it, characterizing the "average" opinion as in the middle would be inappropriate; in such a case, a key point would be the polarized nature of the distribution.

Unrealistic Contrasts

Avoid calculating the effect of changing some variable more than it has been observed to vary in real life. Remember, a variable is unlikely to take on the full range of all possible values. Although tape measures include the measurement zero inches, you'd be hard pressed to find anyone that short in a real-world sample. Instead, pick the lowest value found in your data or a low percentile taken from a standard distribution to illustrate the minimum.

If you use the observed highest and lowest values, explain that those values represent upper and lower bounds, then include a couple of smaller contrasts to illustrate more realistic changes. For instance, the reproductive age range for women is biologically fixed at roughly ages 15 to 45 on average. However, a woman considering childbearing can realistically compare her current age only with older ages, so for women in their 20s, 30s, or 40s, the younger end of that range isn't relevant. Even among teenagers, for whom that entire theoretically possible range is still in their future, few will consider delaying childbearing by 30 years. Hence, comparing the effects of having a child at ages 15 versus 45 isn't likely to apply to many people. A more reasonable contrast would be a five-year difference — age 15 versus 20, or age 30 versus 35, for example.

Out-of-Range Values

Take care when using example values that fall outside the range of your data. This issue is probably most familiar for projecting future

values based on historical patterns. Accompany your calculations
with the assumptions and data upon which they are based.

> "The 'medium' population projection assumes an annual rate
> of growth based on trends in fertility, mortality, and migration
> during the preceding decade (U.S. Census Bureau 2000a)."

Decimal System Biases

Ours is a decimal (base 10) oriented society: people tend to think
in increments of one or multiples of 10, which may or may not correspond to a realistic or interesting contrast. Before you reflexively use
a one or 10- or 100-unit difference, evaluate whether that difference
suits your research question, taking into account theory, the previous
literature on the subject, your data, and common usage. Frequently,
the "choice" of comparison unit is made by the statistical program
used to do the analysis because the default increment often is 1-unit
or 10-unit contrasts.

Single-Unit Contrasts

Even if you have concluded that a 1-unit change is realistic, other
contrasts may be of greater interest. Showing how much more food an
American family could buy with one dollar more income per week
would be a trivial result given today's food prices. An increment of
twenty-five or fifty dollars would be more informative. Even better,
find out how much a proposed change in social benefits or the minimum wage would add to weekly income, then examine its effects on
food purchases. However, as always, context matters: if you were
studying the United States in the early twentieth century or some less
developed countries today, that one-dollar contrast in weekly income
would be well fitted to the question.

Ten-Unit Contrasts

Some analyses, such as life table calculations, use 10-unit contrasts as the default — a poorly suited choice for many research questions. For instance, infant mortality declines precipitously in the
hours, days, and weeks after birth. Ten-day age intervals are too wide
to capture mortality variation in the first few weeks of life and too
narrow in the months thereafter. For that topic, more appropriate
groupings are the first day of life, the rest of the first week (6 days),
the remainder of the first month (21 days), and the rest of the first year
(337 days; table 8.2). Although these ranges are unequal, mortality is

Table 8.2. Example of unequal width contrasts to match substantive and empirical criteria

Infant mortality by age, United States, 1999

Age (days)	Average daily death rate per 1,000
<365	0.02
<1	2.92
1–6	0.16
7–27	0.05
28–364	0.01

Source: Centers for Disease Control 2002.
Note: In the United States in 1999 there were a total of 27,937 infant deaths and 3,819,903 live births, for an infant mortality rate of 7.3 per 1,000 live births.

relatively constant within each interval, satisfying an important empirical criterion. Those age ranges also correspond to theory about causes of infant mortality at different ages (Puffer and Serrano 1973; Mathews et al. 2002). Before you choose your contrasts, investigate the appropriate increment for your research question and do the calculations accordingly.

Digit Preference and Heaping

Another issue is digit preference, whereby people tend to report certain numeric values more than others nearby because of social convention or out of a preference for particular units. In decimal-oriented societies, folks are apt to prefer numbers that end in 0 or 5 (Barclay 1958), rounding actual values of variables such as weight, age, or income to the nearest multiple of 5 or 10 units. When reporting time, people are inclined report whole weeks or months rather than exact number of days; or quarter, half, or whole hours rather than exact number of minutes. These patterns result in "heaping" — a higher than expected frequency of those values at the expense of adjacent ones (figure 8.1).

If you have pronounced heaping in your data, treating the heaped responses and those on either side as precise values may be inap-

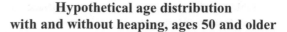

Hypothetical age distribution
with and without heaping, ages 50 and older

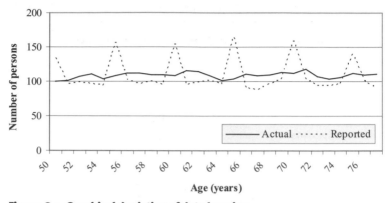

Figure 8.1. Graphical depiction of data heaping

propriate. Instead, analyze data that are grouped into ranges around those preferred digits. For example, if many people who earn between $23,000 and $27,999 report their income as $25,000, looking at small changes within that range may not make sense. Graphs or tabular frequency distributions can help evaluate whether heaping or digit preference is occurring.

Units or Categories of Measurement

Suitable comparisons also are constrained by how your data were collected. With secondary data you are forced to use someone else's choices of level of aggregation and definitions of categories, whether or not those match your research question. If income data were collected in ranges of $500, you cannot look at effects of smaller changes. Even if you pick values such as $490 and $510 that happen to cross category limits, the real comparison is between the two entire categories (<$500 versus $500–$999), not the $20 difference you appear to be contrasting.

■ CHECKLIST FOR CHOOSING EFFECTIVE EXAMPLES AND ANALOGIES

- Select analogies or metaphors to fit each intended audience.
    Take into account their knowledge of the topic and
        concepts.
    Choose familiar ideas and vocabulary.
- Tailor each numeric example to fit its objective.
    Establish the importance of the topic.
    Compare against previous findings.
    Interpret your statistical results.
    Demonstrate substantive significance of your findings.
- Consider your numeric contrasts.
    Do they fall within the observed range of values in your
        data?
    Are they theoretically plausible?
    Are they substantively interesting — neither too big nor too
        small for real-world conditions?
    Do they apply conventional standards or cutoffs used in
        the field?
    Do they correspond to likely uses of the results?
- Specify whether the values you present are typical or unusual.
- Evaluate your contrasts.
    Check comparability of context (W's) and units.
    Present one or two selected dimensions of quantitative
        comparison to assess the difference across values.
- For a sensitivity analysis, explain the alternative assumptions
    or definitions.

Pulling It All Together

PART III

In the preceding chapters, I described a series of tools and principles for writing about numbers. In practice, rarely will you use these elements piecemeal. Instead, you will integrate them to create a compelling explanation of the issues you address, complete with the quantitative evidence needed to evaluate those questions. The next few chapters show how to do just that, starting with illustrative "poor/better/best" descriptions of distributions and associations, then progressing to full paragraphs from a general-interest article and examples of introductory, data and methods, results, and concluding sections of a scientific paper. I also demonstrate how to design slides and accompanying notes for a speech about a quantitative analysis — another common and challenging way to present numeric information. I return often to considerations of audience and kind of work to show how to modify your writing to suit varied purposes.

Writing about Distributions and Associations

Writing about numbers often involves portraying the distribution of a variable or describing the association between two or more variables. These tasks require several of the principles and tools introduced in the preceding chapters: specifying direction and magnitude of association (chapter 2), considering statistical significance (chapter 3), considering types of variables, units, and distribution (chapter 4), using quantitative comparisons (chapter 5), and organizing the text to coordinate with a table or chart (chapters 6 and 7). In this chapter, I explain how to combine these concepts to write about distributions and associations for both academic and general audiences, and I describe common types of univariate, bivariate, and three-way patterns. See Moore (1997), Utts (1999), or another statistics text for more background on the underlying statistical concepts.

Information on distributions of values for single variables or associations among two or three variables provides the foundation of "results" sections in scientific articles and is included in many general-interest articles. In a story about elementary education, for instance, you might describe the distribution of class sizes, then show how class size, expenditures per student, and student achievement are related to one another. In a basic statistical analysis or report about experimental data, descriptions of distributions and bivariate or three-way associations often constitute the entire analysis. For more advanced statistical analyses, such as multivariate regressions, this information helps demonstrate why a more complex statistical technique is needed (see "Building the Case for a Multivariate Model," in Miller, forthcoming).

■ UNIVARIATE DISTRIBUTIONS

Univariate statistics provide information on one variable at a time, showing how cases are distributed across all possible values of that variable. In a scientific paper, create a table with summary information on each variable, then refer to the table as you describe the data. In a general-interest article, report the mean or modal values of your main variables in prose, substituting "average" for "mean" and "most common" for "modal."

If you will be comparing across samples or populations, report the frequency distribution using percentages to adjust for differences in the sizes of the samples. One hundred passing scores among a sample of one thousand students reflects a very different share than one hundred passing scores among several million students, for example.

The information you report for a univariate distribution differs for continuous and categorical variables. The type of variable also affects your choice of a chart type to present composition or distribution; see table 7.1 for guidelines.

Categorical Variables

To show composition of a categorical variable, present the frequency of each category as counts (e.g., number of registered Democrats, Republicans, and Independents) or percentages (e.g., the percentage of all registered voters belonging to each party). Report the modal category; the mean (arithmetic average) is meaningless for categorical variables: the "average region" or "mean political affiliation" cannot be calculated or interpreted. If the variable has only a few categories, report numeric information for each category in the text (see examples below).

For variables with more than a handful of categories, create a chart or table to be summarized in the text. Also consider whether two or more small categories might be combined into a larger category without obscuring a group of particular interest to your analysis.

- In some instances, these combinations are based on conceptual similarity. For example, in a comparison of public, private, and parochial schools, you might combine all parochial schools into a single category regardless of religious affiliation.
- In other instances, these combinations are done to avoid tabulating many rare categories separately. For example, you might combine a disparate array of infrequently mentioned ice cream flavors as "other" even though they share little other than their rarity. In these cases, either explain that "other" includes all categories other than those named elsewhere in the table or chart, or include a footnote specifying what the "other" category includes.

The order in which you mention values of a categorical variable depends on your research question and whether that variable is nominal or ordinal. The criteria described on the next few pages also work for organizing descriptions of bivariate or higher-order associations involving categorical variables (see "Associations" below).

Nominal variables

For nominal variables, such as political affiliation or category of federal budget outlays, use principles such as frequency of occurrence or theoretical criteria to organize numbers within a sentence. Often it makes sense to mention the most common value and then describe where the other values fall, using one or more quantitative comparisons to assess difference in relative shares of different values.

Poor: "The distribution of U.S. federal budget outlays in 2000 was 61% for human resources, 12% for interest, 16% for national defense, 6% for other functions, and 5% for physical resources (figure 7.2)."
This sentence simply reports the share of federal outlays in each category, requiring readers to do their own comparisons to identify the largest category and to assess the size of differences in the shares of different categories. The categories are inexplicably listed in alphabetical order — a poor choice of organizing principle for most text descriptions.

Better: "As shown in figure 7.2, over 60% of U.S. federal budget outlays in 2000 were for human services, with national defense a distant second (16%), and net interest third (12%). The remaining outlays were roughly equally divided between physical resources and other functions."
This description uses modal category, rank, and relative share to convey comparative sizes, reporting numbers only to illustrate relative sizes of the three largest categories.

If a particular category is of special interest, feature it early in your description even if it isn't the modal value. For example, in a story on the share of interest in the federal budget, highlight that category although it ranks third among the categories of outlays.

Ordinal variables

For ordinal variables, the natural sequence of the categories frequently dictates the order in which you report them: young, middle-aged, and elderly age groups, for example. Sometimes, however, you

want to emphasize which group is largest or is of particular importance in your analysis, suggesting that you mention that group first
even if that goes against the normal, ranked sequence of categories.
For an article about the influence of the baby boom generation at the
turn of the millennium, for instance, discuss that cohort first even
though its members are in the middle of the age distribution.

In those situations, begin with a general description of the pattern,
using descriptors such as "bell-shaped" (figures 4.3a and b), "uniform" (figure 4.3c), "U-shaped" (figure 4.3d), or "skewed to the right"
(figure 4.3e). Then report frequency of occurrence for the groups you
wish to highlight.

Poor: "The age distribution of U.S. adults in 2000 was 8.6% ages
20−24, 8.8% ages 25−29, . . . , and 1.9% ages 85 and older (U.S.
Census Bureau 2002d)."
*A lengthy list in the text is overwhelming and a poor way to describe the
overall distribution. To present values for each age group, put them in a
table or chart.*

Poor (version 2): "The percentage of U.S. adults who were aged 35−
39 was larger than the percentages aged 30−34 or 40−44 (10.3%,
9.3%, and 10.1%, respectively). That age group was also much
larger than the oldest age groups (those 80 to 84 and 85+, 2.2%
and 1.9%, respectively). Age groups 20−24, 25−29, 45−49 . . .
and 75−79 were in between (U.S. Census Bureau 2002d)."
Comparing many pairs of numbers is inefficient and confusing.

Better: "In 2000, the age distribution of U.S. adults was roughly
bell-shaped between ages 20 and 55, reflecting the dominant
presence of the baby boom cohorts born in the late 1940s
through the 1950s (figure 9.1). The largest cohorts were ages 35−
39 and 40−44, with 10.3% and 10.1% of the adult population,
respectively. After age 55, the age distribution tails off rapidly,
revealing the combined effects of mortality and smaller birth
cohorts (U.S. Census Bureau 2002d)."
*This description uses a familiar shape to summarize the age distribution.
By naming the baby boom age groups and mentioning birth cohort size
and mortality, it also explains some of the underlying factors that
generated the age distribution.*

Continuous Variables

For continuous variables such as price, height, or age, create a table
to report the minimum and maximum values, pertinent measure of

Age distribution of U.S. adults, 2000

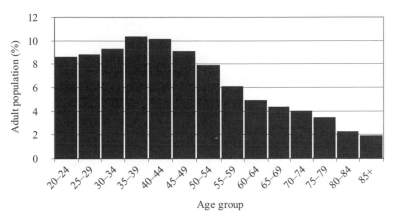

Age group

Figure 9.1. Age distribution illustrated with a histogram.
Source: U.S. Census Bureau 2002d.

central tendency, and standard deviation or interquartile range for the variables used in your analysis. In the prose, give summary statistics rather than reporting information on each case or each value unless there are very few cases. To report kindergarten class size in a school with four kindergarten classes, for instance, you might list the number of students in each class, followed by the overall average:

"Kennedy Elementary School opened its doors with kindergarten classes of 21, 24, 27, and 28 students, for a mean class size of 25 students."

To describe kindergarten class size for all public schools in a large city, report the range and the mean or median class sizes:

"On opening day in New York City, kindergarten class sizes ranged from 17 to 31 students, with an average class size of 22.1."

To provide more detail on the distribution of a continuous variable, create a histogram (to report frequencies for fewer than 20 values) or simple line chart (for 20 or more values). Then portray the general shape of the distribution and report specific values of interest as explained above under "ordinal variables."

Comparing values of a continuous variable against a reference value or cutoff is often informative.

"New York City schools are making progress toward the city and state goal of limiting classes in the youngest grades to 20 pupils, but more than one-fourth of children in kindergarten through third grade are in classes with more than 25 (Medina 2002)."

■ ASSOCIATIONS

Most quantitative analyses examine patterns of association between two or more variables. Bivariate patterns describe an association between two variables, such as mean class size by type of school (e.g., public, private, and parochial). Three-way associations introduce a third variable — calculating mean class size by geographic region and type of school simultaneously, for instance.

Regardless of the types of variables involved, describe both the direction and magnitude of the association. For scientific audiences, also mention names and results of statistical tests. See Morgan et al. (2001) for an excellent guide to reporting results of many types of statistical tests. For lay publications or nonscientific audiences, omit explicit reference to results of statistical tests. Instead, use statistical concepts to screen what you report and how you describe it (see "Writing about Statistical Significance" in chapter 3).

Purpose of Describing Associations

Associations are used for several different reasons:

- To quantify differences in the outcome variable according to values of a predictor, such as variation in the percentage of children passing a proficiency test according to school type
- To describe patterns of association among predictor variables, such as whether different regions have similar distributions of school types
- To evaluate whether the study sample is representative of the target population, such as whether the demographic composition of students in the study schools is the same as in all schools

Roles of Variables and Causal Language

If you are investigating a potential causal relationship, differentiate between the causal variable (the "predictor" or "independent" variable) and the effect (the "outcome" or "dependent" variable) because those roles affect how the statistics are calculated and described. For example, in the relationship between school type and class size, class size is the outcome and school type is the predictor, so report mean class size by school type, not modal school type by class size. For associations among several similar concepts measured at one point in time (e.g., scores in different academic subjects or several concurrent measures of socioeconomic status) or if the causal relationship is ambiguous, avoid causal language.

Types of Associations

The type of statistical procedure and associated statistical test depend on whether you are describing an association between two continuous variables, two categorical variables, or one of each.

Correlations

An association between two continuous variables (e.g., the poverty rate and the unemployment rate) is measured by their correlation coefficient (denoted r). The value of r ranges from -1.0 (for a perfect inverse association) to 1.0 (for a perfect direct association). Variables that are completely uncorrelated have an r of 0.0. Statistical significance is assessed by comparing the correlation coefficient against a critical value, which depends on the number of cases. To describe a correlation, name the two variables and specify the direction of association between them, then report the correlation coefficient and p-value in parentheses:

"Poverty and unemployment were strongly positively correlated ($r = 0.85$; $p < 0.01$)."

Bivariate correlations among many variables are usually reported in a table (e.g., table 6.7). Unless you are testing hypotheses about specific pairs of variables, summarize the correlation results rather than writing a detailed narrative about each bivariate association.

For a scientific audience: "As expected, the different indicators of academic achievement were highly positively correlated with one another, with Pearson correlation coefficients (r) greater than 0.75 ($p < 0.01$ except between mathematics and language comprehension). Correlations between achievement and aptitude were generally lower."

This description uses theoretical groupings (academic achievement and aptitude) to simplify the discussion. Generalizations about correlations among measures within and across those classifications replace detailed descriptions of each pairwise correlation, and exceptions are mentioned. One or two specific examples could also be incorporated.

For a lay audience: "As expected, children who scored well on one test of academic achievement also typically scored well on achievement tests in other subjects. Correlations between achievement and aptitude were generally lower than those among different dimensions of achievement."
This description is similar to that for a scientific audience but replaces names of specific statistical measures with their conceptual equivalents.

Differences in Means across Groups

An association between a continuous variable and a categorical variable can be assessed using a difference in means or ANOVA (analysis of variance). *T*-statistics and *F*-statistics are used to evaluate statistical significance of a difference in means and ANOVAs, respectively. To describe a relationship between a categorical predictor (e.g., race/ethnicity) and a continuous outcome (e.g., birth weight in grams), report the mean outcome for each category of the predictor in a table or simple bar chart, then explain the pattern in the text.

Poor: "The difference in birth weight across racial/ethnic groups was statistically significant ($p < 0.01$; table 9.1).
This sentence omits the direction and magnitude of the association.
Slightly Better: "Non-Hispanic black infants weighed on average 246 grams less at birth ($p < 0.01$; table 9.1)."
This version reports the direction, size, and statistical significance of the association, but fails to specify the comparison group: less than what (or whom)? As written, this statement could mean that black infants weighed less at birth than at some other age, that birth weight for black infants is less now than a few years ago, or that black infants weigh less than some other group.
Best: "On average, Non-Hispanic black newborns were 246 grams lighter than non-Hispanic white newborns (3,181 and 3,427 grams, respectively; $p < 0.01$; table 9.1)."
This description incorporates the mean birth weight, direction and magnitude (absolute difference), and statistical significance of the birth weight difference. It also identifies the comparison group and units of measurement. For a nonacademic audience, omit the p-value.

To summarize mean outcomes across several related categorical variables, name the categories with the highest and lowest values, then summarize where values for the other categories fall.

"In the Appleville school district, 2001 SAT II achievement scores were highest on the English language test (mean = 530 out

Table 9.1. Cross-tabulations and differences in means for study variables

Mean birth weight and percentage low birth weight by race/ethnicity, United States, 1988–1994

	Non-Hispanic white (N = 3,733)	Non-Hispanic black (N = 2,968)	Mexican American (N = 3,112)	All racial/ ethnic groups (N = 9,813)
Mean birth weight (grams)[a]	3,426.8	3,181.3	3,357.3	3,379.2
% low birth weight[ab]	5.8	11.3	7.0	6.8

Note: Weighted to population level using weights provided with the NHANES III (U.S. DHHS 1997); sample size is unweighted.
[a] Differences across racial/ethnic origin groups were statistically significant.
[b] Low birth weight: <2,500 grams or 5.5 pounds.

of 800 possible points) and lowest in mathematics (mean = 475). Average scores in science (four subject areas) also fell below the 500 mark, while those for foreign languages (five languages) and social studies (three subject areas) ranged from 500 to 525." *To avoid mentioning each of the 14 test scores separately, this description combines two criteria to organize the reported numbers: an empirical approach to identify the highest and lowest scores, and substantive criteria to classify the topics into five broad subject areas. Mentioning the highest possible score also helps readers interpret the meaning of the numbers.*

Use a consistent set of criteria to organize the table or chart associated with your description. To coordinate with the above narrative, create a table that groups the scores by broad subject area, then use empirical ranking to arrange topics within and across those groupings.

Cross-Tabulations

Cross-tabulations illustrate how the distribution of one categorical variable (e.g., low birth weight status) varies according to categories of a second variable (race/ethnicity). Statistical significance of differences is assessed by a chi-square test. In addition to showing what percentage of the overall sample was low birth weight, a cross-tabulation reports the percentage low birth weight for infants in each racial/ethnic group.

Consider this addition to the above description of birth weight patterns by race:

> "These gaps in mean birth weight translate into substantial differences in percentage low birth weight (LBW < 2,500 grams), with nearly twice the risk of LBW among non-Hispanic black as non-Hispanic white infants (11.3% and 5.8%, respectively; $p < 0.01$, table 9.1)."
>
> *The acronym LBW is spelled out and defined at first usage. A ratio is used to quantify the variation in LBW, and the percentage LBW is reported for each group to show which numbers were used to compute that ratio. Finally, non-Hispanic white infants are identified as the comparison group.*

Three-Way Associations

Two common types of associations among three variables are three-way cross-tabulations and differences in means.

Three-way cross-tabulations. Three-way cross-tabulations are used to investigate patterns among three categorical variables. A cross-tabulation of passing a math test (a yes/no variable), region, and school type would produce information about how many (and what percentage of) students in each combination of region and school type passed the test. As with bivariate cross-tabulations, the test statistic is the chi-square.

Differences in means. Differences in means are used to quantify patterns among one continuous outcome variable (e.g., math scores) and two categorical predictors (e.g., region and school type). If there are four regions and three school types, this procedure would yield 12 average math scores, one for each combination of region and school type. Statistical significance of differences across groups is assessed by an F-test from a two-way ANOVA.

Describing associations among three variables is complicated because three dimensions are involved, generating more values and patterns to report and interpret. To avoid explaining every number or focusing on a few arbitrarily chosen numbers, use the "Generalization, Example, Exceptions" (GEE) technique described in chapter 2 and appendix A.

■ "GENERALIZATION, EXAMPLE, EXCEPTIONS" REVISITED

To describe a three-way association, start by identifying the three two-way associations among the variables involved. For example, the relationship between race, gender, and labor force participation (figure 9.2) encompasses three bivariate associations: (1) race and gender, (2) gender and labor force participation, and (3) race and labor force participation. Only if there are exceptions to the general pattern in one or more of those bivariate associations does the three-way association need to be considered separately.

In figure 9.2, gender and race are predictors of labor force participation (the outcome). If the association between the predictors (e.g., the race/gender distribution) is important to your study, explain it before discussing how each of the predictors relates to the outcome. Otherwise, focus on the associations between each of the predictors and the outcome. Begin by describing the race/labor force participa-

Labor force participation
by race and gender, United States, 1998

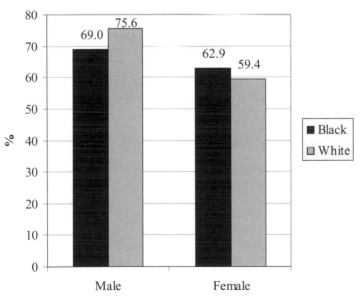

Figure 9.2. Interaction: Exception in direction of association.
Source: U.S. Census Bureau 1999c.

tion relationship and the gender/labor force participation relationship separately, mentioning the three-way pattern only if the two-way associations cannot be generalized:

> "(1) In the United States in 1998, labor force participation rates were higher for males than for females, regardless of race (figure 9.2). (2) However, the racial pattern differed by gender, (3) with higher labor force participation among white than black males (75.6% versus 69.0%), but lower labor force participation among white than black females (59.4% versus 62.9%; U.S. Census Bureau 1999c)."
>
> *The first sentence generalizes the gender pattern in labor force participation, which applies to both races. Phrase 2 explains that the racial pattern cannot be generalized across genders. Phrase 3 describes the three-way association and cites numeric evidence from the chart.*

Interactions

In GEE terms, this difference in how race and labor force participation relate is an exception, because no single description of the race/labor force participation pattern fits both genders. In statistical terminology, situations where the association between two characteristics depends on a third characteristic are known as *interactions* or *effects modifications* (see Miller, forthcoming).

Exceptions in Direction, Magnitude, and Statistical Significance

An exception in the *direction* of an association between two groups is fairly easy to detect from a graph of the relationship, as with the pattern of labor force participation by gender and race shown in figure 9.2. Comparing the heights of the respective bars, we observe that male participation is greater than female for both racial groups, but whether black participation is greater than or less than white depends on gender. Exceptions in direction can also occur in trends (e.g., figure 2.1), with a rising trend for one or more groups and a level or declining trend for others.

Exceptions in *magnitude* of association are more subtle and difficult to detect. Consider the relationship between gender, race, and life expectancy shown in figure 9.3: the interaction occurs in the different sizes of the gaps between the gray and black bars in the clusters for the two genders.

> "Data from 1997 for the United States show that (1) for both genders, whites outlived blacks (figure 9.3). In addition,

Expectation of life at birth
by race and gender, United States, 1997

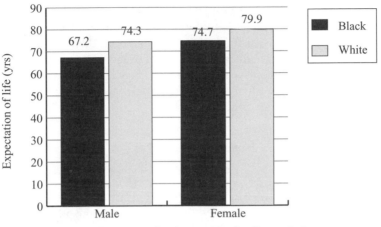

Figure 9.3. Interaction: Exception in magnitude of association.
Source: U.S. Census Bureau 2001c.

(2) females of both races outlive their male counterparts.
(3) However, the racial gap is wider for men than for women.
Among men, whites outlived blacks by 7.1 years on average,
with life expectancies of 74.3 and 67.2 years, respectively.
Among women, whites outlived blacks by 5.2 years (life
expectancies were 79.9 and 74.7 years; U.S. Census Bureau
2001c)."

*In this case, the direction of association in each two-way association can
be generalized: the first sentence explains that in all cases, white life
expectancy is greater than black, while the second sentence explains
that in both races, female life expectancy is greater than male. The third
sentence points out the difference in the size of the two "greater thans."*

For trends, exceptions in size appear as a steeper rise or fall for
some groups than for others.

Generalizations and exceptions also apply to *statistical significance.* If most of the patterns in a table are statistically significant,
summarize that finding and note any exceptions. Conversely, if most
patterns are *not* statistically significant, generalize, identity the few
statistically significant associations as exceptions, and report perti-

nent test statistics or *p*-values in the text. See "Results Section" in chapter 11 for illustrative examples.

Writing about Interactions

The GEE approach is a straightforward way to describe an interaction that is easily understood by most audiences because it emphasizes the substantive patterns before illustrating them with numbers from the associated table or chart. You need not introduce the term "interaction" at all — a genuine advantage if you are writing for people who aren't familiar with the statistical meaning of that word. For a general audience, write:

> "As shown in figure 9.2, the relationship between race and labor force participation depends on gender."

Or

> "As shown in figure 9.2, the relationship between race and labor force participation is different for men than for women."

For an audience that is familiar with the statistical meaning of "interaction," use that term as you introduce your results:

> "Race and gender interact in their relation with labor force participation (figure 9.2)."

Having alerted your audience to the fact that the pattern of association escapes a simple generalization, proceed through the rest of the GEE as in the description of figure 9.2 above. See appendix A for a systematic approach to identifying and describing such patterns.

Phrasing for a GEE

As you write a GEE, choose words that differentiate between broad patterns and exceptions.

Wording for the Generalization

To introduce a generalization, use expressions like "in general," "typically," or "by and large" to convey that the pattern characterizes many of the numbers you are summarizing. Phrases such as "virtually all," "in the majority of cases," or "roughly three-quarters of" can enhance the summary by conveying approximately what share of individuals, places, or time periods are encompassed by that general pattern. Often you can work the numeric illustration into the same sentence as the generalization by placing the specific numeric value in parentheses after the pertinent phrase: "Virtually all respondents (98%) . . ." or "In a majority of cases (59%), . . ."

Wording to Introduce Exceptions
To introduce exceptions, use phrases such as "an exception [to that pattern]" or "on the other hand," varying the wording to add interest to your descriptions.

"In seven out of 10 years studied, [pattern and example.] . . . However, in the other three years, [contrasting pattern]."

If your exception is literally the opposite of your generalization (e.g., falling rather than rising), consider expressions such as "on the contrary" or "conversely." Then describe the shape of the exception:

"Among white persons, male labor force participation exceeded female labor force participation. In contrast, among black persons, female labor force participation was higher than male."

■ **CHECKLIST FOR WRITING ABOUT DISTRIBUTIONS AND ASSOCIATIONS**

To describe univariate distribution or composition, consider the type of variable.
 • For continuous variables, report minimum, maximum, and mean values. For a scientific audience, include measures of variance, e.g., standard deviation.
 • For categorical variables, report modal category and mention selected other categories of interest.
 • Coordinate the order in which you mention categories with their sequence in the associated table or chart, using one or more of the organizing criteria described in chapter 6.
To describe a bivariate association, keep in mind the following:
 • Report direction of association.
 • Use selected quantitative comparisons (e.g., absolute, relative or percentage difference) to convey magnitude of association.
 • For a scientific audience, report results of statistical tests (e.g., chi-square or t-statistics, or the associated p-values).
To describe a three-way association:
 • Use the GEE approach to avoid reporting every number or comparison in the text.
 • Describe exceptions of direction, magnitude, and statistical significance.

Writing about Data and Methods

An essential part of writing about numbers is a description of the data and methods used to generate your figures. This information reveals how well your measures match the concepts you wish to study and how well the analytic methods capture the relationships among your variables — two important issues that affect how your results are interpreted. Suppose you are writing about an evaluation of a new math curriculum. Having explained why students would be expected to perform better under the new curriculum, you report statistics from a sample that includes some students following the new curriculum and some following the old. Because the data are collected in the real world, the concepts you seek to study may not be captured well by the available variables. Perhaps math performance was measured with a multiple-choice test in only a few classes and quite a few children were absent on test day, for example.

In addition, statistical methods require certain assumptions that are not always realistic, thus the methods of analysis may not accurately represent the true relationships among your variables. In an observational study with background information on only a few basic demographic attributes, for instance, the assumption of an experiment-like comparison of the two curriculums is unlikely to be satisfied.

To convey the salience of these issues for your work, write about how the study design, measures, and analytic methods suit the research question, how they improve upon previous analyses of the topic, and what questions remain to be answered with other data and different methods. With this information, readers can assess the quality and interpretation of the numbers you present and understand how your analyses contribute to the body of knowledge in the field.

In this chapter I show how to apply the principles and tools covered in previous chapters to writing about data and methods. In the first section, I discuss how to decide on the appropriate level of detail for your audience and the type of document you are writing. I then give guidelines about the contents of data and methods sections, touching briefly on many aspects of study design, measurement of variables, and statistical analysis. In the interest of space, I refer to other sources on these topics. See Schutt (2001) or Lilienfeld and Stolley (1994) for general references on research design, Wilkinson et al. (1999) for a comprehensive guide to data and methods sections for scientific papers, and Miller (forthcoming) for how to write about data and methods for multivariate analyses. In the final section, I demonstrate how to write about data and methods as you describe your conclusions.

■ WHERE AND HOW MUCH TO WRITE ABOUT DATA AND METHODS

The placement and level of detail about data and methods depend on your audience and the length of your work. For scientific readers, write a dedicated, detailed "Data and Methods" section. For readers with an interest in the topic but not the methods, include the basic information as you describe the findings. Regardless of audience, include a discussion of how these issues affect your conclusions. In the paragraphs that follow, I touch briefly on the different objectives of a data and methods section and the discussion of data and methods in a concluding section. Later in the chapter, I give a more detailed look at the respective contents and styles of those sections.

Data and Methods Sections

For articles or books intended for a scientific audience, comprehensive, precise information on data sources and statistical methods is expected. In a scientific paper, a well-written data and methods section will provide enough information that someone could replicate your analysis: if they were to collect data using your guidelines, they would end up with a comparable study design and variables. If they were to use the same data set and follow your procedures for excluding cases, defining variables, and applying analytic methods, they could reproduce your results.

Data and Methods in the Conclusion

In the concluding section of both lay and scientific papers, emphasize the implications of data and methods for your conclusions.

Discuss the strengths and limitations of the data and methods to place your findings in the larger context of what is and isn't known on your topic. Review the potential biases that affect your data and explain the plusses and minuses of the analytic techniques for your research question and data. In an article for a lay audience, skip the technical details and use colloquial language to describe how your data and methods affect interpretation of the findings.

▧ HOW MUCH TECHNICAL STUFF?

Scientific papers devote an entire section to data and methods, sometimes called just "methods" or "methods and materials." One of the most difficult aspects of writing these sections — particularly for novices — is selecting the appropriate level of detail. Some beginners are astonished that anyone would care how they conducted their analyses, thinking that only the results matter. Others slavishly report every alternative coding scheme and step of their exploratory analysis, yielding an avalanche of information for readers to sift through. A couple of guiding principles will help you arrive at a happy medium.

First, unless explanation of a particular aspect of the data or methods is needed to understand your analyses, keep your description brief and refer to other publications that give the pertinent details. If your document is the first to describe a new data collection strategy, measurement approach, or analytic method, thoroughly and systematically report the steps of the new procedure and how they were developed. If the method has been described elsewhere, restrict your explanation to the aspects needed to understand the current analysis and then cite other works for additional information.

Second, conventions about depth and organization of data and methods sections vary by discipline, level of training, and length of the work. To determine the appropriate style for your work, read examples of similar documents for comparable audiences in your field. Some general guidelines for common types of quantitative writing:

- For general-interest newspaper articles or summaries of research for nontechnical audiences, incorporate the W's (who, what, when, where) and units as you write about the numbers rather than in a separate section, then follow the approach described later in this chapter under "Data and Methods in the Discussion Section" to explain strengths and weaknesses.
- For a journal article or research proposal with a methodological

emphasis, provide details on methods of data collection or analysis that are novel, including why they are needed and the kinds of data and research questions for which they are best suited.

- For a journal article or grant proposal with a substantive emphasis, summarize the data and methods concisely and explain the basic logic of your analytic approach, then return to their advantages and disadvantages in the concluding section. Give less prominence to these issues in both the data and methods and discussion sections than you would in a methodological paper.
- For a "data book" designed to serve as a reference data source, summarize data and methods in the body of the report, with technical information and pertinent citations in appendixes.
- For a book or doctoral dissertation, follow the general guidelines above but take advantage of the additional length to provide more detail and documentation. If quantitative methods aren't a major focus, relegate technical details to appendixes.
- For documentation that accompanies public release of a data set, give a comprehensive, detailed explanation of study design, wording of questions, coding or calculation of variables, imputation, derivation and application of sampling weights, and so forth, accompanied by citations to pertinent methodological documents. Data documentation serves as the main reference source for all subsequent users of those data, so dot all the i's and cross all the t's.

▣ DATA SECTION

More than any other part of a scientific paper, a data and methods section is like a checklist written in sentence form. Organize the description of your data around the W's — who, what, when, where — and two honorary W's, how many and how.

When

Specify whether your data pertain to a single time point (cross-sectional data), to different samples compared across several points in time (repeated cross-sections), or to a sample followed over a period of time (longitudinal data), then report the pertinent dates and units of time.

Where

Identify where your data were collected. For studies of human populations, "where" usually encompasses standard geographic units such as cities, countries, or continents, or institutions such as schools, hospitals, or professional organizations. For ecological, geological, or other natural science studies, other types of places (such as bodies of water, landforms, or ecologic zones) or other geographic and topographic attributes (like latitude, longitude, altitude, or depth) may pertain. If geography is important to your topic, include one or more maps to orient an unfamiliar audience.

If you are using data from a named secondary data source such as the U.S. Census or the National Health Interview Survey, identify that source and provide a citation for published documentation. For nontechnical audiences or brief reports, that citation plus a brief list of who, what, when, and where is sufficient.

Who

"Who" encompasses several dimensions related to how data were collected and whether some cases were omitted from your sample because of missing values on one or more variables. Describe the *final analytic sample* used in your analysis, which may differ from the sample of cases for which data were originally collected.

Universe or Sample?

Some data sources aim to include the full universe of cases in the place and time specified, others a subset of those cases. In your data section, state whether your data include all cases in the specified place and time as in a census, or a sample of those cases, like a 1% poll of prospective voters. See "Study Design" and "Sampling" sections below for related issues.

Characteristics

Some research questions pertain to only some subgroups rather than all possible cases in the time and place specified. If you are using secondary data, you might analyze a subset of cases from a larger study. For example, the study described in box 10.1 focuses only on selected racial/ethnic groups and ages. Indicate whether your analytic sample was restricted to those who meet certain criteria, such as having particular demographic traits, minimum test scores, or a particular disease, and explain why such restrictions suit your research question.

Response Rate

Few studies succeed in collecting data on all the cases they sought to study. For instance, some subjects who are selected for a study cannot be contacted or refuse to participate; censuses and surveillance systems overlook some individuals. Report the response rate for your study as a percentage of the intended study sample and consider representativeness of the sample (see below).

In almost every study, some cases have missing or invalid information on one or more variables. Cases that are missing the outcome variable or a key predictor (birth weight and race/ethnicity, respectively, in the study described below) cannot be used to analyze the association between those variables. Some researchers impute missing values (see "Imputation" below), although this is typically avoided for the main variables in an analysis. See Kalton and Kasprzyk (1986) or Westat (1994).

If you exclude cases with missing values, list the variables that formed the basis for the exclusion and report the number and percentage of cases omitted based on those criteria. If a large percentage of cases that otherwise fit your research question are missing data, discuss whether the retained cases are representative of the population to whom you wish to generalize your results (see "Representativeness" below).

Loss to Follow-Up

Studies that follow subjects across time typically lose some cases between the beginning and end of the study. For instance, studies tracking students' school performance across time lose students who transfer schools, drop out, or refuse to participate. Perhaps you started following a cohort of 500 entering ninth graders, but only 250 remain four years later.

Loss to follow-up, also known as attrition, affects statistical analyses in two important ways. First, the smaller number of cases can affect the power of your statistical tests (Kraemer 1987). Second, if those who are lost differ from those who remain, inferences drawn from analysis of the remaining cases may not be generalizable to the intended universe. For example, dropouts are often weaker students than those who stay in school, yielding a biased look at the performance of the overall cohort.

For longitudinal data, provide the following information, and then discuss representativeness:

- The number of cases at baseline (the start date of the study), following the guidelines for response rate and missing data described above

- The number and percentage of the baseline sample that remained at the latest date from which you use data
- The percentage of initial cases present at each round (if you use data from intervening data collection points, e.g., four sets of observations collected at annual intervals)
- Reasons for dropping out of the study (e.g., moved away, dropped out of school, died), if known, and the number of cases for each
- Whether your analysis includes only cases for which information was available throughout the period of observation or for all cases present at baseline

Outliers

Occasionally, your data will contain "outliers" — values that fall well outside the range of the other values and can substantially affect estimates based on the full sample. To avoid biasing results, outliers are sometimes excluded from an analysis sample. If an NFL first round draft pick happened to be part of your sample of 100 recent college graduates, you would be well justified excluding him from an analysis of income to avoid grossly inflating average income for typical recent graduates. (If your focus were on NFL salaries you would choose your sample differently, but that's another story.)

Any omission of selected cases is an opportunity to "finesse" your data to obtain some desired results — in other words, to lie with statistics — so exercise great care in deciding which cases to exclude and in communicating what you did and why. State how outliers were identified and what criteria you used to exclude cases, then report how many cases were excluded. Finally, report how much the size and statistical significance of associations differ with and without the outliers.

How Many

Once you have identified the "when, where, and who" of your final analytic sample, report the number of cases used in your analysis, overall and for any major subgroups being compared. If there are only a handful of sample sizes to report (e.g., total and for each of four study sites), mention them in the text and in tables that report descriptive statistics or analyses. For larger numbers of subsamples (e.g., each of the 50 states), report the smallest, largest, and average sub-sample sizes, or report subsample sizes in an appendix table. If you are using sampling weights in your analyses (see below), the sample size is the unweighted number of cases.

How

In the data section, "how" encompasses how the data were collected, including data sources, wording and calculation of variables, and how missing values on individual variables were handled. ("How" you analyzed the data is the focus of the methods section; see "Methods Section" below.) State whether your data are primary data (collected by you or someone on your research team) or secondary data (collected by someone else and not necessarily designed with your research question in mind). For primary data collection involving human subjects, give the name of the institutional review board that evaluated the methodology (for general guidelines, see National Institutes for Health 2002).

Study Design

Study designs range from case studies to censuses, from surveys to surveillance systems, from randomized controlled trials to case-control studies, each of which has strengths and weaknesses (Lilienfeld and Stolley 1994; or Schutt 2001). In the data section, specify which type of study design was used to collect your data, and then return to its advantages and limitations in the conclusion.

Indicate whether data were collected cross-sectionally (all variables measured at the same point in time), retrospectively (looking back in time), or prospectively (moving forward in time). State whether the study was a randomized clinical trial or other form of experimental study, a panel study, case-control study, or other type of design. Terminology for study design varies by discipline, so employ the wording used in the field for which you are writing.

Experimental design. If the study involved data from an experiment, explain the experimental conditions:
- Explain how subjects were assigned to the treatment and control groups.
- Describe alternative conditions, whether treatment and control or different treatment variants. For each condition, explain what was done, including total amount of time the experiment

was run, how often observations were made, and other details that would allow readers to replicate the experiment and associated data collection.

- Mention whether placebos were used and whether single- or double-blinding was used.

Sampling. For studies that involve sampling, indicate whether the cases were selected by random sampling, quota sampling, convenience sampling, or some other approach. If random sampling was used, specify whether it was a simple random sample or a more complex design involving stratification, clustering, or disproportionate sampling. For complex sampling designs, explain in your methods section how sampling weights were used (see below) and mention statistical techniques that were used to adjust for the study design (e.g., Westat 1996).

Some types of study design require additional information about identification or selection of cases. Cohort studies sample on the predictor variable, such as selecting smokers and nonsmokers in a prospective cancer study. Case-control studies sample on the outcome, selecting people with and without lung cancer and then retrospectively collecting smoking information. If the study involved matching of cases to controls, describe the criteria and methods.

Data Sources

Specify whether your data came from a questionnaire, interview, surveillance system (e.g., vital registration or cancer registry), administrative records (e.g., medical or tax records, voters' registration), observation of subjects, physical examination, or other sources, and cite associated data documentation. List other attributes of data collection that could introduce sample selection bias, coding mistakes, or other types of errors. These issues vary considerably depending on the mode of data collection, so read the literature on the methods used to collect your data to anticipate what other information is relevant. A few illustrations:

- If the data are from a survey, was the questionnaire self-administered or from an in-person or telephone interview? Were the data collected orally or in written format?
- If information was extracted from existing records, who identified relevant cases and transcribed data from the forms: a few people specifically trained for the task, or people who

normally work with those records but not for research
purposes?

- For scientific measurements, the name and characteristics of
the measuring instrument (e.g., type of scale, brand of caliper
or thermometer) are often required.

What

Finally, having reported the context, study design, and data
sources, describe what variables were measured. If all your variables
come from the same source, summarize the W's in one sentence, and
don't repeat. If more than one data source is involved, generalize as
much as possible about which variables came from which sources.
Use panels within tables or create separate tables to organize variables by topic and source, with information about sources of each
variable in the title or footnotes.

Poor: "Age, sex, race, marital status, number of children, income,
and educational attainment were taken from the demographic
section of the questionnaire. Attitudes about [long list] were
taken from the attitudinal section of the questionnaire. Medical
records provided information about [long list of health items].
Asthma was also asked about on the questionnaire."
*This description is unnecessarily long, repeating information that is far
more easily organized in a table.*

Better: "Demographic characteristics and attitudinal factors (table A)
were drawn from the questionnaire and most health indicators
from the medical records (table B). An exception was asthma, for
which information was available from both sources (see below)."
*This description coordinates with tables (not shown) that organize
variables by data source and major conceptual groupings, eliminating
the need to specify the source for every variable individually.*

Variables

Except for the most detailed scientific texts or data documentation, limit in-depth descriptions of measures to your outcome and
key predictor variables. For other, less central variables, refer to another publication that contains information about their attributes or
mention them as you describe the chart or table in which they are first
shown. The documentation for the NHANES III — the data used in
the birth weight analysis reported here — includes a CD-ROM with
copies of the field manuals used by data collectors, spelling out in

great detail how various aspects of the health examination, nutritional history, and cognitive testing were conducted (NCHS 1994; Westat 1996). Because that information is publicly available, descriptions of the variables in scientific papers that use those data can refer to that source for details.

Raw versus calculated data. Some of your variables may be used exactly as they were collected ("raw data"), others calculated from one or more variables in the raw data. For variables analyzed in the same units or categories in which they were originally collected, mention their source. If the phrasing of a question could affect how subjects interpreted that question, include the original wording either in a short paragraph within the data section or in an appendix that displays the relevant portion of the data collection instrument. Avoid rephrasing the original, such as substituting "better than average" for "excellent" and "very good," or replacing "HIV" for "AIDS," as the specific wording of items can affect subjects' responses. Wording of very short items can sometimes be incorporated into table headings (see table 6.2).

Poor: "One asthma measure was collected on the mother's
   questionnaire, the other from medical records."
   *The questionnaire and medical records could have collected data in any
   of several ways, each of which has different potential biases, so for most
   scientific papers a more precise description is needed.*
Better (for a lay audience): "Two types of asthma measure were
   used. The mother's measure was based on the question 'Have
   you ever been told your child has asthma?', the doctor's measure
   on whether a physician wrote 'asthma' on the medical record or
   checked it on a list of possible diagnoses."
Better (for a scientific audience): "A maternal report of asthma was
   based on the question: 'Have you ever been told your child has
   asthma?' A doctor's report of asthma was based on (1) checking
   that diagnosis on a list of possible diagnoses, (2) listing 'asthma'
   on the open-ended section of the medical record, or (3) listing
   an IDC9 code of 493 on the open-ended section of the medical
   record (NCHS 1995)."

For primary data, indicate whether you adopted or adapted the items or scales from other sources, or developed your own. For either primary or secondary data, explain whether and how items were pretested, and report on reliability and validity (see below).

To address some research questions, new variables must be created from variables in the original data. Examples include calculating a categorical variable from a continuous one (e.g., an indicator of whether blood alcohol level exceeded the legal limit), combining categories (e.g., collapsing 5-year age groups into 10-year groups), creating a summary variable to aggregate information on several related items (e.g., calculating total family income from wages, salary, alimony, Supplemental Security Insurance benefits, etc.), and creating a scale (e.g., the CESD scale from a series of items related to depressive symptoms).

Explain how new variables were calculated, whether by you or in secondary data, and mention whether that approach is consistent with other analyses. State whether the criteria used in those calculations were based on existing standards or cutoffs (such as the legal blood alcohol limit, or the list of income components used to calculate overall income), empirical analysis of your data (such as median income or quartiles of the income distribution), or theoretical criteria, then cite the pertinent literature.

Units and categories. Name the subgroups of each categorical variable and the units of measurement for every continuous variable in each table where that variable is reported. Explain units of measurement in the data section only if they are unusual or complex. Mention variables measured in familiar units as you write up corresponding results. Accompany ordinal values that were created from continuous variables with their numeric equivalents, e.g.,

"'High' and 'low' correspond to the top and bottom quintiles of the income distribution, while 'middle' comprises the middle three quintiles."

If ordinal variables were collected without reference to specific numeric values, list the possible responses exactly as they were worded on the original data collection instrument, e.g.,

"How would you rate your health: excellent, very good, good, fair, or poor?"

Reliability and validity. Indicators of reliability are used to evaluate consistency of alternate measures of the same concept — whether different questions, different observers, or different time points. Measures of validity consider whether a question or scale captures the concepts it is intended to measure, including face validity, concurrent validity, predictive validity, and construct validity. Report standard statistics on the reliability and validity of your key variables. See Schutt (2001) for an overview of reliability and validity; Morgan et al. (2002) for illustrative wording to report the measures.

Missing Values, Again

In most data sets, information is missing on one or more questions for at least some cases: a subject returned the survey but refused to report income, for example, or information on weight was missing from some medical records. In some instances, you will retain cases that are missing information on one or more variables ("item nonresponse") and either create a missing value category or impute missing values. Report frequency of item nonresponse and how you dealt with missing values on individual items (see Westat 1994 for discussion).

Missing value category. One approach to handling missing values for a variable is to create a category of that variable called "missing." This method is best used to avoid excluding cases that lack data on one of several background variables and if only a small share of cases have missing values on any one variable. Report the percentage of cases in the missing value category of each variable in a table of descriptive statistics. Comment on its interpretation in the discussion section if it affects more than a small percentage of cases.

Imputation. Imputation involves filling in values for cases that lack data on a variable based on values of that variable or related variables for cases with valid data. See Miller (forthcoming) or Westat (1994) for a review of imputation processes and evaluation.

Representativeness

Describe how well your sample reflects the population it is intended to represent. Limit this comparison to those who qualify in terms of place, time, and other characteristics that pertain to your research question. For instance, if studying factors that influence urban school performance, don't count students from suburban or rural schools among the excluded cases when assessing representativeness — they aren't part of the population to whom you want to generalize your results.

Depending on your audience and the length of your document, there are several ways to report on representativeness.

- At a minimum, report how many and what percentage of

sampled cases were included. If the response rate is over 85%, no additional discussion of representativeness may be needed.

- Create a table of bivariate statistics comparing known characteristics of included and excluded cases, or, if statistics are available from the census or other sources, comparing the sample (weighted to the population level; see below) to the target population. Statistically significant differences in these traits help identify likely direction of bias, which you can summarize in the concluding section of the paper.
- Write a descriptive analysis of reasons for exclusion or attrition, such as whether those who remained in the sample differed from who were lost from the sample by moving away, dropping out of school, or dying.

Box 10.1 presents an example of a data section for a scientific paper about the birth weight analyses described in chapter 11, numbered to coordinate with the accompanying comments.

■ METHODS SECTION

In the methods section of a scientific paper, explain how you analyzed your data, including what statistical methods were used and why, and whether you used sampling weights. Focus on the logic and strategy of your analytic approach, saving the description of statistical findings for the results section of your work.

Statistical Methods

Name the statistical methods used to analyze your data (e.g., analysis of variance, Pearson correlation, chi-square test) and the type of software (e.g., SAS, SPSS, Stata) used to estimate those statistics.

Sampling Weights

If your data are from a random sample, they usually come with sampling weights that reflect the sampling rate, clustering, or disproportionate sampling, and correct for differential nonresponse and loss to follow-up (Westat 1996, sec. 2). Most analyses of such data use the weights to inflate the estimates back to the population level, for instance, estimating the total number of unemployed persons in the United States based on the number in the study sample. If disproportionate sampling was used, the data must be weighted to correctly represent the composition of the population from which the sample was drawn (e.g., Westat 1996, sec. 1.3). The sample size used

Box 10.1. Example of a Data Section for a Scientific Paper

"(1) Data were extracted from the 1988–1994 *National Health and Nutrition Examination Survey III* (NHANES III) — a cross-sectional, population-based sample survey of the noninstitutionalized population of the United States (U.S. DHHS 1997). (2) To reduce recall bias, birth weight questions were asked only about children aged 0 to 10 years at the time of the survey. (3) Our final sample comprised 3,733 non-Hispanic white, 2,968 non-Hispanic black, and 3,112 Mexican American infants for whom family income and race/ethnicity were known (93% of that age group in the NHANES III). (4) Children of other racial/ethnic backgrounds (mostly Asian) were excluded because there were not enough cases to study them as a separate group.

"(5) All variables used in this analysis were based on information from the interview of the reporting adult in the household. (6) Consistent with World Health Organization conventions (1950) a child was considered to be low birth weight (LBW) if their reported birth weight fell below 2,500 grams or 5.5 lbs. (7) Coding and units of variables are shown in table 6.6, (8) which compares the sample to all U.S. births."

COMMENTS
(1) Names the data source, including dates, and specifies type of study design and target population (where, who), and provides a citation to study documentation.
(2) Mentions potential bias for one of the variables and how it was minimized by the study design (age restrictions).
(3) Reports the unweighted sample size for the three major subgroups in the study, specifies exclusion criteria, and reports the associated response rate.
(4) Explains why children of other racial/ethnic background were excluded from this birth weight analysis. (For other research questions, different criteria would pertain.)
(5) Specifies which sources from the NHANES III provided data for the variables in the analysis. (The NHANES III also included a medical history, physical examination, lab tests, and dietary intake history. Those sources were not used in the birth weight analysis described here.)
(6) Explains how the low birth weight indicator was calculated and gives its standard acronym, with reference to the standard definition and a pertinent reference.

(7) Directs readers to the table of descriptive statistics for details on units and coding of variables, averting lengthy discussion in the text.

(8) Refers to the table with data to assess the representativeness of the sample.

to calculate the standard errors for statistical tests should be the unweighted number of cases; check that your statistical program makes this correction.

Explain when and how you used the sampling weights and refer to the data documentation for background information about the derivation and application of those weights. For analyses of clustered data, name the statistical methods used to correct the standard errors for clustering (e.g., Shah et al. 1996).

Box 10.2 is an illustrative methods section for a scientific paper about the birth weight analysis.

■ DATA AND METHODS IN THE DISCUSSION SECTION

Many of the issues described in the data and methods sections have repercussions for the analysis and interpretation of your results. Explain these points by discussing the advantages and limitations of your data and methods in your concluding section.

Strengths

Remind your audience how your analysis contributes to the existing literature with a brief discussion of the strengths of your data and methods. Point out that you used more recent information than previous studies, data on the particular geographic or demographic group of interest, or improved measures of the key variables, for example. Mention any methodological advances or analytic techniques you used that better suit the research question or data, such as taking a potential confounding variable into account.

Rather than repeating the W's and other technical details from the data and methods section, rephrase them to emphasize specifically how those attributes strengthen your analyses.

Poor: "The experimental nature of the study strengthened the findings by eliminating self-selection."

> **Box 10.2. Example of a Methods Section for a Scientific Paper**
>
> METHODS
> "(1) Bivariate associations among race/ethnicity, socioeconomic characteristics, and birth weight were tested using *t*-tests [for continuous outcomes such as birth weight in grams] and chi-square tests [for categorical outcomes such as low birth weight]. (2) All statistics were weighted to the national level using weights provided for the NHANES III by the National Center for Health Statistics (U.S. DHHS 1997). (3) SUDAAN software was used to adjust the estimated standard errors for complex sampling design (Shah et al. 1996)."
>
> COMMENTS
> (1) Identifies types of statistics used to test bivariate associations. Text shown in brackets clarifies which statistical tests pertain to which outcomes, and would be included only for students of elementary statistics.
> (2) Mentions use and source of sampling weights and cites pertinent documentation.
> (3) Explains what method and software were used to correct for complex study design, with a citation.

This generality about experimental studies doesn't convey how they affected this particular research question and data source.

Better: "Because subjects were randomly assigned to the treatment and control groups, differences in background characteristics of those who elected treatment were ruled out as an explanation for better survival in that group."

This version explains how an experimental design (randomization) improved this study, mentioning the outcome (survival), the predictor (treatment versus control) and potential confounders ("background characteristics").

Limitations

Just as important as touting the strengths of your data and methods is confessing to their limitations. Many neophytes flinch at this suggestion, fearing that they will undermine their own work if they identify its weaknesses. On the contrary, part of demonstrating that you have done good science is acknowledging that no study is perfect for answering all questions. Having already pointed out the strengths of your study, list aspects of your analyses that should be reexamined with better data or statistical methods, and mention new questions raised by your findings. Translate general statements about biases or other limitations into specific points about how they affect interpretation of your findings.

Poor: "The study sample is not representative, hence results cannot be generalized to the overall target population."
This statement is so broad that it doesn't convey direction of possible biases caused by the lack of representativeness.

Better: "The data were collected using a self-administered questionnaire written in English; consequently the study sample omitted people with low literacy skills and those who do not speak English. In the United States, both of these groups are concentrated at the lower end of the socioeconomic spectrum; therefore estimates of health knowledge from this study probably overstate that in the general adult population."
This version clearly explains how the method of data collection affected who was included in the sample and the implications for estimated patterns of the outcomes under study. Jargon like "representativeness" and "target population" is restated in terms of familiar concepts and the concepts related to the particular research question and study design.

Accompany your statements about limitations with reference to other publications that have evaluated those issues for other similar data. By drawing on others' work, you may be able to estimate the extent of bias without conducting your own analyses of each such issue.

Directions for Future Research

Close your discussion of limitations by listing some directions for future research. Identify ways to address the drawbacks of your study, perhaps by collecting additional data, or collecting or analyzing it differently, and mention new questions raised by your analyses. This approach demonstrates that you are aware of potential solutions to your study's limitations and contributes to an understanding of where it fits in the body of research on the topic.

Box 10.3 is an example of a discussion of the advantages and disadvantages of the birth weight data, to follow the concluding section presented in box 11.4. By discussing possible strengths and weaknesses consecutively, the first paragraph helps to weigh their respective influences and provide a balanced assessment of the data quality.

Box 10.3. Data and Methods in the Discussion of a Scientific Paper

"(1) This study of a large, nationally representative survey of U.S. children extends previous research on determinants of low birth weight by including income and maternal smoking behavior — two variables not available on birth certificates, which were the principal data source for many past studies. (2) A potential drawback of the survey data is that information on birth weight was collected from the child's mother at the time of the survey — up to 10 years after the child's birth. In contrast to birth weight data from the birth certificate, which are recorded at the time of the birth, these data may suffer from retrospective recall bias. (3) However, previous studies of birth weight data collected from mothers reveal that they can accurately recall birth weight and other aspects of pregnancy and early infant health several years later (Githens et al. 1993; Olson et al. 1997). (4) In addition, racial and socioeconomic patterns of birth weight in our study are consistent with those based on birth certificate data (Martin et al. 2002) suggesting that the mode of data collection did not appreciably affect results.

"(5) A useful extension of this analysis would be to investigate whether other Latino subgroups exhibit similar rates of low birth weight to those observed among the Mexican American infants studied here. (6) Inclusion of additional measures of socioeconomic status, acculturation, and health behaviors would provide insight into possible reasons for that pattern."

COMMENTS

(1) Identifies an advantage of the current data source over those used in previous analyses.

(2) Points out a potential source of bias in the study data.

(3) Cites previous research evaluating maternal retrospective recall of birth weight to suggest that such bias is likely to be small.

(4) Compares findings about sociodemographic determinants of birth weight from the survey with findings from studies using other sources of birth weight data to further dispel concerns about the accuracy of the survey data, and provides citations to those studies.

(5) Rather than describing the inclusion of only one Latino group in the study sample as a weakness, suggests that expanding the range of Latino groups would be a useful direction for future research.

(6) Identifies additional variables that could shed light on the underlying reasons for the epidemiologic paradox (explained in box 11.4), again suggesting important ideas for later work.

■ CHECKLIST FOR WRITING ABOUT DATA AND METHODS

Consider audience and type of work to determine appropriate placement and detail about data and methods.

- For short, nonscientific papers:

  Integrate the W's into your narrative.

  Name the type of study design.

  Explain briefly how key variables were measured, if this affects interpretation of your findings.

- For scientific papers or grant proposals, include a separate data and methods section.

  Use the W's to organize material on context and methods of data collection.

  Report the analytic sample size, then discuss the response rate, extent of missing values on individual variables, treatment of outliers, and representativeness.

  Define your variables:

     –Include original wording of novel or complex questions, in the text or an appendix for key variables, as you describe results for other variables.

     –Report units, defining them if unusual or complicated.

     –Describe how new variables were created.

     –Report on reliability and validity.

  Name the statistical methods.

  Mention whether sampling weights were used, and if so, their source.

- Where possible, refer to other publications that contain details about the same data and methods.

- Regardless of audience, discuss how the strengths and limitations of your data and methods affect interpretation of your findings.

- For a scientific paper, suggest ways future research could address the limitations of your analysis.

Writing Introductions, Results, and Conclusions

The earlier material in this book laid the foundation for this culminating chapter by introducing and demonstrating the principles and tools used to write about numbers. In this chapter, I show how to put those building blocks together to craft a clear, well-integrated article or paper. In the first section I give an overview of how to organize prose involving quantitative information, constructing a sequential, logical story with numbers used as evidence for the topic at hand. The rest of the chapter illustrates two common types of expository writing aimed at different audiences:

- An article for a general audience that includes numeric facts gleaned from several sources.
- An academic paper, book, or scientific report focusing on the analysis of a single data set. In such works, most of the detailed analysis is presented in a results section, with selected background facts from other sources included in introductory and concluding sections.

Most of the example sentences in this chapter are written in an academic style, incorporating the formal citation of author and date for each fact. To adapt these sentences for a lay audience, replace the citation with the name of the author or source: "A report by the Federal Aviation Administration showed . . ." or "According to statistics from the National Center for Health Statistics . . . ," for example.

■ ORGANIZING YOUR PROSE

Writing about numbers is similar to writing a legal argument. In the opening statement, a lawyer raises the major questions to be addressed during the trial and gives a general introduction to the characters and events in question. To build a compelling case, he then presents specific facts collected and analyzed using standard methods of inquiry. If innovative or unusual methods were used, he introduces experts to describe and justify those techniques. He presents individual facts, then ties them to other evidence to demonstrate patterns or themes. He may submit exhibits such as diagrams or physical evidence to supplement or clarify the facts. He cites previous cases that have established precedents and standards in the field and discusses how they do or do not apply to the current case. Finally, in the closing argument he summarizes conclusions based on the complete body of evidence, restating the critical points but with far less detail than in the evidence portion of the trial.

Follow the same general structure as you write your quantitative story line for a scientific paper or grant proposal. The introduction parallels the opening argument; the data and methods and results sections mirror the evidence portion of the trial; and the discussion and conclusions parallel the closing argument. Open by introducing the overarching questions before describing the detailed numbers, just as a lawyer outlines the big picture before introducing specific testimony or other evidence to the jury. Describe and justify your methods of data collection and analysis. Systematically introduce and explain the numeric evidence in your exhibits — tables, charts, maps, or other diagrams — building a logical sequence of analyses. Close by summarizing your findings and connecting them back to the initial questions and previous studies of related topics.

In a general-interest article, use a less formal structure — perhaps more like a lawyer recounting his case over a few drinks after work — but retain a logical, well-organized approach to introducing, presenting, and interpreting facts. See "General-Interest Articles" below for examples and guidance.

Using Paragraphs to Organize Your Ideas

As in other types of expository writing, introduce the broad topic or question of the work and then organize the factual material into separate paragraphs, each of which describes one major topic or pattern or a series of closely related patterns. Begin each paragraph with a statement of the issue or question to be addressed, write a sentence or two to sketch out the shape of the contrast or pattern with words, then provide and interpret numeric evidence to document that pattern. To portray the size of each pattern, use selected comparisons such as rank, absolute difference, relative difference, or percentage difference.

To describe a table or chart that encompasses more than one type of pattern, organize your narrative into paragraphs, each of which deals with one topic or set of closely related topics. For instance, a description of a chart portraying trends in unemployment over two decades for each of several occupations might be organized into two paragraphs, the first describing trends over time and whether they are consistent for all the occupation categories, the second comparing levels of unemployment across occupational categories at one point in time and whether that pattern is consistent across time.

As you write, select analogies and descriptive words or phrases to convey the context and scale of those differences. Well-chosen verbs, adjectives, and adverbs sharpen the description of the patterns and contrasts and can add considerable texture and interest.

■ GENERAL-INTEREST ARTICLES

In general-interest articles, numeric facts are often used to highlight the importance of the topic, to provide other background information, or to illustrate patterns of distribution or association. If you include charts or tables, keep them simple and focused. Refer to them by name or number as you describe them in the associated narrative.

To illustrate how to apply these concepts, I have included an excerpt from a two-page article in the *New York Times* about the physical impact of the planes that hit the Twin Towers on September 11, 2001 (Lipton and Glanz 2002; box 11.1). The article includes some fairly technical information but is written for an educated lay audience. Accompanying the excerpt are annotations which show how the authors included explanations, charts, and analogies to elucidate numbers and concepts in the article. Some explanations define terms (joules) and concepts (how speed relates to energy on impact); others provide comparisons to clarify what the numbers mean or why certain cutoffs are pertinent. Without that information, readers who aren't familiar with physics, engineering, or airline regulations would find it hard to understand the purpose or interpretation of the numbers in the article. In each comment, I also identify which principle or tool the authors used in the associated sentence. Note that the authors did not name the various principles and tools as they used them, but simply integrated them into the narrative.

■ SCIENTIFIC PAPERS, REPORTS, AND GRANT PROPOSALS

Academic papers, books, or scientific reports that describe analyses of one or more data sets usually follow a prescribed structure,

Box 11.1. Using Numbers in a General-Interest Article:
Impact of the Planes on the Twin Towers, September 11, 2001

" . . . (1) The government's analysis put the speeds [on impact] at 586 m.p.h. for the United flight and 494 m.p.h. for the American one. In both cases, (2) the planes were flying much faster than they should have been at that altitude: The aviation agency's limit below 10,000 feet is 287 m.p.h . . . .

"(3) The energy of motion carried by any object, called the kinetic energy, varies as the square of its velocity, so even modest differences in speed can translate into large variations in what the building had to absorb. (4) That means that while the United jet was traveling only about a quarter faster than the American jet, it would have released about 50% more energy on impact . . . (5) Even at a speed of only about 500 m.p.h., a partly loaded Boeing 767 weighing 132 tons would have created about three billion joules of energy at impact, the equivalent of three-quarters of a ton of T.N.T.

After (6) presenting the respective speeds in a simple bar chart (figure 11.1), the authors explain that (7) both jets were traveling at speeds that exceeded the Boeing design speed limit at 1,500 feet, and the United jet exceeded even the design cruise speed at 35,000 feet. Such speeds threatened the structural integrity of the planes even before they struck the buildings, because "(8) The lower the plane goes, . . . the thicker the air becomes, so the slower the plane must travel to avoid excessive stress."

COMMENTS

(1) Reports the actual speeds of each plane. *Basic principle: Report numbers.*

(2) Compares the planes' speeds with a cutoff: the FAA limit for flights at that altitude. *Basic principle: Compare against a standard to help interpret numbers.*

(3) Explains in lay terms how differences in speed translate into differences in energy on impact, paraphrasing the meaning of "kinetic energy." *Basic principle: Define concepts using simple wording, and avoid or paraphrase jargon.*

(4) Reports results of calculations to illustrate how much more energy the second plane released, applying the general formula given in the preceding sentence. *Basic principle:*

> *Report numbers and results of calculations. Tools: Relative difference and percentage difference.*
>
> (5) Reports results of calculation of absolute energy generated by the second plane. Units of measurement (joules) are compared against a more familiar quantity. *Basic principle: Interpret numbers using analogies or metaphors.*
>
> (6) Uses a bar chart to illustrate speeds of the two planes and how they compare to industry design speeds. *Basic principle: Choose the right tools.*
>
> (7) Explains that the planes were traveling too fast for conditions by comparing their speeds against the design speed limit at both the altitude where the planes were flying and cruise altitude. *Basic principle: Compare against meaningful cutoffs.*
>
> (8) Uses colloquial language to explain the physical principles why the design speed is slower for lower altitudes. *Basic principle: Explain complicated concepts in everyday language.*

Impact speed of 9/11 flights and comparison speeds

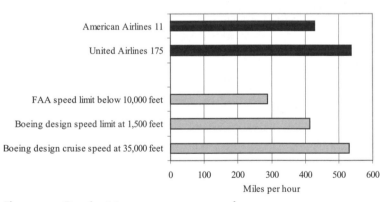

Figure 11.1. Bar chart to accompany a comparison.
Source: Lipton and Glanz 2002.

with the text divided into an introduction, literature review, data and methods, results, and discussion and conclusions (Montgomery 2003; Pyrczak and Bruce 2000). Grant proposals follow a similar structure, substituting a description of pilot studies or preliminary findings for the results section, and replacing the discussion and conclusions with a section on policy, program, or research implications of the proposed project. In the next few pages, I show the structure and contents of introductory, results, and concluding sections of a research paper on the relationships among race/ethnicity, socioeconomic status, and birth weight in the United States.

Introduction

In your introduction, state the topic and explain why it is of interest. After a general introductory sentence, report a few numbers to establish the importance of that topic. Include information on the prevalence of the issue or phenomenon under study, or the consequences of that phenomenon, using one or two selected numeric contrasts to place those statistics in perspective. Cite the source of each fact as you mention it, using the standard citation format for your discipline. End the introduction with a statement of what your study will add to what is already known on the subject, either as a list of questions to be addressed or as one or more hypotheses.

Box 11.2 illustrates how to apply these ideas to the birth weight study that is the theme of this chapter, with comments keyed to numbered sentences within the paragraph.

Literature Review

Academic papers and grant proposals usually include a review of the existing literature on the topic to describe what is already known, provide theoretical background on the hypothesized relationships among variables, and report major quantitative findings for comparison with the current study. In some disciplines, the literature review is a free-standing section or chapter; in others, it is integrated into the introduction. If your literature review is separate from your introduction, place your research questions or hypotheses at the end of the literature review. Having acquainted readers with theory and empirical findings from other studies helps substantiate the reasons behind the specific objectives and hypotheses for your study.

Literature reviews typically emphasize the approximate size (and possibly statistical significance) of associations rather than giving precise measures of magnitude of association, reporting only a few

Box 11.2. Using Numbers in an Introduction to a Scientific Paper or Report

"(1) Low birth weight is a widely recognized risk factor for infant mortality, neurological problems, asthma, and a variety of developmental problems that can persist into childhood and even adulthood (U.S. Environmental Protection Agency 2002; Institute of Medicine 1985). (2) For example, in 1999, U.S. infants born weighing less than 2,500 grams (5.5 pounds) were 24 times as likely as normal birth weight infants to die before their first birthday (60.5 deaths per 1,000 live births and 2.5 deaths per 1,000, respectively; Mathews, MacDorman, and Menacker 2002). Although they comprise about 7.5% of all births, low birth weight infants account for more than 75% of infant deaths (Paneth 1995).

"(3) Costs associated with low birth weight are substantial: in 1995, Lewit and colleagues estimated that $4 billion — more than one-third of all expenditures on health care for infants — was spent on the incremental costs of medical care for low birth weight infants. Higher risks of special education, grade repetition, hospitalization, and other medical costs add more than $85,000 (in 1995 dollars) per low birth weight child to costs incurred by normal birth weight children through age 15 (Lewit et al. 1995).

"(4) Despite considerable efforts to reduce the incidence of low birth weight, the problem remains fairly intractable: between 1981 and 2000, the percentage of low birth weight infants rose from 6.8% to 7.6% of all infants, in part reflecting the increase in multiple births (Martin et al. 2002). (5) Rates of low birth weight among black infants have remained approximately twice that among white infants over the same period (13.0% and 6.5% in 2000, respectively). (6) To what extent is that pattern due to the lower socioeconomic status of black children in the United States? That question is the focus of this analysis."

COMMENTS

(1) Introduces the topic of the paper and gives a general sense of its importance, with reference to major studies on the topic.

(2) Reports statistics on the consequences of low birth weight, using relative risk and percentage share to quantify mortality differences, and citing original sources of the figures used in those comparisons.

(3) Reports estimates from other studies of the costs associated with low birth weight, providing further evidence that the topic merits additional study.

(4) Generalizes about trends in low birth weight over the past two decades and reports numeric facts to illustrate those patterns, with citations of the original data sources.

(5) Presents information about racial differences in low birth weight, providing a transition to the research question for this study (sentence 6).

illustrative numbers. To provide the basis for comparison of results across studies, report numbers in the same style and level of detail as in an introductory section. As with statistics from your own analyses, always report the value as well as quantitative comparisons such as absolute difference, ratio, or percentage change to provide the raw data for those comparisons and help readers interpret the contrasts. Examples of these applications are included in box 11.2.

Results Section

In the results section, report and describe numeric evidence to test your hypotheses, systematically presenting quantitative examples and contrasts. Organize the section into paragraphs, each of which addresses one aspect of your research question. Start each paragraph with a sentence that introduces the topic of that paragraph and generalizes the patterns. Then present numeric evidence for those conclusions. A handful of numbers can be presented in a sentence or two. For more complex patterns, report the numbers in a chart or table, then describe the patterns using the "generalization, example, exception" (GEE) approach. Refer to each table or chart by name as you describe the patterns and report numbers presented therein.

Boxes 11.3a and 11.3b show "poor" and "better" descriptions of table 11.1, which comprises the first step in an analysis of whether socioeconomic or behavioral factors explain racial differences in birth weight. On the pages that follow, I critique the numbered sentences (statements) from those descriptions, identifying the various principles for introducing, organizing, and describing statistical findings. (In the interest of space, I did not include a complete results sec-

Box 11.3a. Description of a Bivariate Table for a Results Section: Poor Version

"(1) (2) Race/ethnicity is strongly related to birth weight and LBW (both $p < 0.01$). Mean birth weight was 3,426.8, 3,181.3 and 3,357.3, for non-Hispanic black, non-Hispanic white, and Mexican American infants, respectively. (3) Average educational attainment, percentage of high school graduates, income, percentage in poverty, percentage of teen mothers, and maternal age are all statistically significant ($p < 0.01$). (4) An interesting finding is that smoking shows the opposite pattern of all the other variables ($p < 0.01$). (5) Table X (not shown) presents incidence of LBW for each racial group and SES combination . . ."

tion for this analysis, as the material shown below illustrates the relevant points.)

Statement 1
Poor: [No introductory sentence.]
  By jumping right into a description of the table, this version fails to orient readers to the purpose of that table.
Better: "Table 11.1 presents weighted statistics on birth weight, socioeconomic characteristics, and smoking for the three racial/ethnic groups, along with unweighted number of cases in each racial/ethnic group. All differences shown are statistically significant at $p < 0.01$."
  The topic sentence names the associated table and introduces its purpose, restating the title into a full sentence. It also specifies which statistics are weighted and which are unweighted. The second sentence generalizes about statistical significance for the entire table, echoing the footnote to the table and eliminating the need to report results of statistical tests for each association.

Statement 2
Poor: "Race/ethnicity is strongly related to birth weight and LBW (both $p < 0.01$). Mean birth weight was 3,426.8, 3,181.3 and 3,357.3, for non-Hispanic white, non-Hispanic black, and Mexican American infants, respectively."

Box 11.3b. Description of a Bivariate Table for a Results Section: Better Version

"(1) Table 11.1 presents weighted statistics on birth weight, socioeconomic characteristics, and maternal smoking for the three racial/ethnic groups, along with unweighted number of cases in each racial/ethnic group. All differences shown are statistically significant at $p < 0.01$. (2) On average, Non-Hispanic white newborns were 246 grams heavier than non-Hispanic black infants and 70 grams heavier than Mexican American infants (3,427 grams, 3,181 grams, and 3,357 grams, respectively). The birth weight difference between Mexican American and non-Hispanic black infants (176 grams) was also statistically significant. These deficits in mean birth weight translate into substantial differences in percentage low birth weight (LBW $< 2,500$ grams), with nearly twice the risk of LBW among non-Hispanic black as non-Hispanic white infants (11.3% and 5.8%, respectively). Mexican American infants were only slightly more likely than whites to be LBW (7.0%; relative risk $= 1.2$; $p < 0.05$).

"(3) In every dimension of socioeconomic status studied here, non-Hispanic black and Mexican American mothers were substantially disadvantaged relative to their non-Hispanic white counterparts. They were twice as likely as white mothers to be teenagers at the time they gave birth and two to three times as likely to be high school dropouts. Mean income/needs ratios for black and Mexican American families were roughly half those of white families. (4) In contrast to the socioeconomic patterns, maternal smoking — an important behavioral risk factor for low birth weight — was more common among non-Hispanic white women (27%) than non-Hispanic black (23%) or Mexican American women (10%).

"(5) Does the lower average socioeconomic status of non-Hispanic black and Mexican American infants explain their higher risks of low birth weight? To answer that question, table X (not shown) presents data on incidence of LBW for the three racial/ethnic groups within each of several socioeconomic strata . . ." (Discussion of those patterns is not shown here, but is summarized in sentence 4 of box 11.4.)

Table 11.1. Descriptive statistics on study sample

Birth weight, socioeconomic characteristics, and smoking behavior
by race/ethnicity, United States, 1988–1994

	Non-Hispanic white (N = 3,733)	Non-Hispanic black (N = 2,968)	Mexican American (N = 3,112)	All racial/ethnic groups (N = 9,813)
Birth weight[a]				
Mean (grams)	3,426.8	3,181.3	3,357.3	3,379.2
% Low birth weight[b]	5.8	11.3	7.0	6.8
Socioeconomic characteristics				
Mother's age				
Mean (years)	26.6	24.2	24.9	26.0
% Teen mother	9.4	22.9	18.4	12.5
Mother's education				
Mean (years)	13.3	11.9	9.1	12.6
% <High school	14.7	30.1	58.4	21.6
% =High school	34.9	41.7	24.5	35.0
Income/needs ratio[c]				
Mean	2.60	1.39	1.34	2.28
% Poor	14.7	48.5	50.7	23.9
Health behavior				
% Mother smoked while pregnant	26.8	22.9	10.1	24.5

Note: Statistics are weighted to population level using weights provided with the
NHANES III (U.S. DHHS 1997); sample size is unweighted.
[a] Differences across racial/ethnic origin groups were statistically significant for all
variables shown; $p < 0.01$.
[b] Low birth weight < 2,500 grams or 5.5 pounds.
[c] The income/needs ratio is family income in dollars divided by the Federal Poverty
Threshold for a family of comparable size and age composition. A family with
income equal to the poverty threshold (e.g., $17,960 for two adults and two
children in 2001; U.S. Census 2002b) would have an income/needs ratio of 1.0.

This sentence reports but does not interpret average birth weight for each racial/ethnic group, adding little to the information in the table. It omits the units in which birth weight is reported. It also presents a string of numbers that is visually difficult to take in. It's always good to separate large numbers with a little text.

Better: "(A) On average, non-Hispanic white newborns were 246 grams heavier than non-Hispanic black infants and 70 grams heavier than Mexican American infants (3,427 grams, 3,181 grams, and 3,357 grams, respectively). The birth weight difference between Mexican American and non-Hispanic black infants (176 grams) was also statistically significant. (B) These gaps in mean birth weight translate into substantial differences in percentage low birth weight (LBW $< 2,500$ grams), with nearly twice the risk of LBW among non-Hispanic black as non-Hispanic white infants (11.3% and 5.8%, respectively). Mexican American infants were only slightly more likely than whites to be LBW (7.0%; relative risk $= 1.2$; $p < 0.05$)."

The first and second sentences (A) report direction and size of differences in mean birth weight across racial/ethnic groups using absolute difference to assess size, and reporting the units of measurement. The last two sentences (B) quantify differences in low birth weight across racial/ethnic groups using relative risk, and report the numbers for that calculation. The LBW acronym and definition of low birth weight are repeated from the methods section to remind readers of their meaning.

Statement 3

Poor: "Average educational attainment, percentage of high school graduates, income, percentage poor, percentage of teen mothers, and maternal age are all statistically significant ($p < 0.01$)."
This seemingly simple sentence is plagued by numerous problems.

- Results are listed without differentiating between the outcome (birth weight) and predictor variables or drawing a distinction between socioeconomic status (SES) and behavioral characteristics. Combined with the absence of an introductory sentence, this lack of explanation leaves the results almost completely disconnected from the research question.
- This sentence does not explain that the statistical tests are for differences *across racial/ethnic groups* in each of the SES variables. Because race is not mentioned, readers may

mistakenly think that the tests are for association among the SES variables.

- Both the continuous and categorical versions of each SES measure are reported (e.g., "income" and "percentage poor") without pointing out that they are merely two different perspectives on the same concept. For example, "% Poor" simply classifies family income into poor and nonpoor.
- The variables are named in a different order in the table and text.

Better: "In every dimension of socioeconomic status studied here, non-Hispanic black and Mexican American mothers were substantially disadvantaged relative to their non-Hispanic white counterparts. They were twice as likely as white mothers to be teenagers at the time they gave birth and two to three times as likely to be high school dropouts. Mean income/needs ratios for black and Mexican American families were roughly half those of white families."

Because most of the remaining numbers in the table deal with associations between race/ethnicity and socioeconomic status, a new paragraph is started to describe those findings. The topic sentence introduces the concepts to be discussed and generalizes the patterns. The next two sentences illustrate the preceding generalization with specific comparisons from the table, using relative differences to quantify racial/ethnic disparities in the three socioeconomic measures.

Statement 4

Poor: "An interesting finding is that smoking shows the opposite pattern of all the other variables."

"Opposite" of what? This sentence does not indicate which patterns smoking is being compared against or mention the direction of any of the patterns. Neither this nor the preceding sentence (statement 3) mentions that the associations are with race/ethnicity, again keeping the description divorced from the main purpose of the analysis.

Better: "In contrast to the socioeconomic patterns, maternal smoking — an important behavioral risk factor for low birth weight — was more common among non-Hispanic white women (27%) than non-Hispanic black (23%) or Mexican American women (10%)."

This version points out an exception to the generalization that people of color are worse off, reporting the higher smoking rates among non-Hispanic whites.

Statement 5

Poor: "Table X presents incidence of LBW for each racial group and SES . . ."

This version does not provide a transition between the first table and a second (hypothetical) table that presents the next step in the analysis, instead simply stating the topic but not the purpose of the second table. By failing to link the description of table 11.1 with the subsequent tables, this description leaves readers without a sense of how the evidence in the two tables fits together or how those analyses relate to the overall research question. This version also uses an acronym without defining it first.

Better: "Does the lower average socioeconomic status of non-Hispanic black and Mexican American infants explain their higher risks of low birth weight? To answer that question, table X (not shown) presents data on incidence of LBW for the three racial/ethnic groups within each of several socioeconomic strata . . ."

These sentences orient readers to the purpose of the different steps in the analysis, summarizing the findings in table 11.1 and introducing the hypothetical subsequent table and discussion that build upon the findings in the first table. By starting a new paragraph, this version provides a segue from the first table — which documented the racial differences in both LBW and socioeconomic status — to another table showing the three-way association among race/ethnicity, socioeconomic status, and LBW.

The rest of that paragraph (not shown) would describe differences in incidence of low birth weight between non-Hispanic black, non-Hispanic white, and Mexican American children of similar socioeconomic status, reporting the direction, size, and statistical significance of those associations.

Discussion and Conclusions

In the discussion and conclusions section, relate the evidence back to the larger research question, comparing broad conclusions against hypotheses posed at the beginning of the work and results from related studies.

Numeric Information in a Concluding Section

In the discussion and concluding section of your work, restate conclusions about the size and statistical significance of associations among the variables in the main research question, and consider extensions that help readers see the importance (or lack of importance) of those findings. To convey the purpose and interpretation of numeric facts or contrasts, introduce them in sentences that place them in their substantive context.

Effect size. Rather than repeating precise numeric estimates and results of statistical tests from the results section, use verbal descriptions or approximate numeric values, rounding to the nearest whole multiple or familiar fraction.

Statistical significance. Rarely is statistical significance discussed explicitly in the concluding section, and then only for key variables in your research question. Use results of statistical tests in conjunction with substantive considerations to assess which findings to emphasize. Instead of reporting standard errors, p-values, or confidence intervals, use phrases such as "were strongly related" or "was not associated."

There are three situations where you should discuss statistical significance in your conclusion:

(1) If your statistical test results *run counter to theoretical expectations,* such as when theory led you to predict a large, statistically significant difference across groups that was not borne out in your study, or vice versa.

(2) If your statistical test results *conflict with those of previous empirical studies.* Perhaps you found statistically significant differences that others had not. Or, others may have found statistically significant differences that were not apparent with your data.

In those instances, explicitly mention the discrepant findings regarding statistical significance, using words rather than detailed numeric results. Explain what these findings imply, relating them back to your original hypotheses and the literature that led you to formulate those hypotheses. Discuss possible explanations for the discrepancy of findings across studies, such as differences in study populations, design, or variables.

(3) The third situation in which statistical significance merits attention in the discussion section is if you observe changes in effect size and statistical significance of key variables in

your model when you introduce measures of potentially mediating or confounding factors, particularly those that were not previously available or were poorly measured in other studies. This kind of issue is often the reason for estimating a multivariate model (see Miller, forthcoming).

Causality and statistical significance revisited. To bring your analysis to a close, describe the implications of the associations reported in the analytic portion of the paper. In analyses that ask cause-and-effect type questions, revisit two issues discussed in chapter 3. First, can the associations be viewed as causal? And second, if so, what is the substantive meaning of the findings? As you describe the relationships in your analysis, choose wording that conveys whether you are interpreting those relationships as causal or merely as associations. To assess how much a pattern matters in the substantive sense, combine estimates from the analytic portion of the paper with information from other sources. Depending on your topic, these calculations might involve cost effectiveness analysis (e.g., Gold et al. 1996), attributable risk calculations (Lilienfeld and Stolley 1994; Miller, forthcoming), or other applicable measures of net benefits, costs, or tradeoffs between alternative proposed solutions.

Citing Other Sources

Unlike the results section, which is devoted almost exclusively to reporting and analyzing data from within the study, a discussion and conclusions section often incorporates numeric information from other studies. There are several reasons to cite other works in the discussion:

- To evaluate whether the current findings are consistent with previous research
- To provide perspective on the importance of the research question
- To apply numbers from other sources of background information that place the findings of the current study in context
- To offer ideas about underlying reasons for observed patterns, generating hypotheses to be tested empirically in later studies (otherwise known as "directions for future research")

Box 11.4 is an illustrative discussion and conclusion section of a scientific paper on racial/ethnic differences in birth weight, summarizing the findings presented in the preceding results section.

Box 11.4. Using Numbers in a Discussion and Conclusion to a Scientific Paper

"(1) Consistent with a large body of previous research (e.g., Institute of Medicine 1985), we found a substantial birth weight disadvantage among black infants compared to infants from other racial/ethnic groups in the United States. (2) Although black infants have on average twice the incidence of low birth weight of white infants, (3) in large part this difference can be attributed to the fact that black infants are more likely to be of low socioeconomic status (SES). Regardless of race, children born into low SES families are at elevated risk of low birth weight (LBW) compared to those born at higher SES. (4) However, differences in family socioeconomic background do not explain the entire difference across racial ethnic groups. At each socioeconomic level, black infants are more likely to be low birth weight than their white counterparts, with particularly marked gaps at higher socioeconomic levels: for infants born to mothers with less than complete high school education, LBW is 30% more common among black infants than among white infants; for those born to mothers who attended college, the excess risk for blacks is 125%. [These conclusions are based on data that would be in the hypothetical second table.]

"(5) The causal role of low socioeconomic status is also brought into question by the relatively low incidence of LBW among Mexican American infants, which is quite close to that of white infants and is far below that of black infants. This phenomenon of relatively good health among Mexican Americans despite their low SES is referred to as the "epidemiological paradox" or "Hispanic paradox" and also has been observed for other health conditions (Franzini et al. 2001; Palloni and Morenoff 2001).

"(6) Other possible mechanisms that have been proposed to explain why black infants are more likely to be low birth weight include less access to health care, higher rates of poor health behaviors, greater social stress (Zambrana et al. 1999), intergenerational transmission of health disadvantage (Conley and Bennett 2000), and other unmeasured factors that affect black people more than those of other racial/ethnic origins.

"(7) Reducing the incidence of low birth weight is a key objective of Healthy People 2010 (U.S. DHHS 2001). (8) If the incidence of low birth weight among black infants had been decreased to the level among white infants, nearly 40,000 of the low birth weight black infants born in 2000 would instead have been born at normal birth weight. That reduction in low birth weight would have cut the black infant mortality rate by more than one-third, assuming the infant mortality rate for normal birth weight infants (Mathews, MacDorman, and Menacker 2002). In addition, an estimated $3.4 million in medical and educational expenses would be saved from that birth cohort alone, based on Lewit and colleagues' estimates of the cost of low birth weight (1995)."

COMMENTS

(1) Generalizes the major finding of the current study and places it in the context of previous research, citing a summary report by a prominent national research institute.

(2) Quantifies the size of the black/white difference in low birth weight with approximate figures ("twice the incidence") rather than reporting exact percentages for each group.

(3–6) The description of the association between race/ethnicity is stated in cause-neutral language ("found a substantial birth weight disadvantage among," sentence 1), leading into a discussion of causal interpretation. In contrast, the hypothesized causal role of socioeconomic characteristics is clearly conveyed using language such as "attributed to" (sentence 3), "do not explain" (sentence 4). The intentional use of causal language continues into the subsequent paragraph with "causal role" (sentence 5), and "possible mechanisms" (sentence 6). (Conclusions summarized in sentence 4 are based on findings that would be presented in the complete results section of this paper but that were omitted to save space.) Sentences 5 and 6 discuss possible explanatory mechanisms linking race and low birth weight, citing published sources of these theories. Sentence 5 mentions the "epidemiological paradox" observed in other health studies and relates it to the current findings. Sentence 6 introduces other theories that can be used to generate hypotheses to be tested in future studies.

(7) Brings the paper full circle, returning to the "big picture" to remind readers of the reasons for addressing this research question. Establishes that lowering the incidence of low birth weight is a major priority identified by experts in the field, citing the pertinent policy document.

(8) Combines statistics on the excess risk of low birth weight among black infants from the current analysis with information from other published sources about infant mortality rates and costs of low birth weight to estimate how many infant deaths could be prevented and how many dollars saved if the incidence of low birth weight among black infants could be reduced to the same level as that among whites. Again, figures are reported in round numbers: phrases such as "nearly 40,000" and "more than one-third" are precise enough to make the point.

■ CHECKLIST FOR WRITING INTRODUCTIONS, RESULTS, AND CONCLUSIONS

- Open your work by introducing the issues to be discussed, with evidence about their importance.
- In the body of the work, systematically introduce and review numeric information from tables and charts that each present data on one aspect of the analysis.
- Close your work by coming full circle, returning in the discussion and conclusions to the questions raised in your introduction.
- Apply the principles for good expository writing:
    Organize ideas into one major topic per paragraph.
    Start each with an introductory sentence that identifies the purpose of that paragraph.
- Mention context (W's) and units.
- Keep jargon to a minimum, defining it when needed.
- Use dimensions of quantitative comparison to interpret numbers. Specify the direction and magnitude of associations.
- Synthesize patterns rather than repeating detailed numbers from associated tables and charts. Refer to charts and tables by name as you discuss them.
- Consider whether you have used an appropriate level of detail for the type of writing and section of the document, saving precise statistical test results for the results sections of scientific papers.

Speaking about Numbers

Speaking about numbers is a common means of communicating quantitative information, whether a lecture in a classroom setting, a short speech to the general public, or a professional conference presentation. Many of the principles described throughout this book apply to speaking about numbers. However, there are a few important modifications that will improve your speeches about quantitative concepts or help you translate written documents into spoken form.

The first section of this chapter includes a quick overview of time and pacing, use of visual materials, and speaker's notes, with an emphasis on aspects of public speaking that pertain specifically to conveying quantitative information. The second section describes how to create slides for a speech, including text, tabular, and graphical slides and their applications. The third section explains how to write speaker's notes to accompany your slides, including my infamous "Vanna White" technique for succinctly but systematically describing a table or chart. The last section provides guidance on rehearsing your speech to make sure it is clear and fits within the allotted time. See also Fink (1995) for guidance on preparing slides, Montgomery (2003) for suggestions on speaking about scientific topics, and Miller (forthcoming) for additional issues related to speaking about multivariate analyses.

■ CONSIDERATIONS FOR PUBLIC SPEAKING

Three factors together determine how you will design and deliver a speech: your topic, your audience, and the time available to you. Leave out any of those elements as you plan and your talk will not be as successful. For example, the appropriate depth, pace, types of materials, and language for describing relationships between exercise and obesity are very different for a 5-minute presentation to your child's fifth-grade class than for a 10-minute talk to the school board or a half-hour presentation to a panel of nutrition experts.

First identify the few key points you want your listeners to understand and remember, taking into account both your topic and audience. Then consider time and pacing before you design the visual materials and speaker's notes.

Time and Pacing

Most speeches have been allocated a specific amount of time, whether 5 minutes, 15 minutes, or an hour or longer. There are trade-offs between the length of time, the amount of material, and the pace at which you must speak. Reduce the range and depth of coverage rather than speeding up your delivery, especially for an audience that is not accustomed to quantitative information. Better to cut detail than to rush an explanation of your central points or fail to leave time for questions and discussion.

In contrast to when they read a written document, members of your listening audience all receive the material at the same rate — the pace at which you show the slides and explain them. During a speech, individuals cannot take extra time to examine a chart or table, or go back to reread an earlier point. Set the tempo to meet the needs of your typical listener rather than aiming to please either the least or most sophisticated members of your audience. Even for scientific audiences, avoid moving at too rapid a clip. If you present many different statistics in a short talk, the findings blur together and the purpose of each gets lost. Decide which results relate to your main objectives, then introduce and explain them accordingly.

Visual Accompaniment

For speeches of more than a few minutes, visual materials focus your audience's attention and provide a structure to your speech. Slides also help listeners recall facts or concepts to which you refer. In the absence of visual reminders, spoken numbers are easily forgotten, so if specific values are important, put them on a slide. This point is doubly true for comparisons, patterns, or calculations: even if you elect not to create slides for every facet of your talk, do provide charts and tables for your audience to follow as you describe key patterns or findings so they don't have to try to envision them as you speak.

A complete set of slides guides you through your material in a logical order and reminds you where you were if you stopped to answer questions from the audience. Some speakers like to create slides for each component of their talk, mixing text slides for introductory, background, and concluding material with charts and tables of results. However, some speakers prefer a less formal approach, with slides only of essential tables and charts. Even if you use a comprehensive set of slides in some situations, you may want only selected slides in others. For example, although I usually create slides for the whole talk for short professional presentations, I rarely use that approach when teaching. I've found that putting every aspect of a lecture on slides discourages student participation, so I generally create slides only of tables, charts, or other diagrams that I plan to discuss. Working from a written outline or notes, I then introduce each topic, interweaving questions that require students to supply details from readings, describe patterns in the charts or tables, practice calculations, or provide illustrative anecdotes for the points under discussion.

To decide among these different approaches, consider the available time and your own experience, style, and desired extent of interaction with your audience.

Speaker's Notes

Effective slides reduce full sentences into short phrases and reduce complex tables and charts into simpler versions. Accompanying speaker's notes include full sentences and paragraphs to introduce, flesh out, and summarize the information on each slide, and to provide the wording of transitions between slides. For a "generalization, example, exception" (GEE) description of a chart or table, speaker's notes are a place to store clear, concise, well-organized descriptions that you have pretested on similar audiences. Notes can prompt you about which aspects of tables or graphs to emphasize. Perhaps most important, speaker's notes are a reminder *not* to simply read the material on your slide out loud — a truly deadening way to give a presentation. More detailed guidelines on writing speaker's notes are given below.

■ SLIDES TO ACCOMPANY A SPEECH

Slides focus and direct your audience and display the facts and patterns mentioned in the speech. With the advent of computerized presentation software such as PowerPoint, it is easy to produce text, tabular and graphical slides, and accompanying speaker's notes. Such software automatically formats the material with large type, bullets, and other features that enhance readability and organization. Once the slides have been created, it is simple to reorganize text within and across slides, adding or removing material to create longer or shorter versions of talks, or making other revisions. Depending upon available audiovisual equipment, these materials can be projected from a computer directly onto an auditorium screen, printed onto overhead transparencies or slides, or printed as paper handouts.

Recently, a backlash has emerged against the use of PowerPoint and other presentation software, stating that these programs have lead to inferior content and organization of slides, overreliance on fancy graphics, and substitution of rote reading of slides for other, more engaging means of presentation (Schwartz 2003). Used poorly, any tool — whether a hammer, paintbrush, or presentation software — can be used to produce substandard work. With appropriate training and good technique, however, these tools can help create exemplary results. Below are guidelines on how to create effective slides for a speech, whether or not you elect to use presentation software.

Organizing Your Talk

For a speech to an academic or professional audience, organize your talk with sections that parallel the sections of a scientific paper: an overview and introduction, review of the key literature, description of your data and methods, results, and conclusions. Below are illustrative slides for the sections of a scientific talk about racial/ethnic and socioeconomic differences in low birth weight based on the material in chapters 10 and 11. For a talk to a lay audience, devote less time to previous literature or data and methods, focusing instead on the purpose, results, and conclusions of your study.

Introduction and Overview

In the introduction, familiarize your audience with your topic: what are the main issues you will be investigating and why are they interesting and important? Incorporate some background statistics about the consequences of the issue under study (figure 12.1) or provide some figures on the frequency with which it occurs (figure 12.2).

For speeches of 20 minutes or more, consider starting with an overview slide which outlines the topics you will touch upon (figure 12.3).

Literature review. Unless you have half an hour or more for your speech, devote much less attention to reviewing the published literature on your topic than you would in a written description of the same study. Often you can incorporate a few important citations in

Consequences of Low Birth Weight

- Low birth weight (LBW) = 2,500 grams (or 5.5 pounds)

- LBW infants more likely to
  - die before their first birthday;
    - 24 times as likely as normal-weight infants to die in infancy.
  - have other health problems in
    - infancy,
    - childhood,
    - adulthood;
  - have developmental problems.

Figure 12.1. Introductory slide: Bulleted text on consequences of issue under study.
Sources: Martin et al. 2002; U.S. Environmental Protection Agency 2002; Institute of Medicine 1985.

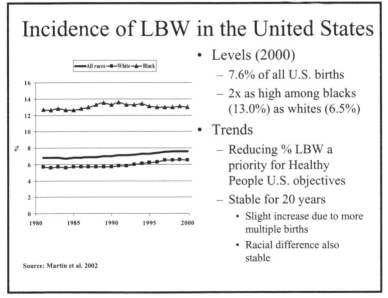

Incidence of LBW in the United States

- Levels (2000)
  - 7.6% of all U.S. births
  - 2x as high among blacks (13.0%) as whites (6.5%)
- Trends
  - Reducing % LBW a priority for Healthy People U.S. objectives
  - Stable for 20 years
    - Slight increase due to more multiple births
    - Racial difference also stable

Source: Martin et al. 2002

Figure 12.2. Introductory slide: Chart and text on incidence of issue under study

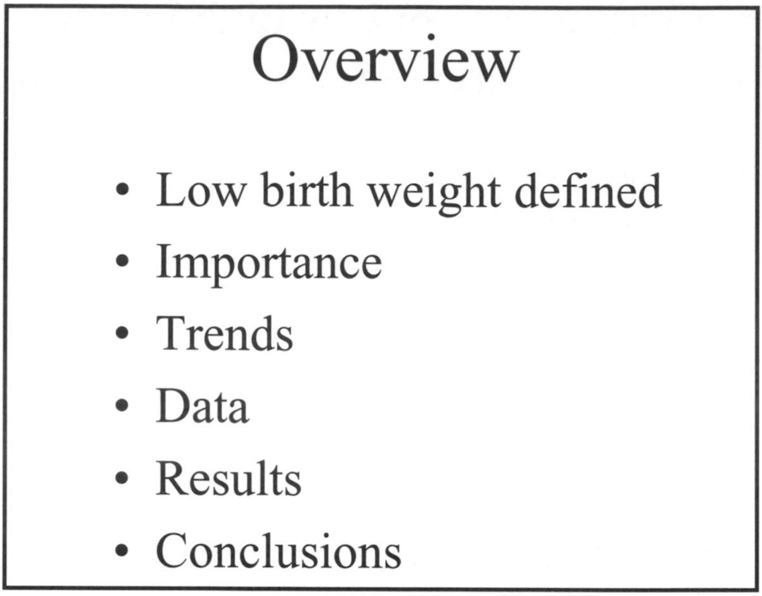

Overview

- Low birth weight defined
- Importance
- Trends
- Data
- Results
- Conclusions

Figure 12.3. Slide outlining contents of speech

your introduction. If a comparison of individual articles is important, consider summarizing their key conclusions on your topic in tabular form (e.g., figure 12.4).

Data and Methods

Introduce your data, starting with the W's (who, what, when, where, and how many), type of study design, response rates for your data sources (figure 12.5), and key variables (figure 12.6).

Break this material up onto several slides to make room for all those topics without creating a cluttered slide. Define your variables on one or more slides in the data and methods section. If you define them as you present the results, viewers tend to focus on the numeric findings rather than listening to how the variables were measured and defined.

Consider including a schematic diagram to illustrate how your variables are hypothesized to relate to one another (figure 12.7) — showing mediating or confounding relations, for example.

See below for guidelines about slides to present your results and conclusions.

Previous Studies of Race & Birth Weight

Article	Type of study & data source	RR† of LBW: black/white	Comments
Smith & Jones (1999)	Sample survey; birth certificates	2.2*	Nationally representative; controlled education
Williams (2000)	Retrospective survey; maternal questionnaires	3.8*	Study in state X; no controls for SES
Travis et al. (1990)	Prospective study; medical records	1.5	Enrolled women in prenatal care clinics in NYC; low SES only

† RR: Relative risk.
* denotes p < .05.

Figure 12.4. Slide with tabular presentation of literature review

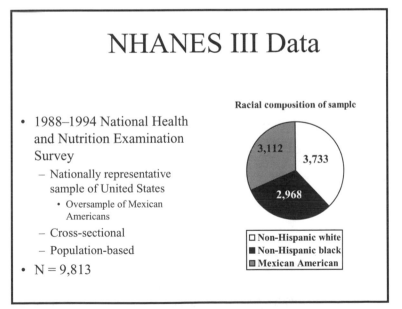

Figure 12.5. Slide describing data source using text and a pie chart

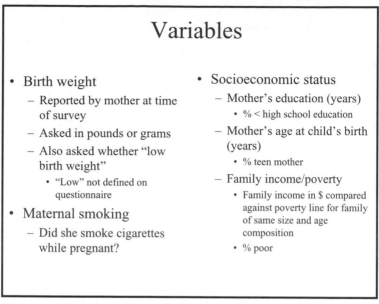

Figure 12.6. Slide describing major variables in the analysis

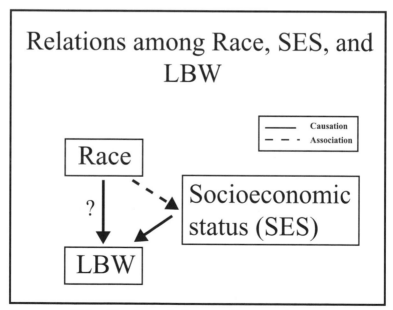

Figure 12.7. Slide with schematic diagram of hypothesized relationship among major variables in the analysis

General Guidelines for Slides

"KISS"

"Keep it simple, stupid," to reiterate one of the principles from chapter 2. Design each slide to concentrate on one or two major points, with title and content to match. Doing so divides your material into small, readily digestible chunks that are easier to organize into a logical, straightforward sequence. Simple, uncluttered slides have another advantage: each can be covered in a minute or two — a much better way to maintain your audience's attention than showing the same crowded slide for several minutes while you slog through each of its contents.

How Many Slides?

Figure on an average of one slide per minute, then err on the low side to avoid rushing and to permit time for questions or discussion. Although a simple text slide can often be covered in 30 seconds, those showing many specific facts or complex patterns may require several minutes apiece. If you are drafting a talk from a written document, start by creating one slide for each major paragraph or topic to be discussed. For short talks, be parsimonious in selecting what material to cover: A five-minute talk obviously cannot accommodate one slide for every paragraph and table in a 20-page document. Determine which parts of the paper are essential for introducing and answering the key points you have identified for your audience and time limit, then design slides accordingly.

Slide Formats

Like written documents, slides can include text, tables, graphs, diagrams, maps, and other types of graphical images. To enhance the visual appeal of your slides and introduce texture into your talk, vary the design of your slides to include a combination of these elements.

Slide Titles

Good titles guide listeners through your talk, introducing the specific purpose of each slide and orienting listeners to the different sections of the talk. To outline a new talk or revise an existing talk for a new audience, write the titles for each of your slides before you fill in the body of the slide. Give each slide a short, specific title to identify the objective or content of that particular slide. General titles such as "Introduction" or "Results" tend to be ignored if they are repeated for several consecutive slides. The title features prominently on each slide — at the top in large type. Take advantage of that size and position: write informative titles! For instance, although the slides shown in figures 12.1 through 12.3 all comprise parts of the introduction, their titles clearly identify which facet of the introductory material is covered in the respective slides.

Some speakers like to title each slide with a concluding point or rhetorical question related to the slide contents. For example, the title to figure 12.2 could be replaced with "LBW Stable over Past Two Decades" or "Has LBW Declined over Time?" Alternatively, put a title such as "Incidence of LBW" on the slide, then paraphrase it into a concluding point or rhetorical question as you introduce the slide.

Text Slides

Text slides can be used throughout a presentation, as an outline (figure 12.3), in the introduction (figure 12.1), in the data and methods section (figure 12.6), and in the discussion and conclusions (figure 12.8). Text slides also work well to summarize a few key points from previous studies, state hypotheses, list major results, or provide an executive summary.

As you design each text slide, put vital numbers in a prominent

---

Conclusions

- Much of racial/ethnic difference in LBW due to SES:
  - Infants of color more likely to be low SES.
  - Low SES infants more likely to be LBW.
  - When SES taken into account, LBW differences narrow.
- Mexican American infants do better than expected despite low SES.
  - "Epidemiological paradox"

Figure 12.8. Text slide summarizing major study conclusions

position in large type, and make sure to report and explain them before they are used in any calculations or discussion. A NASA presentation about possible explanations of damage to the shuttle *Columbia*'s wing during its fatal flight placed critical numeric information in a footnote on the last slide where it was easily overlooked, making it hard to follow the logic of the investigation or understand its conclusions (Schwartz 2003).

Resist the urge to cut and paste sentences from a written document or speaker's notes into your slides. Instead, simplify your paragraphs and sentences into bulleted text phrases, aiming for no more than six bullets per slide and no more than 6 to 10 words or numbers per bullet (Fink 1995). These guidelines force you to plan simple, focused slides, and enhance readability by permitting large type and ample white space.

Bullets. Create a separate bullet for each concept, definition, or fact. For a review of the previous literature, use bullets to organize material from different studies. To revise sentences into bulleted format:

- Include only the essential words from each sentence — nouns, verbs, adjectives, and adverbs.
- Look for commas or the words "and" or "or" to identify clauses or elements of a list, each of which can become its own bullet item.
- Substitute common mathematical symbols such as $<$, $>$, $=$, #, or % for their equivalent phrases.
- Use arrows to convey directionality and causation.
- Eliminate most other words from the slide.
- Cast all bulleted points in the same syntax. If one is a sentence, make all sentences. Make all bullet points either active or passive, and use a consistent tense throughout. It's much easier to take in and remember points conveyed in a consistent, predictable form.

After you have drafted a bulleted version of a sentence or paragraph, review it to see whether more words can be eliminated without loss of meaning, or if additional words are needed to maintain clarity.

Indenting. Use indenting to organize the material on a slide, presenting supporting facts or clusters of related information under one heading. In figure 12.6, socioeconomic status (SES) is one of several conceptual blocks of variables in the analysis. Indented below the bullet "socioeconomic status" is a list of the different SES measures,

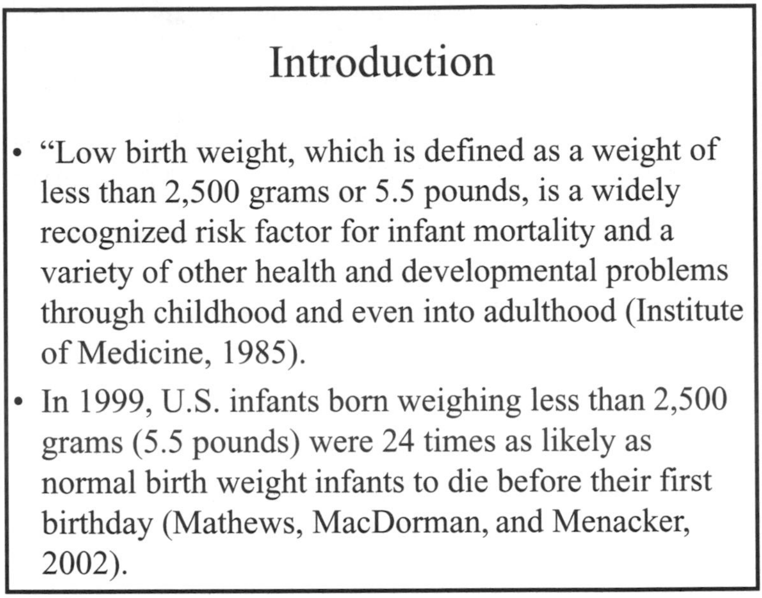

Introduction

- "Low birth weight, which is defined as a weight of less than 2,500 grams or 5.5 pounds, is a widely recognized risk factor for infant mortality and a variety of other health and developmental problems through childhood and even into adulthood (Institute of Medicine, 1985).
- In 1999, U.S. infants born weighing less than 2,500 grams (5.5 pounds) were 24 times as likely as normal birth weight infants to die before their first birthday (Mathews, MacDorman, and Menacker, 2002).

Figure 12.9. Example of a poor introductory slide

with one variable per bullet. Indented yet again beneath each of the SES measures is the categorical version used in this study to indicate low SES.

Observe how these principles improve the introductory slide shown in figure 12.9.

Poor: Figure 12.9.
  The slide includes the full text sentences from the introductory paragraph of the paper upon which the talk is based. Although each sentence is given its own bullet, the full sentences crowd the slide and encourage viewers to read rather than listen. The title of the slide describes its position in the talk but does not identify the contents or issues addressed.
Better: Figures 12.1 and 12.2.
  This version includes the essential information from the "poor" version but is more succinct and better organized. The titles clue listeners into the specific topics and purposes of the slides. Clauses are broken into separate lines, with supporting information indented.

Full-sentences can be used in the accompanying speaker's notes. For an academic audience, mention citations in the bullets or as foot-

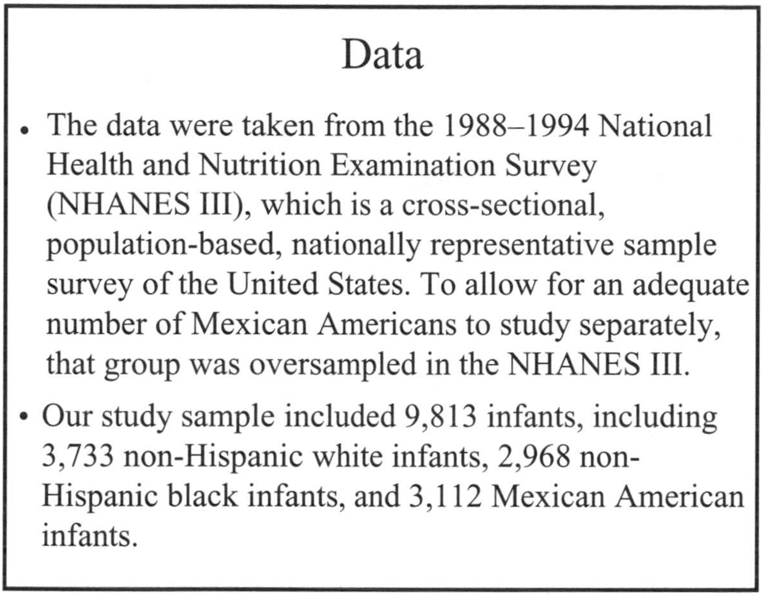

Data

- The data were taken from the 1988–1994 National Health and Nutrition Examination Survey (NHANES III), which is a cross-sectional, population-based, nationally representative sample survey of the United States. To allow for an adequate number of Mexican Americans to study separately, that group was oversampled in the NHANES III.

- Our study sample included 9,813 infants, including 3,733 non-Hispanic white infants, 2,968 non-Hispanic black infants, and 3,112 Mexican American infants.

Figure 12.10. Example of a poor data slide

notes. For lay audiences, omit citations except for public figures or widely recognized authorities (e.g., the Centers for Disease Control).

Another example, this time from the data and methods:

Poor: Figure 12.10
   Again, paragraphs are pasted directly from the paper onto a slide, resulting in an overcrowded slide that is difficult to read.
Better: Figures 12.5 and 12.6.
   The information from figure 12.10 is broken up into manageable pieces. Racial composition of the sample is presented in a pie chart and the W's and other background information on the data source and variables for the analysis are organized using bullets and indenting.

Diagrams, Maps, or Graphic Images
   In many cases a picture is worth a thousand words — a particularly valuable saving in a timed speech. Schematic diagrams can help viewers understand hypothesized relationships among variables (e.g., figure 12.7), using different types of arrows to illustrate association and causation. Timelines can portray the sequence of events under study or illustrate the number and timing of data collection points in

a longitudinal study. If your topic has an important geographic component, include one or more maps to present statistics such as population density or pollution levels for each area, or to show where the sites you discuss are located relative to hospitals, rail lines, or other features that pertain to your research question. Photographs of people or places can provide a richness difficult to capture in words.

Charts and Tables

Use slides with tables, charts, or other graphical material in both brief, general speeches and longer, in-depth presentations. Simple tables of numeric results work well for both scientific and general audiences. For a scientific talk, a table that organizes and compares key previous literature on your topic can be very effective (e.g., figure 12.4).

Adapting tables and charts for slides. Rather than using tables or charts that were designed for a written document, adapt them to suit a slide format. If your table or chart includes information on more than a few variables, it is impossible to discuss all the patterns simultaneously, so don't ask your viewers to ignore most of a large table or complex chart while you describe one portion. Instead, create two or more slides with simpler tables or charts, each of which includes only the information needed for one comparison. Although many publishers set limits on the number of charts or tables in a published document, such restrictions don't affect speeches, so take advantage of that flexibility by creating chart and table slides that focus on one or two straightforward relationships apiece.

First, identify the different patterns you plan to discuss from a given table or chart, then design simplified versions that focus on one or two major points (or one GEE) apiece.

Poor: Figure 12.11

The type for the table, which was copied and pasted directly from a typed document, is far too small for a slide. To describe the many patterns on this slide, you would have to ask viewers to wade through a lot of microscopic numbers and labels to find the three numbers that pertain to each comparison. E.g., "The second row of numbers shows the percentage of low birth weight births in each racial ethnic group . . ." [Description of that pattern.] [Then] "The fourth row of numbers shows the percentage of mothers in each racial/ethnic group who gave birth as teenagers," etc.

Results

Birth weight, socioeconomic characteristics, and smoking behavior by race/ethnicity, United States, 1988–1994

	Non-Hispanic white ($N = 3,733$)	Non-Hispanic black ($N = 2,968$)	Mexican American ($N = 3,112$)	All racial/ ethnic groups ($N = 9,813$)
Birth weight				
Mean (grams)	3,426.8	3,181.3	3,357.3	3,379.2
% Low birth weight	5.8	11.3	7.0	6.8
Socioeconomic characteristics				
Mother's age				
Mean (years)	26.6	24.2	24.9	26.0
% Teen mother	9.4	22.9	18.4	12.5
Mother's education				
Mean (years)	13.3	11.9	9.1	12.6
% < High school	14.7	30.1	58.4	21.6
% High school	34.9	41.7	24.5	35.0
Income/needs ratio				
Mean	2.60	1.39	1.34	2.28
% Poor	14.7	48.5	50.7	23.9
Health behavior				
% Mother smoked while pregnant	26.8	22.9	10.1	24.5

Figure 12.11. Example of a poor results slide using a table directly from the paper.
Source: U.S. DHHS 1997.

Better: Figures 12.12, 12.13 and 12.14

The table from the poor version has been transformed into three separate slides, each of which presents data for one aspect of the story. Although this approach results in more slides, it takes no longer to describe because the amount of material is unchanged. It may even save time, because less guidance is needed to find the pertinent numbers for each comparison. The title of each slide names the variables or relationships in question. Speaker's notes would introduce each slide by identifying the role of the variables before describing the pattern and the findings on the topic at hand.

- Figure 12.12 uses a simple bar chart to show how the outcome — low birth weight — varies by race and ethnicity.
- Figure 12.13 shows how the three socioeconomic variables each relate to race/ethnicity. To facilitate a "generalization, example, exceptions" (GEE) summary, those patterns are presented in one clustered bar chart rather than as three different bar charts each on a separate slide.

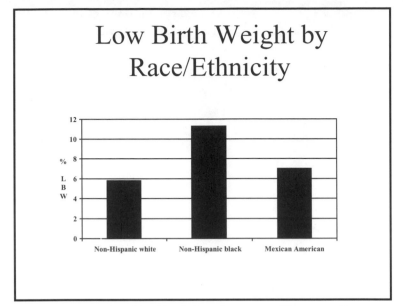

Figure 12.12. Results slide: Simple bar chart created from part of a statistical table.
Source: U.S. DHHS 1997.

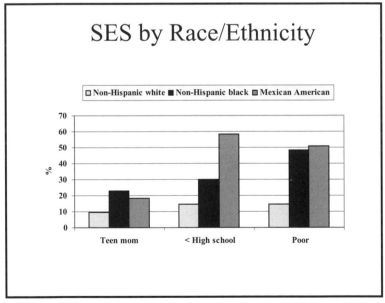

Figure 12.13. Results slide: A clustered bar chart created from part of a statistical table.
Source: U.S. DHHS 1997.

Maternal Smoking by Race/Ethnicity

	Smoked cigarettes (%)
Non-Hispanic white	26.8
Non-Hispanic black	22.9
Mexican American	10.1

Figure 12.14. Results slide: A simple table created from part of a larger table.
Source: U.S. DHHS 1997.

- To emphasize that smoking is a behavior, not a socioeconomic variable, statistics on racial patterns in maternal smoking are shown on a separate slide (figure 12.14).

Although figure 12.14 presents the smoking pattern in tabular form, if I were presenting the material in an actual talk, I would replace the table with a bar chart. Why? Once you have introduced your audience to a certain format — in this case a bar chart — save time and minimize confusion by reusing that format throughout the talk whenever suitable.

Mixed-Format Slides

If your charts or tables are fairly clear-cut (e.g., a 2-by-2 table, or a pie, single-line, or simple bar chart), consider a "chartbook" layout: a table, chart, or other image occupies one side of the slide, with bulleted text annotations on the other side (e.g., figure 12.2 or figure 12.5). Put more complicated tables or charts alone on a slide, then describe the pattern in your speaker's notes or make an additional slide with a short written summary.

Design Considerations

Substance over Style

Don't give in to the temptation to let the features available in presentation software packages carry your show. Fancy, multicolored background designs, animated text, or sound effects might impress your audience for a moment or two, but if they distract from your story line or substitute for correct, clearly presented material, they will do more harm than good. Whatever time you put into creating a dog-and-pony show is taken away from selecting and organizing the information and writing a clear narrative.

Focus on the substance, not the style, of the slides. First, get the content and organization right, just as you would for a written description of the same material. After you have practiced and revised your talk (see below), consider adding a bit of color or animation *only if they enhance your presentation.*

Color

That said, judicious use of color can enhance communication appreciably, giving you another tool for conveying information. For instance, color all of the statistically significant findings in tables or text slides red, leaving nonsignificant effects in a neutral shade. Once you have explained that color convention, your viewers will quickly be able to ascertain results of all your statistical tests without further explanation.

Use a consistent color scheme for all charts within a talk. If the Northeast is represented in green in a pie chart illustrating sample composition, for example, use green for the Northeast in all subsequent charts (whether pie, bar, or line charts) that compare patterns across regions.

A caution about creating handouts from color slides: some color combinations and lighter colors do not reproduce well in grayscale — the typical color scheme for photocopied handouts. To make sure the handouts convey the same information as the projected slides, follow the guidelines in chapter 7 about using color in charts, then review them in black and white on-screen or in print before making copies. Or if your budget and equipment permit, make color handouts.

Type Size

Use a legible font in a large type size on all slides — at least 18 point type — and avoid fussy calligraphic fonts. For your slides to

SPEAKING ABOUT NUMBERS : 257

be of value, they must be readable in the back row. If you aren't sure about the size of the room in which you'll be speaking, err on the generous side when you select your type size (see Zelazny 2001 for specific guidelines). If material you had planned for a single slide will fit only if you use small type, divide that material across several slides until the contents can be displayed with readable type. Ditto for words used to label charts and tables. Even with large type, slides can be difficult to read from the rear of a large auditorium. For such situations, consider printing handouts of your slides; some presentation software can print several slides per page with space for listeners to take notes.

Symbols and Annotations

As you adapt charts or tables for your slides, omit any features such as symbols, reference lines, or other annotations that you don't explain or refer to during your speech. Unless you mention them, they distract your viewers and clutter the slide. Conversely, you may want to add symbols to charts and tables as you modify them for use on slides. For example, your audience won't have time to digest detailed standard errors or test-statistics during your talk, so replace them with symbols for $p < 0.05$ or $p < 0.01$ to save space and reduce the amount of data on the slide.[1] Include footnotes or legends to explain the symbols.

■ WRITING SPEAKER'S NOTES

Having created slides that present the essential textual and graphical elements of your talk, write speaker's notes to fill in the details and transitions among slides. Although you can draw heavily on the content and organization of a full paper or book when formulating these notes, avoid recycling large blocks of text in your speech. Rarely will you have time to read an entire paper in the time available. Even if time permits, reading a document out loud is a poor substitute for a speech.

Speaker's Notes to Suit Your Style

The notes can be adapted to suit your speaking style and level of experience. If you are a novice, are uncomfortable inventing sentences in front of an audience, or have a tendency to be long-winded, you may do best with a full script. The wording for such notes can be pirated largely from the corresponding written paper or article, cutting some of the detail (such as citations) and rephrasing into the first person. For figure 12.5, a script might read:

> "We used data from the 1988–1994 National Health and Nutrition Examination Survey, also known as NHANES III, which is a cross-sectional, population-based, nationally representative sample of the United States. To allow for an adequate number of Mexican Americans to study separately, that group was oversampled in the NHANES III. We excluded infants of racial and ethnic groups not shown on this slide because we did not want to group them with any of these three groups and there were not enough of them to analyze as a distinct group. As shown in the pie chart, our study sample comprised nearly ten thousand infants, approximately equally distributed among the three racial/ethnic groups studied."

If you are at ease speaking extemporaneously and are able to keep yourself on schedule, you may need only a list of additional points to make or items to underscore. For the same slide, such notes might read:

> "To allow for an adequate number of Mexican Americans to study separately, that group was oversampled in the NHANES III."

> "As shown in the pie chart, our study sample comprised approximately equal numbers of the three racial/ethnic groups studied."

Before reading those notes, restate the information in the title and bullets into two or three complete sentences. Using selected reminders takes more practice than working from notes that comprise the full speech because you must remember where each typed note fits within the overall description of each slide. Key your notes to your slides to coordinate the spoken and visual components of your speech. Some presentation software programs allow you to type speaker's notes for each individual slide. If you write your notes longhand or in a word processor, write the number of the slide, table, or chart in the margin next to the associated text to remind yourself when to change slides. Do yourself a favor and print your speaker's notes in large type so you won't have to squint to read them as you deliver your speech.

Explaining a Chart "Live"

Tables, charts, maps, and other diagrams offer real advantages for presenting numeric patterns. Unfortunately, many speakers devote far too little time to describing such slides. They put up the slide, state "as you can see, . . ." and then describe the pattern in a few seconds before moving on to the next slide. As the slide disappears, many listeners are still trying to locate the numbers or pattern in question and have not had time to digest the meaning of the statistics. This disease plagues rookie and veteran speakers alike: Beginners may not want to spend very long on a chart out of fear that they will run out of time (or because they just want to get their talks over with). Experts forget that not everyone is conversant with their chart or table layouts or may be too uppity to explain such rudiments.

Although it may appear to save time, failing to orient your listeners to your charts or diagrams reduces the effectiveness of your talk. If you designed the chart and wrote the accompanying talk, you know it well enough to home in quickly on the exact number or table cell or trend line you wish to discuss. Give your audience the same advantage by showing them where to find your numbers and what questions they address before you report and interpret patterns.

Steps to Explaining a Chart or Table

Follow these three steps to explain a chart or table in a speech.

Introduce the topic. First, state the topic or purpose of the table or chart, just as you do in the introductory sentence of a written paragraph. Rather than reading the title from the slide, paraphrase it into a full sentence or rephrase it as a rhetorical question. For figure 12.13:

> "This slide examines racial and ethnic patterns in each of three indicators of low socioeconomic status. In other words, 'Does socioeconomic status vary by race?'"

Explain the layout. Second, explain the layout of the table or chart. Don't discuss any numbers, patterns, or contrasts yet. Just give your audience a chance to digest what is where. For a table, name what is in the columns and rows. For a chart, identify the concepts and units on the different axes and in the legend, mentioning the color or shading of bars or line styles that correspond to each major group you will discuss. For maps or other diagrams, point out the location of different features and explain the meaning of legend items or other elements such as arrows, symbols, or scales.

Use a "Vanna White"[2] approach as you explain the layout, literally pointing out the applicable portion of the table or chart as you mention it. Point with a laser pointer, pen, or finger — it doesn't matter. The important thing is to lead your viewers' eyes across the key features of the slide before reporting or interpreting the information found there. At first this may seem silly or awkward, but most audiences follow and retain the subsequent description much more easily than if you omit the guided tour.

Below, I use bracketed comments to describe the Vanna White motions that accompany the surrounding script; they are there to guide you, not to be spoken as part of the presentation. For figure 12.13:

"Across the bottom [wave horizontally at the x axis], there is one cluster for each of the three socioeconomic characteristics — teen motherhood, incomplete high school, and poverty [point quickly at each label in turn]. Each racial/ethnic group [point to the legend] is displayed with a different color bar, and the height of a bar [gesture vertically along the y axis] shows the percentage of that racial or ethnic group with the associated characteristic."

In the next step, you will give a specific example and introduce the bar colors for each subgroup. For lay audiences, "x axis" and "y axis" may be fuzzily recalled jargon. Instead, use phrases like "across the bottom" or "on the vertical axis," respectively.

If you are explaining a chart with more than three or four nominal variables or categories, mention the organizing principle you have used rather than simply naming each of the categories. As always, coordinate the narrative with the layout of the chart.

"In figure 7.6, the different AIDS transmission topics are shown on the horizontal axis [point] grouped into "likely" modes on the left [wave at that group of clusters] and "unlikely" modes on the right [gesture]. Within those groupings, the topics are arranged in descending order of average score [wave along the tops of the bars within one group of clusters]."

Describe the patterns. Finally, having introduced your audience to the purpose and layout of the table or chart, proceed to describe the patterns it embodies. Use the GEE approach, starting with a general descriptive sentence followed by specific numeric examples and exceptions (where pertinent). Again, gesture to show comparisons and point to identify specific values, naming the associated colors or shading schemes for each group the first time you mention it, as shown in the following description of figure 12.13.

> "Regardless of which dimension of socioeconomic status we examine, non-Hispanic black infants, illustrated with the black bar, and Mexican American infants — the dark gray bar [point at legend] — are far more likely than their non-Hispanic white counterparts, in light gray [point at legend element], to be born into low SES families. The black and dark gray bars are higher than the light gray bar in each of the three clusters. For example [gesture at the right-most cluster], infants of color are more than three times as likely to be poor as their white counterparts [point to the respective bars as you mention them]."

As you describe your charts, tables, or other graphics, point to and explain any features such as reference lines or regions, symbols, colors, or other annotations. For example,

> "As you can see, recessions, which encompass the years in the gray-shaded bands in figure 7.13 [gesture at the range of shaded dates], coincided with a notable increase in poverty [wave along the line showing the trend in poverty]."

> "In table YYY, relationships that were statistically significant at $p < 0.05$ are shown in orange and are marked with asterisks [point to the footnote on the slide that defines the asterisk]. For example, the difference in average math scores between boys and girls was statistically significant [point to pertinent cells], but most other comparisons in the table were not."

Until you are confident that you can recall your Vanna White description, include it in your speaker's notes, either in full sentences or as circles and arrows on a hardcopy of the chart, numbered to help you recall the order in which you plan to explain each feature.

■ PRACTICE, PRACTICE, PRACTICE

After you have drafted your slides and accompanying notes, practice your presentation, first alone and then with a test audience. If someone else wrote the speech and made the slides, all the more reason to review and practice. Rehearsal is particularly important for slides involving tables or charts, which are usually more complex than simple text slides. Likewise for slides explaining methods, especially if you have not worked previously with those methods or explained them to a similar audience.

Time how long the entire talk takes, anticipating that you will become somewhat faster with practice (and adrenaline). If you will be using a Vanna White approach, rehearse speaking and gesturing at the associated chart until you are comfortable coordinating those two actions. Evaluate the order in which you've covered the material, making sure you define terms, acronyms, and symbols before you use them and that your results are in a logical order with good transitions to convey where they fit in the overall story.

If you exceeded the allotted time by more than a minute or two, identify which sections were too long and assess what can be condensed or eliminated. Some sections will require more time than others, so you may have to omit detail or simplify explanations in other parts of your talk, taking into account what your audience knows (and needs to know). If you finished well under time, think about where additional material or explanation would be most useful. If you were under time but rushed your delivery, slow down.

Revise the coverage, level of detail, and order of material to reflect what you learned from your dry run. If you make substantial revisions, practice on your own again before you enlist a test audience. To assist yourself in pacing your talk, insert reminders in your speaker's notes to indicate where you should be at certain time points so you can speed up or slow down as necessary during your talk.

Dress Rehearsal

Once you have a draft of slides and notes that you are comfortable with, rehearse your talk in front of a colleague or friend who represents your audience well in terms of familiarity with your topic, data, and methods of analysis. If you differ substantially from your prospective listeners on those dimensions, it is difficult to "put yourself in their shoes" to identify potential points of confusion. A fresh set of eyes and ears will be more likely to notice such issues than someone who is jaded from working closely with the material while writing the paper or drafting the slides and talk.

Elements to Listen For

Before you begin your dress rehearsal, ask your guinea pig audience to make notes on the following aspects of your talk:

- Were the objectives of your talk plainly identified?

- Were the purpose and interpretation of your numeric examples evident?
- Were your definitions of terms and concepts easy to grasp? Did you define terms before you used them?
- Did you use jargon that could be replaced by terms more familiar to this audience?
- Were your descriptions of tables or charts clear and not too rushed? Was it easy to see where your numeric examples came from in those tables or charts? To follow the patterns you described?
- If you were over time, what material could be omitted or explained more briefly? If under time, where would more information or time be most beneficial?
- Was the amount of time for each section about right? If not, which sections need more or less emphasis?

Go over your reviewer's comments with them, then revise your talk and slides accordingly. Practice yet again if you make appreciable changes.

■ CHECKLIST FOR SPEAKING ABOUT NUMBERS

Before you plan your speech, consider your topic, audience, and amount of time, pacing the talk for the average listener and allowing time for questions and discussion.

- Slide format and content: adapt material from your paper, following the same sequence of major topics.
    For a scientific audience, include an introduction, literature review, data and methods, results, discussion, and conclusions.
    For lay audiences, omit the literature review and condense the data and methods.
    Write a simple, specific title for each slide.
    Replace full sentences with bullets.
    Simplify tables and charts to focus on one major question per slide.
    Create no more than one slide per minute, fewer if slides involve tables or charts.
- Speaker's notes: decide whether you need a full script or selected notes. In either case, follow these steps:
    Write an introductory sentence.

Note aspects of the slide you want to emphasize.

Include analogies or examples you use to flesh out the material.

Write a Vanna White description of charts or tables.

–Paraphrase the purpose of the slide.

–Explain the layout of the table (contents of rows and columns) or chart (axes, legend), with notes about which elements to point to for each sentence.

–Describe the pattern, listing which illustrative numbers you will point to as you speak.

Write a summary sentence.

Insert a transition to the next slide.

- Other design considerations:

Use at least 18 point type for titles and text; smaller for footnotes.

Consider using color to emphasize selected points or terms, or to indicate statistical significance.

- Rehearsing your talk. First alone, then with a critic familiar with your intended audience, evaluate the following:

Order and relative emphasis of topics

Definitions of terms

Level of detail

Introductions and explanations of charts and tables

Coordination of spoken and visual materials

Time to complete the talk

APPENDIX A
Implementing "Generalization, Example, Exceptions" (GEE)

One of the basic principles for describing a relationship among two or more variables is to summarize, characterizing that association with one or two broad patterns. In chapter 2, I introduced a mantra, GEE, for "generalization, example, exceptions," to use as a guide on how to write an effective summary. Generalize by stepping back to look at the forest, not the individual trees, describing the broad pattern rather than reporting every component number. Illustrate with representative numbers to portray that general pattern. Finally, if the general pattern doesn't fit all your data, identify and portray the exceptions. For inexperienced writers, this can seem like a daunting task.

In this appendix, I sketch out six steps to guide you through implementing a GEE. After creating a chart or table to present data on the variables in the pattern, proceed through several intermediate steps to identify and characterize the patterns for your final written description. The notes, calculations, and scribbles generated in those steps will not appear in the final written narrative, but are an important part of the analytic process involved in writing a succinct but thorough summary.

■ STEP 1: DISPLAY THE DATA IN A TABLE OR CHART

Create a table and chart to display your data. Even if you plan to use a table or prose in your document, the chart version may help you see patterns in your data more easily as you write your GEE. It doesn't have to be pretty — even a hand-drawn version will work fine for this purpose — as long as it is an appropriate type of chart for the task, is drawn to scale, and is labeled well enough that you can recognize the variables and assess approximate numeric values.

■ STEP 2: IDENTIFY THE DIMENSIONS OF THE COMPARISON

Identify the dimensions of the comparison — one for each variable or set of variables in your table or chart. In a table, the rows and columns each comprise one dimension; panels of rows or spanners across columns often indicate the presence of additional dimensions.

Median sales price of new single-family homes, by region, United States, 1980–2000

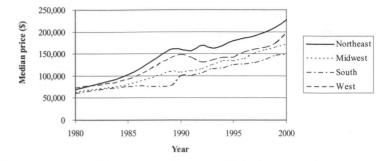

Figure A.1. Summarizing patterns from a multiple-line trend chart.
Source: U.S. Census Bureau 2001a.

In a chart, the axes and legends each comprise one dimension. Vary only one dimension of the chart or table at a time, keeping the others constant.

In a multiple-line trend chart like figure A.1, there are two separate comparisons:

(1) *Moving left to right along one line.* In figure A.1, this comparison shows how the variable on the *y* axis (price of housing) varies with time (the *x* variable), within one region (value of the *z* variable, shown in the legend).

(2) *Moving (vertically) across lines.* This comparison shows how price (the *y* variable) varies across regions (the *z* variable) at one time point (value of the *x* variable).

In a three-way table, there are two comparisons:

(1) *Moving down the rows within one column.* Table A.1 shows how AIDS knowledge (in the interior cells) varies by row (topic) within one language group (column).

(2) *Moving across the columns within one row.* Table A.1 shows how AIDS knowledge varies by column (language of respondent) for one topic (row).

■ STEP 3: CHOOSING A REPRESENTATIVE EXAMPLE

Having identified each of the dimensions of comparison, choose one representative example as the basis for each generalization.

- For a comparison across a series of related outcomes a good starting point is a summary measure (e.g., in table A.1, the mean percentage of "likely" questions correct) that combines results for the various component variables. Lacking a summary measure, pick a value of particular interest or start at one end of the axis, column, or row (the best-answered or worst-answered topic, in table A.1).

- For a comparison across groups, a good starting point for a representative value is the overall sample (e.g., all language groups combined). Alternatively, use the modal (most common) group — English speakers, in table A.1 — or a group of particular interest for your research question.

Follow steps 4 and 5 to ensure that your example is in fact representative of a general pattern. If not (e.g., if it turns out to be an ex-

Table A.1. Generalizing one pattern within a three-way table

Percentage of respondents answering AIDS transmission questions correctly, by language spoken at home and language used on the questionnaire, New Jersey, 1998

Mode of transmission	English	Spanish/ English ques.	Spanish/ Spanish ques.
		Language spoken at home and language used on questionnaire	
Likely modes of transmission			
Sexual intercourse with an infected person	93.6	87.5	95.0
Sharing needles for IV drug use*	92.4	90.6	65.0
Pregnant mother to baby*	89.5	75.0	80.0
Blood transfusion from infected person*	87.5	81.3	60.0
Mean percentage of "likely" questions correct*	91.7	83.6	75.0

Source: Miller 2000a.
* Difference across language groups is significant at $p < 0.05$.

Box A.1

Generalization 1: Down the rows. On the summary measure of knowledge of "likely" modes of AIDS transmission, English speakers score higher than Spanish/English speakers, who in turn score higher than Spanish/Spanish speakers. The difference in mean percentage of "likely" questions correct is statistically significant, as indicated by the asterisk at the end of the row label (see note to table).

Check: Does the pattern in the row showing mean percentage correct apply to the other rows? In other words, does the generalization from the summary row fit each of the component questions?

Answer: The generalization fits all but the sexual intercourse question, for which the Spanish/Spanish group did best. In addition, the difference across language groups in knowledge of sexual intercourse as a likely means of AIDS transmission is not statistically significant. Hence that question is the exception to the general pattern, in terms of both direction and statistical significance.

Generalization 2: Across the columns. Among English speakers, the best understood "likely" AIDS transmission topic was transmission via sexual intercourse, followed by sharing IV needles, transmission from pregnant mother to baby, and blood transfusion. (Note that the question topics were arranged in the table in descending order of correct answers for the English-speaking group, facilitating this description.)

Check: Does this same rank order of topics apply to the other language groups? In other words, does the generalization from the summary column fit each of the other columns?

Answer: Spanish/English speakers did best on the needles question and least well on mother to baby. Among Spanish/Spanish speakers, the rank order of the two middle questions is reversed. In this analysis, number of Spanish speakers is small, so these exceptions would not be emphasized.

ception), try again with a different example until you've found one that is generalizable.

■ STEP 4: CHARACTERIZING THE PATTERN

Using your example value, describe the shape of the pattern, including direction, magnitude, and for a scientific audience, statistical significance. Make notes in the margins of your table or chart or on an accompanying page. Don't worry about writing complete sentences at this stage. Abbreviate concepts to use as a basis for your written description with short phrases, upward or downward pointing arrows and $<$, $=$, or $>$ to show how values on different categories, topics, or time points relate to one another.

Direction

For *trends* across values of an interval or ordinal variable such as time, age, or price, describe whether the pattern is
- level (constant) or changing;
- linear (rising or falling at a steady rate), accelerating, or decelerating;
- monotonic or with a change of direction (is there a notable "blip" or other sudden change?).

For *differentials* across categories of a nominal variable such as religious affiliation, political party, or gender, indicate which categories have the highest and lowest values and where other categories of interest fall relative to those extremes, as explained in chapter 9.

Magnitude

Use one or two types of quantitative comparisons (chapter 5) to calculate the size of the trend or differential. If the calculations involve only a few numbers and basic arithmetic (e.g., a ratio of two numbers or simple percentage change), include those calculations in your notes, including units. For more complex or repetitive calculations, such as confidence intervals for each of a dozen predictor variables, save your work in a spreadsheet, then annotate it to indicate which calculations correspond to which aspects of the GEE for your own future reference.

Scribble down descriptive words or phrases to depict the size of the variation. Is the trend steep or shallow? Is the differential marked or minuscule?

Statistical Significance

Note patterns of statistical significance on your table or chart, particularly if it does not include symbols to indicate which results are statistically significant. Are most of the associations in the table statistically significant? If so, generalize that finding. If most are not, the lack of statistical significance is your generalization. Finally, if only some portions of your table or chart have statistically significant findings, try to identify what they have in common so you can summarize the patterns to the extent possible.

■ STEP 5: IDENTIFYING EXCEPTIONS

If parts of your table or chart depart appreciably from the generalization you have made in the steps above, they are exceptions. Exceptions come in three flavors: direction, magnitude, and statistical significance. A few more illustrations:

Exceptions in Direction

In figure A.1, median sales prices dipped in the early 1990s in the West, but continued upward or remained level in the other regions — an example of a different direction of trend. The West was the exception. In 1980, sales prices in the Northeast were slightly below those in the West ("Northeast < West"), an example of a contrasting direction of a differential (cross-sectional comparison). In all subsequent years, the Northeast had the highest prices ("Northeast > West"). The year 1980 was the exception.

Exceptions in Magnitude

In figure A.2a, the difference across racial groups is much larger among the nonpoor than in the other two income groups (compare brackets 2 and 3 to bracket 4). Generalize based on the two income groups for which the racial gap in ER use is similar (poor and near poor), and then point out that the nonpoor are the exception.

Exceptions in Statistical Significance

In table A.1, the sexual intercourse question is the only one for which the language difference is not statistically significant. For that table, statistical significance is the rule (generalization) and lack of statistical significance is the exception.

On the printed copy of your table or chart, circle or otherwise mark exceptions to your general pattern. If your table or chart is complicated, consider using color coding (highlighter) to shade which parts share a common pattern and which deviate from that pattern.

■ STEP 6: WRITING THE DESCRIPTION

Working from your notes and calculations, write a systematic description of the patterns. For relationships among three or more

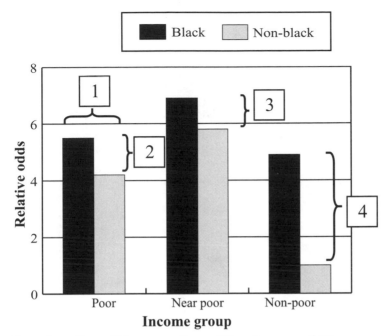

a. Relative odds of emergency room visits for asthma, by race and income, United States, 1991

Figure A.2a. **Generalizing one pattern within a three-way chart: Within clusters.**

Source: Miller 2000b.

Note: Difference across income groups significant at $p < .05$ for non-blacks only; difference across racial groups within income group significant at $p < .05$ for non-poor only.

Box A.2a

Generalization: Among the poor (the left-most cluster), use of the emergency room is greater for blacks than non-blacks (bracket 1).

Check: Does the same pattern apply in the other clusters? Does that description fit the near poor? The non-poor?

Answer: Yes, ER use is higher among blacks than non-blacks in all three income groups. However (exception), the racial difference is much smaller among the poor and near poor (brackets 2 and 3) than among the non-poor (bracket 4) and is only statistically significant among the non-poor (see figure footnote).

b. Relative odds of emergency room visits for asthma, by race and income, United States, 1991

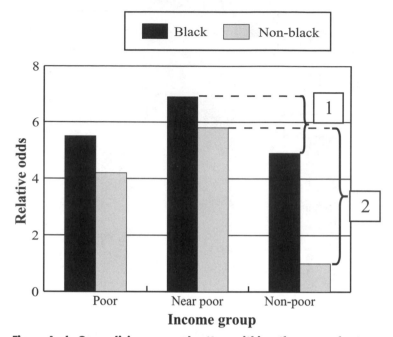

Figure A.2b. Generalizing a second pattern within a three-way chart: Across clusters.

Source: Miller 2000b.

Note: Difference across income groups significant at $p < .05$ for non-blacks only; difference across racial groups within income group significant at $p < .05$ for non-poor only.

Box A.2b

Generalization: Among blacks (the black-shaded bars), emergency room use is highest among the near poor and lowest among the non-poor.

Check: Does that pattern apply to non-blacks (the other bar color) as well?

Answer: Yes, the non-blacks exhibit the same income/ER use pattern as blacks. However (exception), the drop in ER use between near poor and non-poor is much smaller among blacks (bracket 1) than among non-blacks (bracket 2), and is only statistically significant among non-blacks (see figure footnote).

variables, organize the GEE into one paragraph for each type of comparison — e.g., one for the pattern "across the columns," another for "down the rows."

Start each paragraph with a topic sentence that identifies the main concepts or variables in the comparison. Provide a verbal sketch of the general pattern, selecting verbs and adjectives to convey direction and magnitude. Follow with one or more sentences with the results of your quantitative comparisons, reporting the raw data from which they were calculated or (if many numbers are involved), referring to the associated table or chart. Finally, describe and document any exceptions. See chapter 9 for suggested wording to differentiate general patterns from exceptions.

Figures A.2a and b, table A.1, and the associated text boxes illustrate how to identify the dimensions, select a starting point for each generalization, and test the generalization for exceptions of direction and magnitude.

NOTES

CHAPTER 2

1. See Best 2001.
2. See chapter 3 for further discussion of various dimensions of "significance" that come into play when assessing quantitative relations.
3. Another aspect of association — statistical significance — is covered in chapter 3.

CHAPTER 3

1. The fifth criterion — specificity — is most applicable to the study of infectious disease. It concerns the extent to which a particular exposure (e.g., the measles virus) produces one specific disease (measles).
2. Strictly speaking, a 95% confidence interval is the estimate ± 1.96 times the standard error, but for most purposes, ± twice the standard error gives a good approximation (and is much easier to calculate).
3. Other width confidence intervals can also be calculated. For example, a 99% CI (equivalent to testing whether $p < 0.01$) is calculated as the estimate ± 2.58 times the standard error.

CHAPTER 4

1. Temperature in degrees Kelvin has a meaningful absolute zero value and can be treated as a ratio variable, but is rarely used by anyone other than physical scientists in technical documents.
2. When categorical variables are entered onto a computer, each group is often assigned a numeric code as an abbreviation. Do not treat those values as if they had real numeric meaning. It makes no sense to calculate "average gender" by computing the mean of a variable coded 1 for male and 2 for female. For categorical variables, the appropriate measure of central tendency is the mode, not the mean.
3. Order of magnitude refers to multiples of 10. E.g., one thousand is an order of magnitude greater than one hundred, which is an order of magnitude greater than 10.
4. To generalize, "__ % of [concept in the denominator] is [concept in the numerator]."
5. Although the "middle category" can be identified with an ordinal variable having an odd number of values, taking the mean of the two "middle values" with an even number of categories cannot. Hence the median often doesn't work for interval variables.
6. In the phrase "significant digits," the term "significant" has a different meaning from the statistical interpretation discussed in chapter 3. Here, it

refers to precision of measurement and how that affects the appropriate number of digits in measured values (raw data) and calculations.

7. Leading zeros are those found to the right of the decimal point, before the first "significant" (nonzero) numeral, e.g., the five zeros between the decimal point and the 2 in the numeral "0.0000023". They serve as placeholders which convey the scale or units of the number, in this case, millionths. Likewise "trailing zeros" are placeholders for thousands, millions, or billions. For example, the six zeros used to convey the scale in "285,000,000" rarely reflect an exact count down to the single unit. Eliminate them by rounding to that scale — just write "285 million."

CHAPTER 5

1. For authors working with multivariate analyses, some additional types of comparison are needed. See Miller (forthcoming) for a detailed discussion of these calculations and their interpretation.

2. Changing the reference group in a two-group calculation merely involves "flipping over" the ratio to calculate its reciprocal: a ratio of 1.43 southerners per midwesterner is equivalent to 0.70 midwesterners per southerner.

3. With negative growth rates (yes, they are called that, not "shrinkage rates"!), the base population, or principal, becomes successively smaller across time.

4. For annual compounding, calculate the annual interest rate (r) using the formula $\log(1 + r) = \log(P_2/P_1)/n$, where P_1 and P_2 are the populations at times 1 and 2 respectively, n is the number of years between P_1 and P_2, and "log" indicates base 10 logarithms. For continuous compounding use $r = \ln(P_2/P_1)/n$, where "ln" indicates natural logarithms (Barclay 1958; Nicholson 1985).

5. A Likert scale is a common way of collecting attitudinal data on surveys. Subjects are asked to express agreement or disagreement on a five-point scale.

CHAPTER 6

1. Breakdowns of non-Hispanic blacks and non-Hispanics of other races could likewise be indented under the respective headings. Those data were not available in the current source (U.S. Census Bureau 1998).

2. For example, there were 34,385,000 people aged 65+ in the United States in 2002, of whom 10.4% were poor. Hence 34,385,000 × .104 = 3,576,000 elderly persons were poor in 2002.

3. Place the category that combines "all other" values at the bottom of the table body, before the "total" row. Frequently, it is not ranked with specifically named categories, as it combines several values.

4. However, if a response is missing for a substantial share of cases, show the distribution of both "yes" and "no," as well as "don't know" or other missing values.

CHAPTER 7

1. A pie chart can present two categorical variables simultaneously by cross-tabulating them first. For example, a single pie showing gender and age distribution might have slices for males under 20, males 20+, females under 20, and females 20+, four mutually exclusive categories. Univariate slices (e.g., <20 and "male") cannot be shown in the same pie chart because some people are both <20 and male.

CHAPTER 12

1. For audiences interested in standard errors or other ways of presenting statistical significance that allow them to make their own comparisons (see Miller forthcoming), hand out the full statistical table at the end of the speech for readers to peruse on their own time. If you give it out during the talk, they'll pay attention to it, not you, and may ask distracting questions about specific numbers unrelated to your main points.

2. The "Vanna White" moniker is in honor of the longtime hostess of the TV game show *Wheel of Fortune* who gestures at the display to identify each item or feature as it is introduced.

REFERENCE LIST

Abramson, J. H. 1994. *Making Sense of Data: A Self-Instruction Manual on the Interpretation of Epidemiologic Data.* 2nd ed. New York: Oxford University Press.

Agresti, Alan, and Barbara Finlay. 1997. *Statistical Methods for the Social Sciences.* 3rd ed. Upper Saddle River, NJ: Prentice Hall.

Allison, Paul D. 1999. *Multiple Regression: A Primer.* Thousand Oaks: Sage Publications.

Alred, Gerald J., Charles T. Brusaw, and Walter E. Oliu. 2000. *Handbook of Technical Writing.* 6th ed. New York: St. Martin's Press.

Anderson, Robert N. 2001. "Deaths: Leading Causes for 1999." *National Vital Statistics Reports* 49 (11). Hyattsville, MD: National Center for Health Statistics.

Anderson, Robert N., and Harry M. Rosenberg. 1998. "Age Standardization of Death Rates: Implementation of the Year 2000 Standard." *National Vital Statistics Report* 47 (3). Hyattsville, MD: National Center for Health Statistics.

Autoweb.com. 2000. "Information on 2000 and 2001 Model Cars." Available online at http://www.autoweb.com/. Accessed August 2000.

Barclay, George W. 1958. *Techniques of Population Analysis.* New York: John Wiley and Sons.

Benson, Veronica, and Marie A. Marano. 1998. "Current Estimates from the National Health Interview Survey, 1995." *Vital and Health Statistics* 10 (199). Hyattsville, MD: National Center for Health Statistics.

Best, Joel. 2001. *Damned Lies and Statistics.* Berkeley: University of California Press.

Centers for Disease Control. 1999. "Notice to Readers: New Population Standard for Age-Adjusting Death Rates." *Morbidity and Mortality Weekly Review* 48 (06): 126–27. Available at http://www.cdc.gov/mmwr/preview/mmwrhtml/00056512.htm.

———. 2002. "Compressed Mortality File: U.S. 1999."

Centers for Medicare and Medicaid Services, Office of the Actuary, National Health Statistics Group, Department of Health and Human Services. 2004. "Table 1. National Health Expenditures, Aggregate and Per Capita Amounts, Percent Distribution, and Average Annual Percent Growth, by Source of Funds: Selected Calendar Years 1980–2002." Available at http://cms.hhs.gov/statistics/nhe/historical/t1.asp.

Chambliss, Daniel F., and Russell K. Schutt. 2003. *Making Sense of the Social World: Methods of Investigation.* Thousand Oaks, CA: Sage Publications.

Citro, Constance F., Robert T. Michael, and Nancy Maritano, eds. 1996.

Measuring Poverty: A New Approach. Table 5–8. Washington DC: National Academy Press.

Conley, Dalton, and Neil G. Bennett. 2000. "Race and the Inheritance of Low Birth Weight." *Social Biology* 47 (1–2): 77–93.

Davis, James A. 1985. *The Logic of Causal Order.* Quantitative Applications in the Social Sciences 55. Thousand Oaks, CA: Sage Publications.

Davis, James A., Tom W. Smith, and Peter V. Marsden. 2003. *General Social Surveys, 1972–2000: Computer Codebook.* 2nd ICPSR version. Chicago, IL: National Opinion Research Center.

Eaton, Leslie. 2002. "Job Data May Show a False Positive." *New York Times,* February 10, sec. 10.

Fink, Arlene. 1995. *How to Report on Surveys.* Thousand Oaks, CA: Sage Publications.

Franzini, L., J. C. Ribble, and A. M. Keddie. 2001. "Understanding the Hispanic Paradox." *Ethnicity and Disease* 11 (3): 496–518.

Githens, P. B., C. A. Glass, F. A. Sloan, and S. S. Entman. 1993. "Maternal Recall and Medical Records: An Examination of Events during Pregnancy, Childbirth, and Early Infancy." *Birth* 20 (3): 136–41.

Glanz, James, and Eric Lipton. 2002. "The Height of Ambition." *New York Times,* September 8, sec. 6.

Gold, Marthe R., Joanna E. Siegel, Louise B. Russell, and Milton C. Weinstein, eds. 1996. *Cost-Effectiveness in Health and Medicine.* New York: Oxford University Press.

Health Care Financing Administration, Department of Health and Human Services. 2000. "Highlights: National Health Expenditures, 1998." Available online at http://www.hcfa.gov/stats/NHE-OAct/hilites.htm; or in *Health Affairs* (Jan./Feb. 2000). Accessed June 2001.

Hoaglin, David C., Frederick Mosteller, and John W. Tukey. 2000. *Understanding Robust and Exploratory Data Analysis.* New York: John Wiley and Sons.

Institute for Democracy and Electoral Assistance. 1999. *Voter Turnout from 1945 to 1998: A Global Participation Report.* Available online at http://www.int-idea.se/Voter_turnout/northamerica/usa.html. Accessed January 2003.

Institute of Medicine, Committee to Study the Prevention of Low Birthweight. 1985. *Preventing Low Birthweight.* Washington, DC: National Academy Press.

Jochim, Jennifer. 1997. "Generation X Defies Definition." *Outpost.* Available online at http://www.jour.unr.edu/outpost/specials/genx.overvw1.html. Accessed February 2002.

Kalton, G., and D. Kasprzyk. 1986. "The Treatment of Missing Survey Data." *Survey Methodology* 12 (1), 1–16.

Kolata, Gina. 2003. "Hormone Studies: What Went Wrong?" *New York Times,* April 22, Science sec.

Kornegay, Chris. 1999. *Math Dictionary with Solutions: A Math Review.* 2nd ed. Thousand Oaks, CA: Sage Publications.

Kraemer, Helena C. 1987. *How Many Subjects? Statistical Power Analysis in Research.* Thousand Oaks, CA: Sage Publications.

Kuczmarski, Robert J., et al. 2000. "CDC Growth Charts: United States." *Advance Data from Vital and Health Statistics.* No. 314. Hyattsville, MD: National Center for Health Statistics.

Lanham, Richard. 2000. *Revising Prose.* 4th ed. New York: Longham.

Levy, Helen, and Thomas DeLeire. 2002. "What Do People Buy When They Don't Buy Health Insurance?" Northwestern University/University of Chicago Joint Center for Poverty Research Working Paper 296 06–26–2002.

Lewit, Eugene, L. Baker, Hope Corman, and P. Shiono. 1995. "The Direct Cost of Low Birth Weight." *The Future of Children* 5 (1).

Lilienfeld, David E., and Paul D. Stolley. 1994. *Foundations of Epidemiology.* 3rd ed. New York: Oxford University Press.

Lipton, Eric, and James Glanz. 2002. "First Tower to Fall Was Hit at Higher Speed, Study Finds." *New York Times,* February 23.

Logan, Ralph H. 1995. "Significant Digits." Available online at http://members.aol.com/profchm/sig_fig.html. Accessed January 2003.

Maciejewski, Matthew L., Paula Diehr, Maureen A. Smith, and Paul Hebert. 2002. "Common Methodological Terms in Health Services Research and Their Symptoms." *Medical Care* 40: 477–84.

Mack, Tim. No date. "Plagues since the Roman Empire." Available online at http://www.ento.vt.edu/IHS/plagueHistory.html#justinian. Accessed January 2002.

Martin, Joyce A., Brady E. Hamilton, Stephanie J. Ventura, Fay Menacker, and Melissa M. Park. 2002. "Births: Final Data for 2000." *National Vital Statistics Reports* 50 (5).

Mathews, T. J., and Brady E. Hamilton. 2002. "Mean Age of Mother, 1970–2000." *National Vital Statistics Report* 51 (1). Hyattsville, MD: National Center for Health Statistics.

Mathews, T. J., Marian F. MacDorman, and Fay Menacker. 2002. "Infant Mortality Statistics from the 1999 Period Linked Birth/Infant Death Data Set." *National Vital Statistics Reports* 50 (4). Hyattsville, MD: National Center for Health Statistics.

Medina, Jennifer. 2002. "Report Finds Drop in Average City Class Size." *New York Times,* September 20, sec. B.

Miller, Jane E. 2000a. "Differences in AIDS Knowledge among Spanish and English Speakers by Socioeconomic Status and Ability to Speak English." *Journal of Urban Health* 77 (3): 415–24.

———. 2000b. "Income, Race/Ethnicity, and Early Childhood Asthma Prevalence and Health Care Utilization." *American Journal of Public Health* 90 (3): 428–30.

————. Forthcoming. *The Chicago Guide to Writing about Multivariate Analyses.* Chicago: University of Chicago Press.

Monmonier, Mark. 1993. *Mapping It Out: Expository Cartography for the Humanities and Social Sciences.* Chicago: University of Chicago Press.

Montgomery, Scott L. 2003. *The Chicago Guide to Communicating Science.* Chicago: University of Chicago Press.

Moore, David S. 1997. *Statistics: Concepts and Controversies.* 4th ed. New York: W. H. Freeman and Co.

Morgan, Susan E., Tom Reichert, and Tyler R. Harrison. 2002. *From Numbers to Words: Reporting Statistical Results for the Social Sciences.* Boston: Allyn and Bacon.

Morton, Richard F., J. Richard Hebel, and Robert J. McCarter. 2001. *A Study Guide to Epidemiology and Biostatistics.* 5th ed. Gaithersburg, MD: Aspen Publishers.

Navarro, Mireya. 2003. "Going beyond Black and White, Hispanics in Census Pick 'Other.'" *New York Times,* November 9.

NCHS (National Center for Health Statistics). 1994. "Plan and Operation of the Third National Health and Nutrition Examination Survey, 1988–1994." *Vital and Health Statistics* 1 (32).

————. 1995. "International Classification of Diseases, Ninth Revision, Clinical Modification." 5th ed. NCHS CD-ROM no. 1. DHHS pub. no. (PHS) 95–1260.

————. 2002. "Policy on Micro-data dissemination." Available online at http://www.cdc.gov/nchs/data/NCHS%20Micro-Data%20Release%20Policy%204-02A.pdf. Accessed January 2003.

Nicholson, Walter. 1985. *Microeconomic Theory.* New York: Holt, Rinehart and Winston.

NIST (National Institute of Standards and Technology). 2000. "Uncertainty of Measurement Results." In *The NIST Reference on Constants, Units, and Uncertainty.* Available online at http://physics.nist.gov/cuu/Uncertainty/index.html. Accessed January 2004.

National Institutes for Health, Office of Human Subjects Research. 2002. *Regulations and Ethics.* Available online at http://206.102.88.10/ohsrsite/guidelines/guidelines.html. Accessed January 2003.

Nicol, Adelheid A. M., and Penny M. Pexman. 1999. *Presenting Your Findings: A Practical Guide for Creating Tables.* Washington, DC: American Psychological Association.

Olson, J. E., X. O. Shu, J. A. Ross, T. Pendergrass, and L. L. Robison. 1997. "Medical Record Validation of Maternally Reported Birth Characteristics and Pregnancy-Related Events: A Report from the Children's Cancer Group." *American Journal of Epidemiology* 145 (1): 58–67.

Omran, Abdel R. 1971. "The Epidemiologic Transition: A Theory of the Epidemiology of Population Change." *Milbank Memorial Fund Quarterly* 49 (4): 509–38.

Palloni Alberto, and J. D. Morenoff. 2001. "Interpreting the Paradoxical in the Hispanic Paradox: Demographic and Epidemiologic Approaches." *Annals of the New York Academy of Sciences* 954: 140–74.

Paneth, Nigel. 1995. "The Problem of Low Birth Weight." *The Future of Children* 5 (1).

Peters, Kimberley D., Kenneth D. Kochanek, and Sherry L. Murphy. 1998. "Deaths: Final Data for 1996." *National Vital Statisitcs Report* 47 (9). Available online at http://www.cdc.gov/nchs/data/nvsr/nvsr47/ nvs47_09.pdf. Accessed January 2003.

Pollack, Andrew. 1999. "Missing What Didn't Add Up, NASA Subtracted an Orbiter." *New York Times,* October 1.

Population Reference Bureau. 1999. "World Population: More than Just Numbers." Washington DC: Population Reference Bureau.

Preston, Samuel H. 1976. *Mortality Patterns in National Populations.* New York: Academic Press.

Proctor, Bernadette D., and Joseph Dalaker. 2002. "Poverty in the U.S., 2001." *Current Population Reports.* P60–219. Washington, DC: U.S. Government Printing Office.

———. 2003. "Poverty in the United States: 2002." *Current Population Reports.* P60–222. Washington, DC: U.S. Government Printing Office.

Puffer, Ruth R., and Carlos V. Serrano. 1973. *Patterns of Mortality in Childhood.* Washington, DC: World Health Organization.

Pyrczak, Fred, and Randall R. Bruce. 2000. *Writing Empirical Research Reports.* 3rd ed. Los Angeles: Pyrczak Publishing.

Quality Resource Systems, Inc. 2001. *Area Resource File.* Available online at http://www.arfsys.com/.

Radloff, L. S., and B. Z. Locke. 1986. "The Community Mental Health Assessment Survey and the CES-D Scale." In *Community Surveys of Psychiatric Disorders,* edited by M. M. Weissma, J. K. Myers, and C. E. Ross. New Brunswick, NJ: Rutgers University Press.

Schutt, Russell K. 2001. *Investigating the Social World: The Process and Practice of Research.* 3rd ed. Boston: Pine Forge Press.

Schwartz, John. 2003. "The Level of Discourse Continues to Slide." *New York Times,* Week in Review, September 28.

Shah, B. V., B. G. Barnwell, and G. S. Bieler. 1996. *SUDAAN User's Manual, Release 7.0.* Research Triangle Park, NC: Research Triangle Institute.

Slocum, Terry A. 1998. *Thematic Cartography and Visualization.* Upper Saddle River, NJ: Prentice Hall.

Snow, John. 1936. *Snow on Cholera.* New York: The Commonwealth Fund.

Strunk, William, Jr., and E. B. White. 1999. *The Elements of Style.* 4th ed. Boston, MA: Allyn and Bacon.

Tufte, Edward R. 1990. *Envisioning Information.* Cheshire, CT: Graphics Press.

———. 1997. *Visual Explanations: Images and Quantities, Evidence and Narrative.* Cheshire, CT: Graphics Press.

———. 2001. *The Visual Display of Quantitative Information.* 2nd ed. Cheshire, CT: Graphics Press.

Tukey, John W. 1977. *Exploratory Data Analysis.* New York: Addison-Wesley Publishing Co.

University of Chicago Press. 2003. *The Chicago Manual of Style: The Essential Guide for Writers, Editors, and Publishers.* 15th ed. Chicago: University of Chicago Press.

U.S. Bureau of Labor Statistics. 2002a. "U.S. Economy at a Glance." Available online at http://www.bls.gov/eag/eag.us.htm. Accessed March 2002.

———. 2002b. "Consumer Price Indexes: Frequently Asked Questions." Available online at http://www.bls.gov/cpi/cpifaq.htm. Accessed March 2002.

U.S. Bureau of Labor Statistics and U.S. Census Bureau. 2002. "Table 1. Age, Sex, Household Relationship, Race, and Hispanic Origin: Poverty Status of People by Selected Characteristics in 2000." In *Current Population Survey: Annual Demographic Survey.* Available online at http://ferret.bls.census.gov/macro/032001/pov/new01_001.htm. Accessed March 2002.

U.S. Census Bureau. 1998. "Households by Type and Selected Characteristics: 1998." Available online at http://www.census.gov/population/socdemo/hh-fam/98ppla.txt.

———. 1999a. "Comparison of Summary Measures of Income by Selected Characteristics: 1989, 1997, and 1998." Available online at http://www.census.gov/hhes/income/income98/in98sum.html.

———. 1999b. "State Population Estimates and Demographic Components of Population Change: April 1, 1990, to July 1, 1999." Available online at http://www.census.gov/population/estimates/state/st-99-2.txt.

———. 1999c. "Table 650. Civilian Labor Force Participation and Rates, with Projections, 1970–2006." *Statistical Abstract of the United States, 1999.* Available online at http://www.census.gov/prod/99pubs/99statab/sec13.pdf.

———. 2000a. "Annual Projections of the Total Resident Population as of July 1: Middle, Lowest, Highest, and Zero International Migration Series, 1999 to 2100." Washington, DC: Population Estimates Program, Population Division. Available online at http://www.census.gov/population/projections/nation/summary/np-t1.pdf.

———. 2001a. "Table 940. Median Sales Price of New Privately Owned One-Family Houses Sold by Region, 1980–2000." *Statistical Abstract of the United States, 2001.* Available online at http://www.census.gov/prod/2002pubs/01statab/construct.pdf.

———. 2001b. "Money Income in the United States: 2000." *Current Population Reports.* P60–213. Washington, DC: U.S. Government Printing Office.

————. 2001c. "Table 118. Expectation of Life and Expected Deaths by Race, Sex, and Age: 1997." *Statistical Abstract of the United States, 2000.* Available online at http://www.census.gov/prod/2001pubs/statab/ sec02.pdf. Accessed

————. 2002a. "Poverty 2001." Available online at http://www.census.gov/ hhes/poverty/threshld/thresh01.html. Accessed October 2002.

————. 2002b. "No. 310. Drug Use by Arrestees in Major United States Cities by Type of Drug and Sex, 1999." *Statistical Abstract of the United States, 2001.* Available on-line at http://www.census.gov/prod/2002pubs/ 01statab/stat-ab01.html. Accessed January 2004.

————. 2002c. "Table 611. Average Annual Pay, by State, U.S. 1999 and 2000." *Statistical Abstract of the United States, 2002.*

————. 2002d. "2000 Detailed Tables: Sex by Age, U.S. Summary File SF1." Available online at http://factfinder.census.gov/. Accessed September 2002.

U.S. DHHS (Department of Health and Human Services). 1991. *Longitudinal Follow-up to the 1988 National Maternal and Infant Health Survey.* Hyattsville, MD: National Center for Health Statistics.

————. 1997. *National Health and Nutrition Examination Survey, III, 1988– 1994.* CD-ROM Series 11, no. 1. Hyattsville, MD: National Center for Health Statistics, Centers for Disease Control and Prevention.

————, Centers for Disease Control and Prevention, 2002. *Z-score Data Files.* Hyattsville, MD: National Center for Health Statistics, Division of Data Services. Available online at http://www.cdc.gov/nchs/about/major/ nhanes/growthcharts/zscore/zscore.htm. Accessed January 2003.

————, Office of Disease Prevention and Health Promotion. 2001. *Healthy People 2010.* US GPO Stock no. 017-001-00547-9. Washington DC: U.S. Government Printing Office. Available online at http://www.health.gov/ healthypeople/. Accessed September 2002.

U.S. Environmental Protection Agency. 2002. *Cost of Illness Handbook.* Available online at http://www.epa.gov/oppt/coi/. Accessed September 2002.

U.S. National Energy Information Center. 2003. "Crude Oil Production. Table 2.2. World Crude Oil Production, 1980–2001." http://www.eia.doe .gov/pub/international/iealf/table22.xls. Accessed January 2004.

U.S. Office of Management and Budget. 2002. *Budget of the United States, Fiscal Year 2003, Historical Tables.* Table 3.1. Available online at http:// w3.access.gpo.gov/usbudget/fy2003/pdf/hist.pdf. Accessed June 2002.

Utts, Jessica M. 1999. *Seeing through Statistics.* 2nd ed. New York: Duxbury Press.

Ventura, Stephanie J., Joyce A. Martin, Sally C. Curtin, and T. J. Mathews. 1999. "Births: Final Data for 1997." *National Vital Statistics Report* 47 (18). Hyattsville, MD: National Center for Health Statistics.

Westat. 1994. "National Health and Nutrition Examination Survey III, Section 4.1: Accounting for Item Non-Response Bias." *NHANES III*

Reference Manuals and Reports. Washington, DC: U.S. Department of Health and Human Services, Public Health Service, Centers for Disease Control and Prevention, National Center for Health Statistics.

———. 1996. "National Health and Nutrition Examination Survey III, Weighting and Estimation Methodology." In *NHANES III Reference Manuals and Reports.* Hyattsville, MD: U.S. Department of Health and Human Services, Public Health Service, Centers for Disease Control and Prevention, National Center for Health Statistics.

Wilkinson, Leland, and Task Force on Statistical Inference, APA Board of Scientific Affairs. 1999. "Statistical Methods in Psychology Journals: Guidelines and Explanations." *American Psychologist* 54 (8): 594–604.

Wolke, Robert L. 2000. *What Einstein Told His Barber: More Scientific Answers to Everyday Questions.* New York: W. W. Norton.

———. 2002. *What Einstein Told His Cook: Kitchen Science Explained.* New York: W. W. Norton.

World Bank. 2001a. "Health, Nutrition, and Population Statistics." Available online at http://devdata.worldbank.org/hnpstats/. Accessed February 2002.

———. 2001b. *2001 World Development Indicators: Health Expenditure, Service, and Use.* Available online at http://www.worldbank.org/data/ wdi2001/pdfs/tab2_15.pdf. Accessed January 2002.

World Health Organization. 1995. *Physical Status: Use and Interpretation of Anthropometry.* WHO Technical Report Series, no. 854. Geneva: WHO.

———, Expert Committee on Maternal and Child Health. 1950. *Public Health Aspect of Low Birthweight.* WHO Technical Report Series, no. 27. Geneva: WHO.

www.fueleconomy.gov. 2002. "1985–2001 Buyer's Guide to Fuel Efficient Cars and Trucks." Available online at http://www.fueleconomy.gov/feg/ index.htm. Accessed October 2002.

Young, L. R., and M. Nestle. 2002. "The Contribution of Expanding Portions Sizes to the US Obesity Epidemic." *American Journal of Public Health* 92 (2): 246–49.

Zambrana, R. E., C. Dunkel-Schetter, N. L. Collins, and S. C. Scrimshaw. 1999. "Mediators of Ethnic-Associated Differences in Infant Birth Weight." *Journal of Urban Health* 76 (1): 102–16.

Zelazny, Gene. 2001. *Say It with Charts: The Executive's Guide to Visual Communication.* 4th ed. New York: McGraw-Hill.

Zinsser, William. 1998. *On Writing Well: The Classic Guide to Writing Nonfiction.* 6th ed. New York: HarperCollins Publishers.

INDEX